EMBRACING A CITY

THE KRESGE FOUNDATION IN DETROIT

1993–2017

Tony Proscio and Myron Farber

The Kresge Foundation
3215 W. Big Beaver Road
Troy, MI 48084
Kresge.org

ISBN: 978-0-9839654-7-3

Printed by Clark Graphics (Warren, MI) USA

Every effort has been taken to minimize the environmental footprint of this publication. The soy- and vegetable oil-based inks used in printing are 95% free of volatile organic compounds. This report was printed on Neenah Environment Bright White Cover and Finch Fine Opaque White Text papers, which are Forest Stewardship Council® certified.

Book Design: Meaghan Barry and Lilian Crum of Unsold Studio
Cover Art: Installation view *Neighborhood Detroit*, a commissioned artwork for The Kresge Foundation's midtown Detroit Office
Artist Credit: Clinton Snider
Photo Credit: Tim Thayer Photography

TABLE OF CONTENTS

FOREWORD

Major foundations occupy a unique place in modern American society. Often guided by the most general of mission statements (in the case of the Kresge Foundation, it is "to promote human progress"), these institutions stand astride the other spheres of more specialized human activities: governmental, commercial, academic, educational, religious, journalistic, and civic. The most important question any foundation faces, therefore, is what role will it assume in relation to the constellation of actors in these other spheres? Should it be solely supportive, taking the world as it is and awarding grants to enhance the capacity of worthy institutions to operate in their spheres? Should it deploy the foundation's resources to influence, even reform, how other actors behave? Or, most dramatically, should the foundation develop its own agenda for making an impact in the world and then identify the actors best able to serve as partners in implementing that vision?

These are not easy issues to resolve. Faced with the distinctive challenges ccompanying each approach, we have seen a trend over the past half century for foundations to elect the more activist, purposive role. The decision to pursue that ambitious direction, however, carries with it a variety of significant pitfalls. The first is the debilitating belief that your vision and approach are always correct, a bias often confirmed by resource-limited applicants all too ready to validate your wisdom. Related to this concern, it is easy to squander the foundation's precious resources by promoting actions that end up being of limited consequence, a mistake to be avoided at all costs given the many urgent problems we face. And, finally, there is the familiar institutional misstep of veering from one problem to the next, as new boards and presidents come and go each with their own individual pet missions.

A truly great modern foundation must live comfortably in all three possible realms. Most of all, it must understand that it has the advantage of being able to develop a very special kind of knowledge about the world and its needs but that it will only succeed by working collaboratively with other institutions and actors, who generate their own distinctive knowledge. Moreover, working collectively is the only way to magnify available resources, financial and otherwise, at a scale comparable to the challenges to be met. The good foundation recognizes in its heart that to be truly effective, it must operate on the principle that the world would be better off if the foundation were eventually able to disappear from the scene.

When the Kresge Board of Trustees appointed Rip Rapson as President in 2006, the Kresge Foundation was at the beginning of its journey as a modern foundation of great consequence. Rip led the transition of the then eight-decade-old institution in a way that will make all those involved with the Kresge Foundation forever proud. The exquisitely complex and highly delicate balance that was required to fulfill the Foundation's goals was met with a continuous interaction of vision, experimentation, and self-criticism. This work was conducted in the context of the deeply distressed and magical City of Detroit, with quite stunning and, we hope, ultimately joyous results.

As Edmund Burke said, "To be attached to the subdivision, to love the little platoon we belong to in society, is the first principle (the germ as it were) of public affections." The "subdivision," the "platoon," Kresge chose to belong to, first and foremost, was Detroit. This volume is the story of one major American foundation finding its way in the modern landscape of foundations and of how, with many partners, it could "promote human progress" in its home of Detroit.

Lee Bollinger
President of Columbia University in the City of New York, and
former Kresge Foundation Trustee (2001—2017)

ACKNOWLEDGMENTS

The research and writing of this book were supported by The Kresge Foundation. The Foundation also provided generous access to its records, archives, staff, and grantees. Nonetheless, the authors retained editorial control, and any errors or omissions are solely their responsibility.

The information presented here comes from three main sources. The first is an exhaustive review of The Kresge Foundation's written record on its efforts in Detroit, including strategy papers, annual reports, staff memos, speeches and publications by Kresge executives, grant recommendations, and periodic program reviews and assessments. These documents amount to many thousands of pages in all. The second source of information is roughly four dozen interviews with civic, philanthropic, and community leaders and Detroit residents, and with members of Kresge's Detroit staff. Some of these interviews were conducted on the condition that the source not be identified. Wherever the source of a quotation is not otherwise noted, it came from one of these interviews. A third source of information was media coverage of Detroit and its efforts at recovery, including news publications and online and social media. Most of this text was written between January 2016 and November 2017, a time of change and challenge in Detroit. There is no reason to believe that these changes have ended, or even have slowed. Therefore, many statements throughout this history must be understood as snapshots of a particular moment and reflections on a recent past that will remain open to interpretation — and re-interpretation — long after these pages are published.

The text of this book was expertly edited, and in a great many places improved, by Merrill Perlman, an award-winning editor and journalist. The process of assembling and interpreting the documents, hunting down facts, and locating interviewees was aided enormously by Kresge's Detroit team, particularly its former Managing Director Laura J. Trudeau, and its current Managing Directors, Wendy Lewis Jackson and Benjamin S. Kennedy, as well as former Senior Program Officer George C. Jacobsen and Program Officers Bryan P. Hogle and Neesha B. Modi. Senior Communications Officer W. Kim Heron offered valuable insight, and Marcus L. McGrew, director of Program Operations and Information Management, fielded multiple requests for data and helped with their interpretation.

Throughout the long months of research and writing, Senior Program Team Assistant Krista Lowes and former Detroit Office Fellow Alycia Socia endured constant requests for advice, documents, contact information, and internal resources at the Foundation, always responding with skill, patience, and grace and, most remarkably, without complaint.

Rip Rapson, president of The Kresge Foundation.
Photo Credit: Steve Cohn Photography

The imperturbable Sharon Zimmerman, assistant to Kresge's president and director of the Executive Office, carefully shepherded the text through months of final revisions, gap-filling, and fact-checking, brokering connections with staff and outside reviewers and protecting the authors from any number of embarrassments. She and External Affairs and Communications Director Jennifer Kulczycki assembled illustrations and graphics and managed the entire process of publication and design.

Our gratitude to all of these staff members, and to the presence of Great Lakes Coffee beneath the Kresge office in Detroit, can never be sufficient.

TAP232

Chapter 1

A SHARED COMMUNITY VISION

"Make no little plans; they have no magic to stir men's blood and probably themselves will not be realized. Make big plans; aim high in hope and work, remembering that a noble, logical diagram once recorded will never die, but long after we are gone will be a living thing, asserting itself with ever-growing insistency."

— Daniel H. Burnham, 1907[1]

The Alley Project community art-making workshop. Photo Credit: Erik Howard

For close to 50 years, Detroit has held a peculiar fascination for American philanthropy. The prospect of reversing a steep and accelerating decline, a cause at once tantalizing and forbidding, has drawn a number of foundations into repeated, often unsatisfying, efforts at novel civic-philanthropic initiatives there. Like Kafka's castle, the city's unique history of triumphs and crises has loomed on the philanthropic horizon as alluring yet stubbornly impenetrable.

Millions of charitable dollars have been ventured to various ends in Detroit, including education reform, the arts, regional cooperation, nutrition and health, neighborhood redevelopment, economic revitalization, juvenile justice, and many others. Some of these contributed to improvements here and there, though for most of this history only a very few led to any fundamental shift in conditions that average Detroiters would experience. Several efforts flared and sputtered without leaving much of a trace.

Perennially wary of political entanglements and public controversy, funders not rooted in the city tended for decades to focus their projects narrowly, concentrating on just one or two aspects of urban life, such as health or urban planning or after-school programs. They hoped, in these circumscribed areas, to find a critical lever or "root cause" that, if set to rights, might weaken or blunt some of the forces of decline. But they generally sought the comfort of coalitions, banding with other funders, public and private, to share the risks. And they often pulled the plug when conditions failed to change significantly — as the Robert Wood Johnson Foundation did with its Urban Health Initiative, or the Ford Foundation with its Neighborhood and Family Initiative, or the Annie E. Casey Foundation with its "Making Connections" community revitalization effort.[2]

With little staff to devote to Detroit's complex environment, where face time and trust-building are indispensable elements of any program of change, foundations sought, as one veteran Detroit grantmaker put it, "very narrow portals for support, so that it was easy to close the portal if things didn't go well. They tended to be funders, not partners. And

they set predetermined time horizons — three to five years, typically" within which to succeed or, more often, to make a swift and silent exit.

This sensitivity to risk, as it applied to Detroit, was rooted in decades of foundation orthodoxy that discouraged making grants in desperate environments. When the Ford Foundation set out in the late 1970s to draw conclusions from its previous 20 years of urban philanthropy — from programs encompassing community development, school reform, and fair housing and lending — senior executives repeatedly invoked the metaphor of triage: Foundations should concentrate on a middle band of need, places that were neither advantaged nor collapsing (one signature Ford program had actually been called "Gray Areas"), where resources and opportunities were still plentiful enough to offer a tangible prospect of success.

As a key policy paper summed it up, smart philanthropy "should avoid areas affluent beyond the need for intervention as well as those devastated beyond hope."[3] One senior officer at the time was more specific: "You can't get bogged down in the South Bronx or Camden or Gary." (As it happens, Ford soon changed its opinion of the South Bronx, where it contributed to an extraordinary, and widely praised, revitalization program in partnership with enterprising community organizations using massive city and state subsidies. But even that experience was viewed as evidence that only a gigantic commitment of public dollars could make a foundation initiative successful in such a place. Camden and Gary remained off-limits.)

Yet as Detroit's distress descended into disaster in the late decades of the 20th century, the sheer scale and urgency of the problems proved hard for foundations to ignore. After all, this was not just any industrial-age city fallen on hard times; this was *Detroit,* once the Arsenal of Democracy, cradle of the African-American middle class. Though it had become an encompassing tragedy, it was also a place with unmistakable assets, including a strong (if battered) local culture and

Above: Detroit, the Arsenal of Democracy: Constructing Consolidated B-24 Liberators at Willow Run, 1944.
Photo Credit: Detroit Historical Society

sense of identity, a determined resident population, an assortment of local and nearby universities and hospitals, a committed civic leadership, and a healthy regional economy. Seen in a certain way, it was the kind of place for which philanthropy was designed: important, beleaguered, resolute, and — surely, somehow — primed to revive.

Detroit is also home to several foundations of its own, which could exert leadership, test emerging ideas, and serve as the local funding partners on which outside institutions prefer to rely. These resident institutions, such as the Skillman, McGregor, and Hudson-Webber foundations and the Community Foundation for Southeast Michigan, were dedicated entirely or primarily to the Detroit area as part of their founding missions. They could be depended on to cultivate Detroit grantees, persevere through setbacks, and struggle for even small signs of success, with which they might then hope to attract bigger partners.

Through most of the 20th century, however, national funders tended to choose their targets in Detroit more warily, set tight boundaries on the scope of their involvement, and proceed only when the potential losses seemed manageable. That was true even for those foundations as close by as Kresge (Troy), Kellogg (Battle Creek), or Mott (Flint), and certainly those headquartered farther away like Ford (New York), Casey (Baltimore), or Knight (Miami).

Opposite Top: An unused Grand Trunk Railroad line, circa 2007, before it was redeveloped into an urban recreational pathway called the Dequindre Cut Greenway. Photo Credit: Corine Vermeulen

Opposite Bottom: The Dequindre Cut Greenway, a popular recreational walking and biking path in downtown Detroit. Photo Credit: Detroit Riverfront Conservancy

A period of optimism, a new commitment

This pattern began to change slightly in the mid-1990s, when the national economy swelled with the technology boom and Detroit government seemed poised for a long-delayed modernization and housecleaning. With the retirement, after two decades, of Mayor Coleman A. Young, a sense of optimism greeted the 1994 arrival of the more open, pragmatic Dennis W. Archer, widely regarded as a bridge-builder between potential investors and Detroit's capital-wary political establishment. Although Archer's two terms produced only modest reforms to most city services, the strong economy and general sense of political change drew new interest from investors and foundations.

By 1998, nearly 4,000 new housing units were planned or under construction in central Detroit, and the software developer Compuware, with $1 billion in annual revenue, announced that it was moving its headquarters downtown — the first major business to locate there in decades.[4] New casinos, a signature Archer initiative, were under development and promised to add as much as $200 million a year in new revenue to cash-starved city coffers. In 1996, with funding from The Kresge Foundation, the Archer team began a sweeping neighborhood planning process, aimed at setting priorities for commercial development, reconstruction, demolition, and maintenance.[5] The spell of economic and political sunshine in these years gave rise to a multitude of green shoots: falling crime, poverty, and unemployment (though these remained high by national standards); rising property values; an uptick in new businesses and lending; and consequently a growing sense of opportunity for national foundations, several of which launched major initiatives in Detroit during this period.

Among these was The Kresge Foundation — a funder of national scope and stature, one of the 20 largest private foundations in the United States, headquartered 23 miles outside the city — which devoted close to $50 million to Detroit projects during the Archer years. Amid its roughly $100 million in average annual giving at the time, the Foundation had always made grants in Detroit. But the

GROW

SHED 3

creation of a dedicated Detroit Initiative in 1993 was a sharp departure for a foundation that had long regarded its terrain as the entire country, and that focused on promising projects rather than preferred places.

At first, the Detroit Initiative was launched quietly, at the instigation of a core group of board members. It seemed to grow less out of a sense of strategic potential than out of duty to the city where the Foundation's wealth had been created. But any reticence soon gave way to a more confident feeling of rising opportunity, brought about by the economic and political thaw. "The snow has finally melted as this is written," Foundation President John E. Marshall III wrote at the beginning of one of his annual report essays.[6]

Still, even amid the increasing optimism, Kresge's approach remained cautious. It hewed close to two core principles that, from the Foundation's inception, had underlain almost all of its grants nationwide: It would primarily support capital projects, and it would require a significant matching contribution from other funders for every dollar it disbursed. Consequently, much of its grantmaking in those years was for buildings or infrastructure, funded in close partnership with other funders, usually Detroit-based. One example was a $10 million grant for Detroit GreenWays, a project championed by the Community Foundation for Southeast Michigan that aimed to create a network of bike and hiking paths across the region.[7] Kresge's contribution for the initiative was eventually matched nearly seven to one by other public and private donors.[8]

Although the Detroit Initiative constituted a serious commitment to the city and its region, Kresge's program also reflected a bit of philanthropy's general pattern of approach-avoidance in Detroit: The Foundation would commit large amounts of money, often to bold and important efforts, but only after others had done so. ("We expect that an organization will come to us with several of the larger gifts needed for a successful [capital] campaign already committed," Marshall told Philanthropy News Digest in 2006.[9]) And it concentrated on the kind of projects that could be completed in a discrete period of time, where risks would be borne mostly by others, and where success would be measurable in bricks laid, rather than lives altered.

To be sure, these projects were highly significant — not just in the context of the times, but even in as much as 20 years' hindsight. Surely the most farsighted, and still the most celebrated, was the Detroit RiverWalk, a broad esplanade that stretches more than five miles along the waterfront. The eventual Kresge contribution to the RiverWalk, totaling $50 million, was a huge commitment for the Foundation — in fact, its largest commitment to a single project up to that date — but it was intentionally overmatched by funds from other participants that had paved the way. Nonetheless, as Marshall accurately observed in 2003, "The Kresge Foundation's expressed interest in making an extraordinary grant provided encouragement and endorsement that gave this project and its stakeholders momentum."[10]

Other significant capital projects downtown drew support from Kresge in much the same way: Civic and public interest built a head of steam and drew some initial expressions of corporate and government support; then Kresge made a major commitment with matching requirements, which helped galvanize the remainder of the funding needed to bring a project to fruition. This was the story behind the redevelopment of Campus Martius Park, the nucleus of downtown Detroit's hub-and-spoke street plan, of the newly built downtown YMCA, and of renovations to Orchestra Hall, the Detroit Institute of Arts, and Eastern Market. These developments remain signature assets of a resurgent urban core a decade or more after they were completed.

Yet the very success of these ventures suggested to some members of the Kresge Board that the Foundation could be playing a bigger, or at least more versatile, role in helping to revitalize Detroit. The capital challenge grant had proved its value as a philanthropic tool, but was it the *only* tool, or even the best one, that the Foundation should be using as an investor in Detroit's redevelopment? Three decades of large-scale physical developments had proved that the city

Opposite: Detroit's Eastern Market. The Kresge Foundation funded revitalization of several Market sheds. Eastern Market remains one of Detroit's signature assets of a resurgent urban core.

Following Page: Re-imagining Detroit 2020: Rip Rapson's working drawing of the nine building blocks essential for the city's long-term growth.

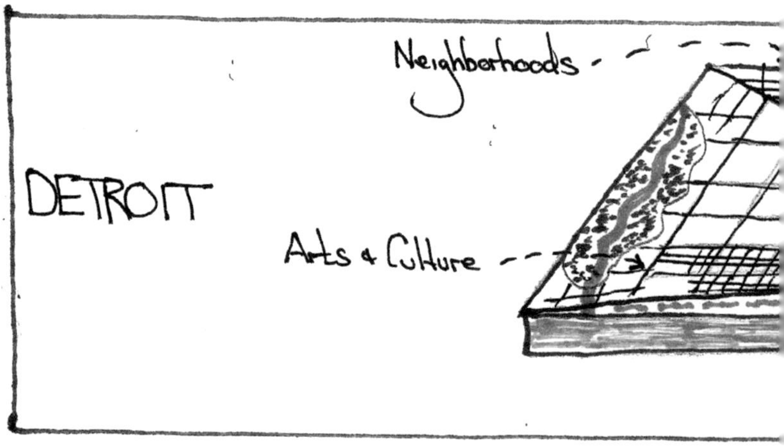

was not going to rebound solely on the strength of giant capital projects alone. Should the Foundation then take no major role in other areas of demonstrable need, such as workforce development, health, education, neighborhood improvement, or entrepreneurship and small businesses?

The capital challenge grant was far from risk free, but it was a good deal less risky than making operating grants to nonprofits working in areas such as these, where success might take years to materialize, if at all. Should the Foundation accept greater risk of possible failure, futility, or controversy, in the hope of participating more broadly and creatively in building the city's future?

Questions like these represented an important shift — subtle at first, but increasingly pronounced — in the way The Kresge Foundation viewed itself, its approach to philanthropy, and its role in Detroit. By 2006, as John Marshall was preparing to retire after 13 years as Foundation president, the Board began to re-examine, in fundamental terms, the way it approached its grantmaking, both in Detroit and nationally. "We wanted to do more, to do it better, and to have a more significant impact," Board Chair Elaine D. Rosen wrote in the Foundation's annual report the following year.

Among other things, she continued, big projects with blue-ribbon financial backing would not be the only eligible grantees: "[S]mall, medium, and large organizations are now on equal footing as they apply for funding." To carry out this more varied, complicated, and admittedly riskier approach, the Board chose as its next President Rip Rapson, a seasoned strategist in both philanthropy and government. He had recently stepped down as president of the McKnight Foundation in Minneapolis, an institutional standard-bearer for diversified, collaborative urban grantmaking.

The change was immediately apparent in Kresge's vision for Detroit. Having previously focused on "strengthening Detroit's civic institutions and public gathering spaces," Rapson wrote in 2007, the Foundation had now "broadened

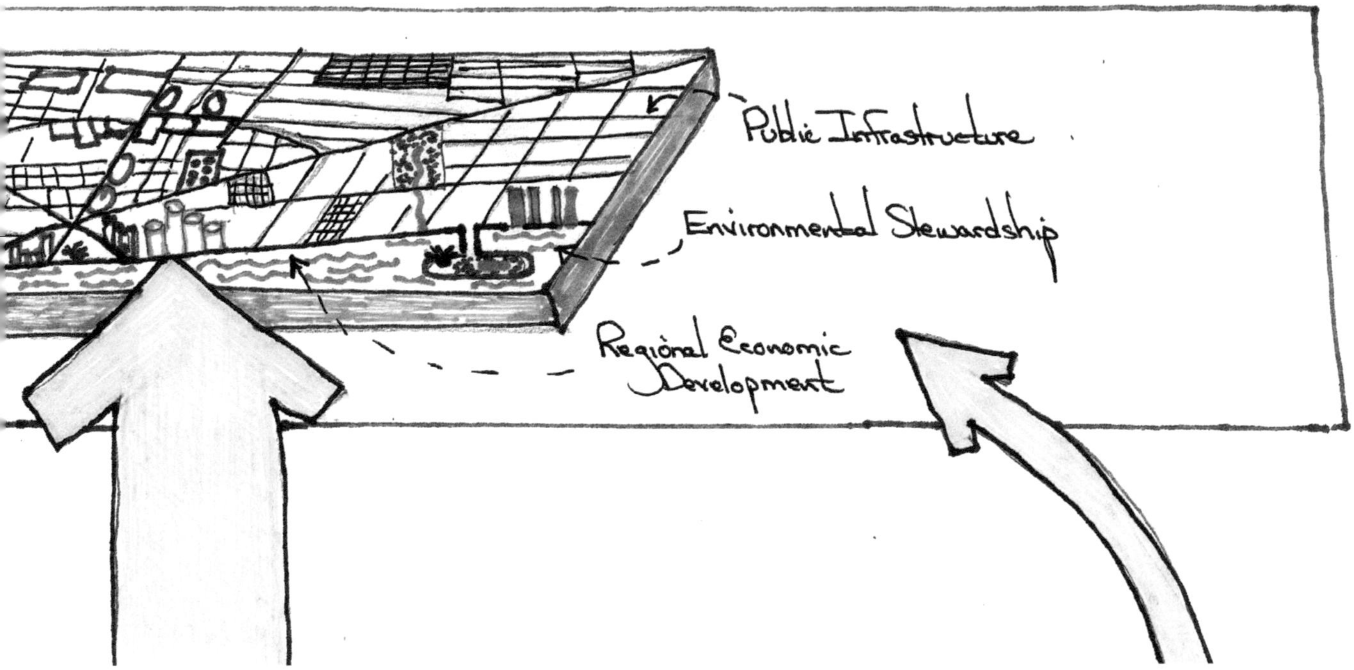

that emphasis to encompass a five-part strategic framework: revitalizing the downtown, recalibrating the regional economy, stabilizing neighborhoods, enhancing the natural environment, and promoting a robust arts and culture ecosystem." Average grant outlays for Detroit more than quadrupled, from less than $8 million a year through 2005 to more than $33 million from 2006 through 2013.

Re-imagining Detroit

The new framework had little time to blossom before disaster struck. The international financial meltdown of 2008 hit Detroit with particular ferocity, and the city then found itself embroiled in additional crises of more local origin. In September 2008, just as the markets were decimating the city's property values, tax receipts, pension funds, and ability to deliver even the most basic public services, the charismatic young mayor, Kwame Kilpatrick, who had succeeded Dennis Archer in 2002, resigned after two years of mounting scandals and an eventual guilty plea on two felony counts. More charges followed, and 32 of the mayor's associates were eventually convicted of crimes including extortion, bribery, and fraud.[11] Not long after Kilpatrick's downfall, another casualty of the global financial implosion, Detroit's two resident automakers, GM and Chrysler, headed for bankruptcy.

In a matter of months, the city had become both economically and politically rudderless. It bore all the earmarks of what the Ford Foundation had once described as "devastated beyond hope": a tidal wave of foreclosures and abandonment, one of the worst violent crime rates in the nation, streetlights blinking out across the city. Forbes magazine was only slightly more blunt than other media when it declared Detroit in 2008 to be America's Most Miserable City.[12]

Undeterred, Kresge unveiled in its 2008 annual report a raft of new initiatives for its Detroit portfolio that would have been all but inconceivable just a few years earlier. "Three years ago, when we began a recalibration of our grantmaking," Rapson wrote in early 2009, "our perspective was embedded

Above: Portion of one of Rip Rapson's working drawings illustrating the Foundation's approach to philanthropy in its hometown. Photo Credit: Courtesy of the National Museum of American History of the Smithsonian Institution

more in a sense of gradualism — of expanding our grant-making in ways that would ensure continuity and build on the strengths of our past work. Today, that perspective has shifted to a heightened sense of urgency."[13] As if to spotlight the scope of Kresge's vision for the city in the midst of "unprecedented stress and hardship,"[14] the Annual Report for 2008 referred, for the first time, to "re-imagin[ing] Detroit," a phrase that would soon become the masthead of the Foundation's approach to philanthropy in its home town.

Among the larger Detroit projects unveiled in 2008, several have ballooned and become even more significant. Prominent among these was the Detroit Neighborhood Forum, conceived jointly by the Skillman and Kresge foundations, where foundations, banks, nonprofits, and government exchange ideas and coordinate joint efforts in outlying residential and commercial districts. Sizable foundation grants in that year also bore lasting fruit, including major grants for the GreenWays initiative, for an entrepreneurial incubator, and for expanding the College for Creative Studies. Kresge made a $25 million contribution to the New Economy Initiative (NEI), a fund for workforce development, innovation, and entrepreneurship organized by the Community Foundation for Southeast Michigan.

A series of grants to the Detroit Economic Growth Corporation included support for the creation of an Office of Foreclosure Intervention and Response — an unprecedented arrangement in which private philanthropy would, in effect, pay for the operation of what normally would be a municipal agency. Million-dollar grants in 2008 also went to the Detroit branch of the Local Initiatives Support Corp. (LISC), the largest national organization supporting neighborhood revitalization, and to Shorebank, a national community development bank with a property redevelopment program tailored to Detroit.

A somewhat smaller grant, of $500,000 to the business and civic alliance known as the Downtown Detroit Partnership, would eventually grow to have large and long-term consequences. It provided "preliminary engineering and administrative planning for the creation of a light-rail system on lower Woodward Avenue"[15] — a seeming pie-in-the-sky vision for a destitute city, steeped in automobile culture, with decades of adamant resistance to all forms of mass transit. In fact, Detroit's only visible dalliance with a big public transportation project, its downtown elevated People Mover, had been a colossal disappointment. The chronically underused system, which opened in 1987, was all that remained of what had once been an ambitious push in the 1970s for regionwide transportation, a push that collapsed amid an all-too-common breakdown in regional cooperation.

Yet despite that troubled history, and at a time when the city was unable to collect all its trash, keep its streetlights lit, and plow its snowy roads, here was a proposal to rip up part of its central artery and install a rail line. The sheer audacity of the idea proved, in time, to be one of its strengths — it was the first step in a sweeping vision for modernizing the region's transportation, the kind of "big plan" favored by the legendary architect Daniel Burnham. But at the moment of inception, it was far from an obvious idea and sorely needed the backing of a credible and well-heeled institution. Kresge's grant came with the promise of $35 million more if the plan led to a feasible project. To at least some observers, this seemed to take the "imagination" factor in "re-imagining Detroit" almost to the level of fantasy.

The following year, The Kresge Foundation formally branded its view of the city's future as "Re-imagining Detroit 2020," and it laid out a schematic picture of philanthropic investment in a single place at a scale that neither the city nor the Foundation had ever experienced. Its purpose was nothing less, Rapson wrote, than "to change the trajectory of Detroit, a city that has simultaneously suffered massive disinvestment by the private sector, witnessed the near-death experience of its dominant industry, and been bludgeoned by the foreclosure crisis."[16]

The new plan of action, he continued, would expand on the five-part framework of 2007 and would now encompass "nine building blocks essential for the city's long-term health."[17]

These were:

- Greening the economy, workforce, and public policy
- Cultivating entrepreneurship
- Fostering innovation in health care
- Reconceiving land use
- Building a vibrant "Creative Corridor"
- Creating mass transit
- Developing "neighborhoods of choice"
- Redesigning education
- Nurturing an arts and culture ecosystem

There was a sweep to this vision that seemed almost deliberately intended to flout the conventions of urban grantmaking. "Philanthropy has certainly enjoyed success in countless individual projects," Rapson told an audience at the University of Minnesota in 2008. "But taking on entire cities? Another matter altogether. At that scale, we begin to implicate a very different kind of politics, a very different interplay of sectors, a very different set of market dynamics." Dealing with the whole complex interplay of health and housing, economic development, transportation, culture and employment, he posited, might be "a good job description for the public sector, one would think. The problem is that in too many cities and towns in America, the public sector no longer has the capacity to do it. Too few resources, too little vision, too limited a skill set. ... [B]udgets are being balanced through short-term gimmickry, thoughtful discourse is being strangled by partisan bickering, and substantive action is being dwarfed by opportunistic gesture politics. Foundations have no choice but to step forward."[18] He did not mention Detroit by name, but the description fit perfectly.

Even so, Rapson carefully framed this all-embracing mission not as a summons to Kresge alone, but to philanthropy writ large, forming a concerted team effort with government, business, and civic leadership. By 2009, a constructive partnership with government was seeming more feasible than at any time in the past decade, since the beginning of the Archer years. The turmoil in Detroit City Hall had eased with the election of the steel entrepreneur and former Detroit Pistons guard Dave Bing, a soft-spoken moderate equally respected among the city's grassroots activists and corporate elite. Although his lack of experience in politics eventually took its toll, most of the city's corporate and philanthropic leaders in 2009 believed, with Rapson, that "there is a new day in this town," and that Mayor Bing could be relied on to tackle the city's mass of difficulties "professionally; he'll do it competently; he'll do it transparently; and he'll do it with a high sense of urgency."[19]

Forging a common agenda

Besides a desired new relationship with City Hall, each of Kresge's nine building blocks, called modules, was designed to be shepherded by one or more funders, with Kresge taking the lead on the green economy, transit, and arts and culture, and a large but supporting role in most of the others. The Skillman Foundation had long been at the forefront of education reform and would be expected to set the pace there. The new Neighborhood Forum, including Skillman and Kresge, would presumably coordinate efforts on "neighborhoods of choice." The Community Foundation had instigated the New Economy Initiative with the Ford Foundation, and both would continue to play a major role in the entrepreneurship effort. As part of that body of work, the Ewing Marion Kauffman Foundation would bring its program of training for new or aspiring entrepreneurs, called FastTrac, to Detroit in 2009. The Hudson-Webber Foundation was a leader in the Creative Corridor initiative, and a coalition of corporate, city, and state players was committed to working on the streetcar project. At Kresge's invitation, the national urban funders' coalition known as Living Cities agreed to shepherd a multiparty investment partnership to ensure that local residents would benefit from development in the area anchored by Wayne State University and the city's major medical centers.

Despite the continued fallout from the market crash, Detroit's civic and economic scene in 2009 was not without its kernels of hope. Most remarkably, Dan Gilbert, founder of the mortgage giant Quicken Loans, was preparing to move his company's headquarters and 1,700 of its employees to downtown Detroit within a year. (The company's downtown

Following Page: Re-imagining Detroit 2020: Rip Rapson's working drawing of the nine building blocks essential for the city's long-term growth.

Overarching Objectives:

1. Create a blueprint for a re-imagined Detroit – its infrastructure, human development systems, economy, & cultural environment
2. Position the re-imagined Detroit as a model for the revitalization of older industrial cities
3. Make tangible progress in each of the nine modules of reinvention

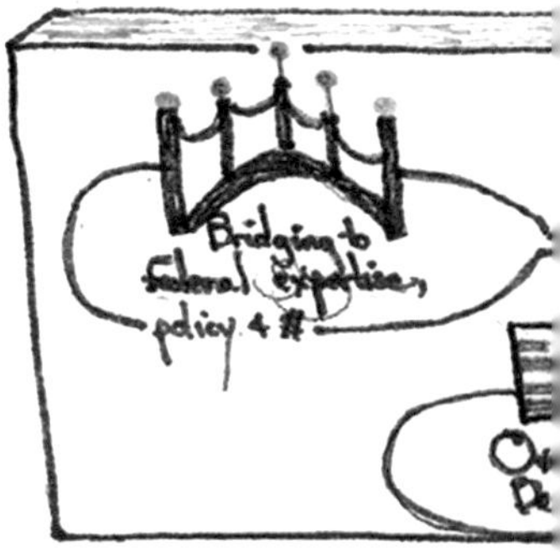

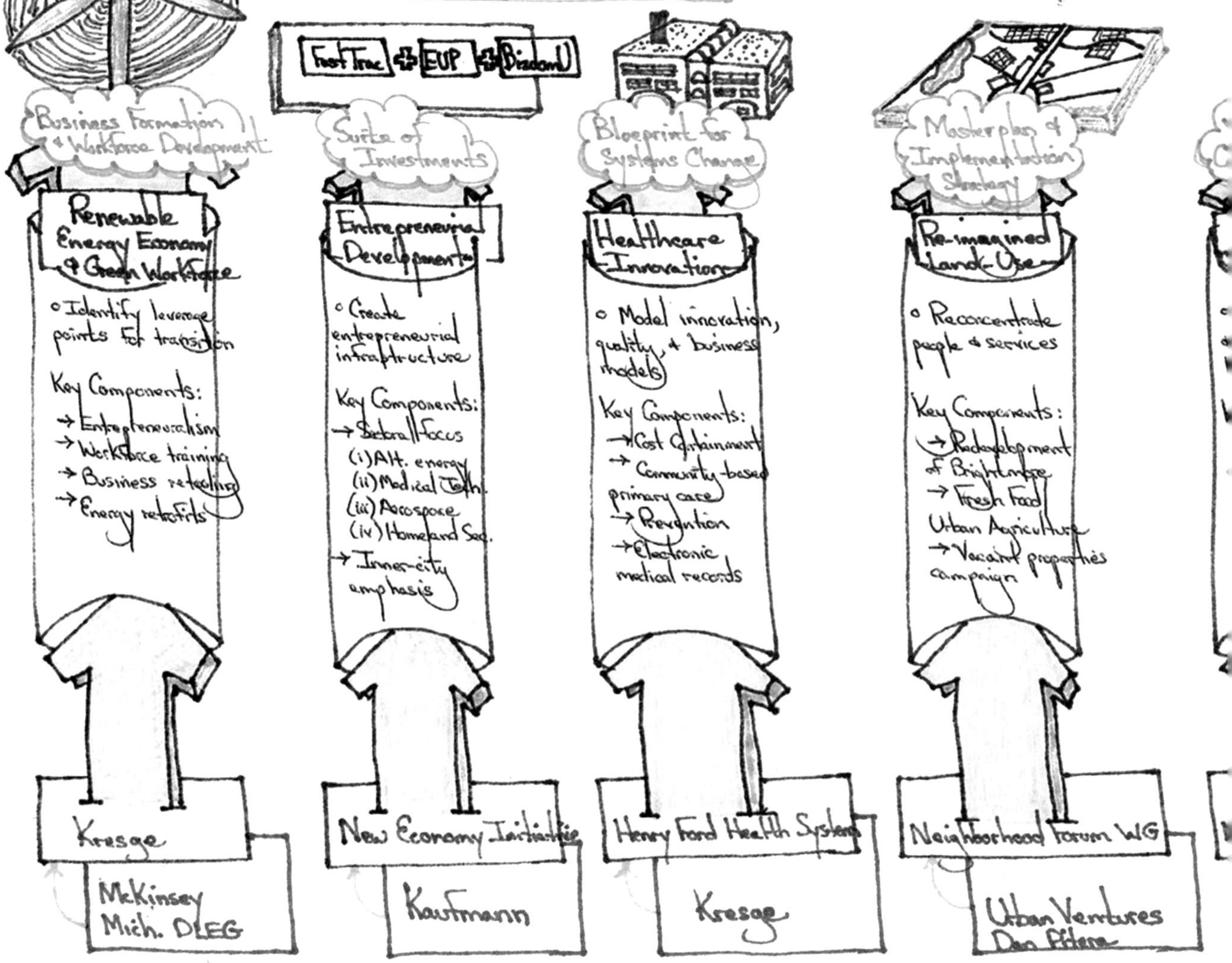

Overarching Questions:

1. What are we being "hired" to do – what are the outcomes we seek?
2. What is the critical path to achieving these outcomes?
3. What are the most significant obstacles?
4. What role can/should philanthropy play?
5. Who are the essential stakeholders?
6. What aspects are attractive to the federal government and what role should it play?

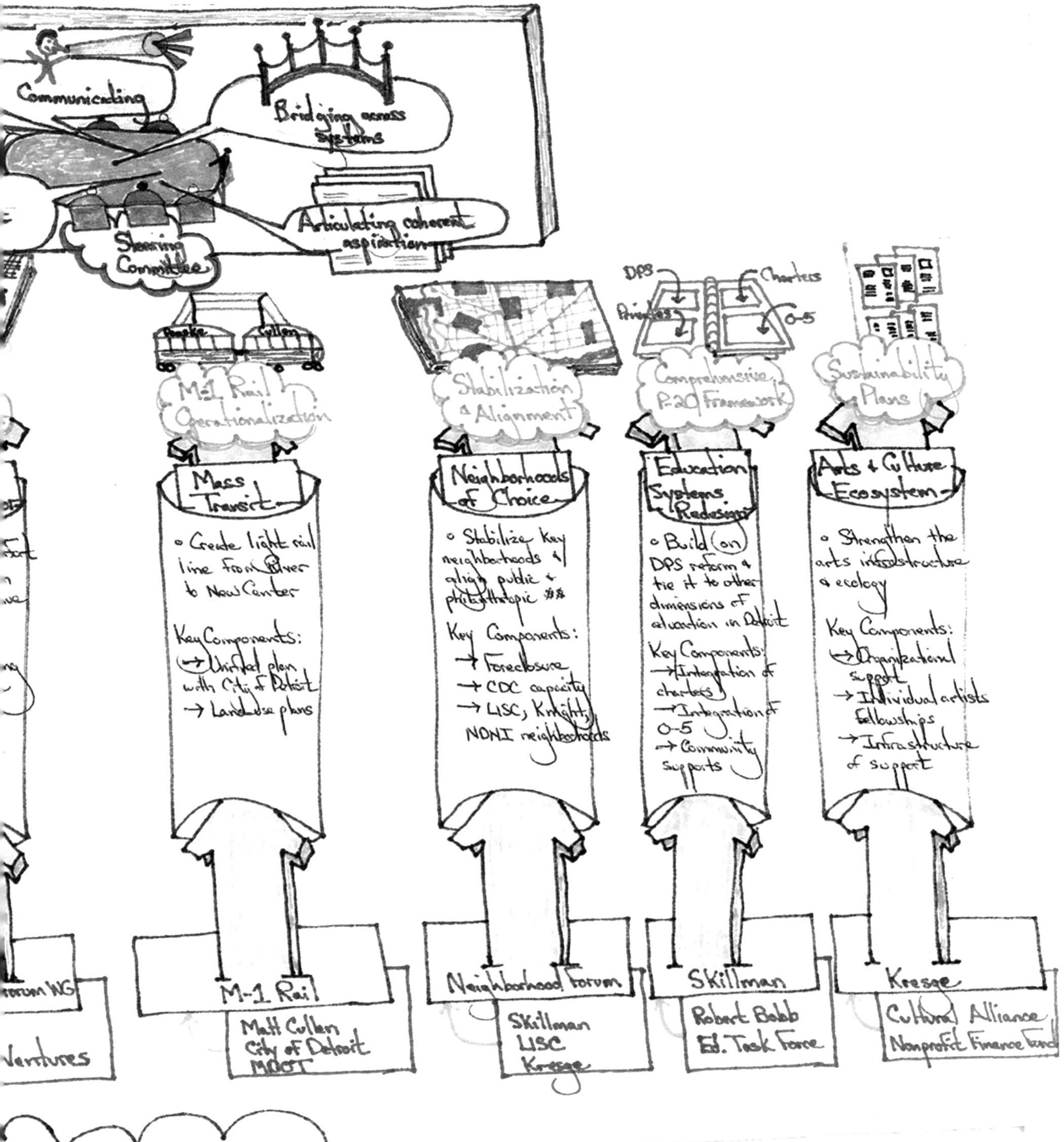

Overarching Principles:

1. The re-imagination must be comprehensive, yet targeted
2. Each module must build on pre-existing energy & capacity
3. Each module should contain the potential for both long-term repositioning and short-term advances
4. The modules are interdependent
5. The aggregate weight of the modules is a fundamentally re-imagined city

Pip Rapsen
7.29.09

workforce doubled in the following months, and eventually rose to more than 17,000.) He would soon recruit, as head of his nonlending ventures, Matthew Cullen, a Detroit corporate and civic eminence who had been the top GM executive most recently responsible for the renovations to the Renaissance Center and its connection to the RiverWalk. Together with the automotive and racing entrepreneur Roger Penske, a longtime champion of Detroit's economic development, and the Detroit Tigers and Red Wings owner Mike Ilitch, founder of Little Caesars Pizza and a major downtown landowner*, plus a handful of other business figures, Gilbert and Cullen were about to become critical partners in the new rail line and in the expanding ambitions of the downtown-to-Midtown economic district.

Even amid the web of alliances and shared responsibilities integrated into "Re-imagining Detroit 2020," it was hard to evade the reality that the framework was Kresge's, and that the complete picture, with all its partners and modules and goals, had come to life primarily in the mind of Rip Rapson. (In fact, the word "picture" is meant literally: Rapson, son of a noted architect, laid out his ideas in a series of illustrated diagrams, in which each of the nine elements was portrayed as a kind of smokestack, with the leading participants shown as engines below, initiatives and component projects lining its walls, and the desired outcomes billowing from the top.)

For this idea to be associated too exclusively with one foundation would surely be counterproductive — more likely to alienate other foundations and public officials than to entice them into closer cooperation. Though Rapson and his colleagues were keenly aware of that risk, and took pains to note that most of the nine elements represented the efforts and imagination of other players, not Kresge, they decided not to shrink from it. Someone needed to put something broad and well-integrated on the table. Until that happened, it would be too easy for all the disparate projects to struggle along separately, without reinforcing one another and without rallying the mass of political support, resources, and energy that a crisis of Detroit's scale demanded.

Some kind of overarching strategy, with a common understanding of goals, responsibilities, and priorities, was therefore an indispensable first step. "The absence of a shared community vision," Rapson said in 2011,

> has been *the* defining problem of our community. It crashes into daily life in the most tangible and harmful ways — immobilizing investors, making it impossible for public officials to describe coherently their intentions to improve community life, befuddling a federal administration that genuinely wants to help.
>
> About a year ago, it struck us that there was, in fact, an emerging coherence to the disparate energies underway in Detroit. I sought to capture those energies in a drawing on a single sheet of paper. It described nine discrete, yet tightly interrelated, bodies of work currently underway in Detroit — from creating transit along Woodward Avenue to promoting entrepreneurialism through the New Economy Initiative; from implementing an anchor-institution investment strategy in Midtown to strengthening the city's arts and cultural ecology; from birthing a "green and sustainable city" agenda to aligning neighborhood investments among banks, foundations, and public agencies through the Detroit Neighborhood Forum.
>
> Called Re-imagining Detroit 2020, this framework has largely accomplished its original purpose. It has become a form of common vocabulary. It has crystallized a sense of urgency. It has provided a scaffolding for various actors to build out work plans for each of the nine modules. And it has cemented a close working relationship with Mayor Bing's administration.[20] [italics in the original]

Planning the Future City

The particulars of Re-imagining Detroit changed over time, with some elements modified and others added. One goal

*Mike Ilitch died in February 2017; his businesses, including the Tigers and the Red Wings, continue under his family's ownership.

not explicitly part of the original nine modules at all, but implicit in them all, was improving city government's ability to deliver on its fundamental responsibilities.

Decades of shrinking population and tax base, dwindling budgets, rising costs, underfunded pension obligations, deferred maintenance, cronyism, and other ills — external or self-inflicted — had left the city barely able to perform even elementary, lifesaving functions like law enforcement and emergency response. Mayor Bing, in a desperate effort to right the ship, adopted a half-dozen ambitious administrative reform goals, including fiscal stability, integrity, and public safety. But with revenues continuing to plummet, most of these lay beyond his reach. By late 2011, he projected that the city could run out of cash in as little as six months. Still, the mayor's reform principles resonated with Kresge and, by incorporating them into the broader framework, Rapson signaled that Re-imagining Detroit was in harmony, and not competing, with the mayor's agenda. He eventually added Bing's goals to his drawings of Re-imagining Detroit, represented as six pillars holding up the framework's nine smokestacks.[21]

In 2010, a Bing priority got an especially warm reception at Kresge and among a handful of other foundations, when the mayor proposed a new round of citywide land-use planning, to be named the Detroit Works Project. Along with the Ford and W.K. Kellogg foundations, Kresge agreed to underwrite the cost of professional planners to inform and guide local deliberations in every neighborhood of the city. It was, in some ways, a do-over of Dennis Archer's 1996 neighborhood planning effort, which had produced reams of community wish lists but little if any way to raise money and organize efforts to implement the plans. This time, however, with the market crash emptying out city neighborhoods at an unprecedented pace (auctions of foreclosed property in 2009 were nearly five times as many as in 2007[22]), the stakes would be much higher.

Above: Detroit's sprawling geographic footprint, which could fit all of Boston, Manhattan, San Francisco, with room to spare.

By the end of 2009 — in a city whose population had shrunk to fewer than 700,000, from close to 2 million residents 60 years earlier — at least 20 square miles of habitable land were vacant,[23] and 17 percent of all city addresses were unoccupied.[24] Dwindling tax revenues from this shrinking base could not support adequate city services across all of Detroit's 139 square miles — a geographic area that could fit all of Boston, San Francisco, and Manhattan with room to spare. Something would need to be done with the expanses of urban prairie, pockmarked with rubble and dotted with the occasional solitary, intact home, that separated one still-viable neighborhood from the next. The time for wish lists had long passed; the questions now concerned survival.

The foundations' goals, as Rapson put it in early 2011, were conditioned "not on *what* the future form and function of Detroit's land must be, because we don't know that, but instead on the *way* the work is to be done." Foundation money would pay for a "platform of empirical analysis and scenario development" — staffed by researchers to assemble data on every neighborhood and led by a consultant, the Harvard urban-design professor Toni Griffin, coordinating teams of government and private planners — all of which would provide communities with information, forecasts, and possible scenarios to inform and flesh out their choices.

Next would come funding for a series of quick projects that could produce "short-term wins" — confidence-building developments that arise from the plans and lend them credibility.[25] A successful effort of this kind in post-Katrina New Orleans, prominently funded and encouraged by the Rockefeller Foundation, had provided a useful model for combining pragmatic, professional planning with genuine leadership from neighborhood residents and organizations.

Once again, as with its funding of the city's foreclosure office, philanthropy in Detroit Works was attempting to build what would, in any healthier municipality, be a purely government function. Yet as Rapson saw it, the distinction was irrelevant in a crisis of these proportions. "If there was ever an issue in Detroit in which philanthropy could play a critical role," he said during the early months of Detroit Works, "it is here. Land use is the third rail of municipal politics; political folks can't get near this and live to tell about it."[26] In yet another departure from the traditional philanthropic canon, Rapson's principle seemed to be that foundations should step in where politicians fear to tread.

It wasn't long before at least one part of Rapson's analysis proved all too correct. Although Dave Bing hardly fit the ordinary image of a politician — his whole claim to public trust was that he had come from far outside Detroit's political battlegrounds and was refreshingly unrehearsed in his public conduct — he had every reason to fear the "third rail" of urban land-use planning. The earliest town-hall gatherings intended to solicit ideas and concerns from rank-and-file Detroiters devolved into a chaos of complaints and accusations that accomplished little. When, in an ill-considered remark, the mayor referred to "depopulating" and eliminating public services in some neighborhoods, residents responded with protests and stinging comparisons to the obliteration of historic African-American neighborhoods in earlier decades.

Initial problems with the organization and logistics of the planning sessions led to further discontent, and to strains between the Foundation and city government. But after several attempts over nine months to restart the process, with a strong, local partner leading the community engagement, it resumed in late 2011. This time, with better outreach and more channels for community participation, the results were more fruitful: a compendium of plans, options, and principles officially designated the Detroit Strategic Framework. The highlights were published in January 2013 in a richly illustrated volume titled "Detroit Future City."

For Kresge, the bumpy learning curve and the complexities of the process, plus the lingering dissatisfaction of some residents and community leaders with the quality of participation they were offered,[27] were all worth the trouble. The whole Re-imagining Detroit framework, Rapson said in 2011, "pivots on land use. The investments and practices we pursue in each of the nine bodies of work are driven by, and in turn themselves drive, the choices we make about the City's physical configuration."[28] And for all its ups and downs, the Detroit Works process did, in reality, end up touching on virtually all of the framework's nine pillars. Environmentally sustainable and healthy uses of vacant property were at the core of the emerging plan. Opportunities for business and job growth, ways of galvanizing the stronger neighborhoods as desirable places to live and work, improvements to public transportation and schools, an expansion of community arts and culture, and ways of harnessing the economic strengths and anchor institutions of central Detroit — all factored prominently in community discussions and the resulting plan. A team was assembled to start implementing parts of the framework, and to ensure that future land-use decisions followed its principles. In 2016, the team became an incorporated nonprofit called Detroit Future City.

Another critical asset for a reviving Detroit also gathered strength from the planning exercise: A team that contributed data on city neighborhoods to inform Detroit Works quickly proved to be a resource of lasting value for all kinds of public purposes, far beyond planning. Nearly two years before Detroit Works, Kresge had joined the Skillman Foundation in supporting a fledgling project known as the Detroit Data Partnership to help it develop into a solid organization with expert staff capable of supplying essential data for the Neighborhood Forum, for city planning, and for other civic endeavors. By 2010, the partnership had been renamed Data Driven Detroit, or D3, and had been transformed into a scrupulously nonpartisan, neutral source of reliable data on Detroit's physical and economic condition. It became a valuable channel of basic data for the Detroit Works planning sessions. But more fundamentally, it proved to be an unprecedented asset for a city where, only a few years earlier, municipal records on delinquent, city-owned property were still being maintained on index cards, most of them out of date.

Assembling engines (literal and figurative) of growth

Meanwhile, through grants, loans, and mission-related investments, Kresge was financing a mounting portfolio of physical redevelopment projects, from small-scale neighborhood restoration efforts to larger, mixed-use and mixed-income developments by local and national real estate enterprises, including the pre-eminent affordable-housing firm McCormack Baron Salazar. Other major Kresge-financed projects included manufacturing, tech, and retail facilities in Midtown, downtown, and around the wholesale and retail fresh-food enterprises of Eastern Market. Kresge support followed that of the Hudson-Webber Foundation in sponsoring the community economic development organization Midtown Detroit Inc., a merger of two north-of-downtown community organizations that has become a powerful engine of growth — and a vital link between investors and neighborhood residents — in the surging business and institutional center.

Connecting the hub of growth in Midtown with the city's economic nucleus, the rapidly repopulating downtown, was an increasingly obvious challenge. Between the Midtown boomlet, anchored by Wayne State University and the nearby hospitals, and the downtown recovery, driven mainly by large real estate and corporate investors like Gilbert and Ilitch, lay a patch of underused territory, running more than a mile along either side of Woodward Avenue, that could, with help, draw greater strength from the activity at either end. But that would require some means by which people doing business in one or the other growth center could easily move between them.

What was needed was a ready means of travel from a downtown office tower or restaurant or stadium to a home or shop or business farther north, continuing northward to the university or medical center or business incubator or cultural institution in Midtown, all as part of a single, seamless experience at the heart of Detroit's resurgence. To counter the inward gravitational pull of casinos, stadiums, and office towers, an easy-on, easy-off streetcar could invite Detroiters and visitors alike to venture abroad in the heart of the city, treating its various central assets as equally accessible and inviting. What had been two separate nodes of development would surely be stronger if linked by rail into a single business-residential-creative-retail-health-education-tech district — and their surroundings would likely be stronger as well.

The idea germinated soon after Kresge began its expanded engagement in Detroit. A Foundation memo in 2008 described a rail line that would run north on Woodward from downtown to Midtown, connecting various transportation hubs and points of interest and eventually stimulating the development of more mass transit. The concept of a Woodward rail line had originated with the region's lead transportation planner, John Hertel, and got a significant boost in a fertile conversation between Rapson and Roger Penske, the transportation entrepreneur and dean of the city's civic leadership. The Foundation soon made a half-million-dollar grant to the Downtown Detroit Partnership, which Penske then chaired, to support "preliminary engineering and advance planning."[29] The federal offer of $35 million more would be available if the plans and funding prospects showed promise.

The project weathered multiple deaths and rebirths. But it crossed the goal line when the first paying passenger stepped aboard on Sept. 6, 2017. Its momentum was sustained through a gantlet of crises and setbacks by the combined sponsorship and funding of The Kresge Foundation, the prominent corporate leadership of Penske, Gilbert, and Ilitch, and later, significant contributions from federal and state government. The streetcar, Rapson wrote in an early assessment of the concept, would be "the signature physical development in our [Detroit] program" and "the intersection of all of our strategic objectives to strengthen neighborhoods, the regional economy, arts, downtown, and the environment."

'Scaffolding' a city in crisis

While the scope and price of a possible streetcar system were being explored, revised, and re-revised, the city was sinking ever deeper into insolvency. In December 2012, just as the new rail line was navigating one of its periodic planning crises, a state-appointed Financial Advisory Board revealed that City Hall barely had enough money to start the new year. Within three months, Michigan Gov. Rick Snyder declared a financial emergency and placed Detroit under the near-total control of an emergency manager, the Jones Day attorney Kevyn D. Orr.

Although Orr initially drew up a plan to avoid bankruptcy, it took him little more than a month to determine that the city would not meet its financial obligations under any reasonable scenario. Detroit's debt — including a bundle of exotic financial instruments intended to restructure the city's pension funds, negotiated by an increasingly desperate Kwame Kilpatrick in 2005 — was starving the city of money for even the most essential operations. The only route to a revived city, he concluded, ran through Chapter 9. On July 18, 2013, Detroit filed the largest municipal bankruptcy in American history.

Even amid the storm clouds, Kresge was essentially doubling down on its support for the city. In 2012, with state government plainly signaling an intent to take control of Detroit, the Foundation provided $3.7 million to complete the strategic land-use framework that was to become Detroit Future City, and to establish the office to implement it. Kresge expanded its arts funding, committing several million to help stabilize the city-owned Detroit Institute of Arts (which would, in less than a year, be under serious threat of liquidation to pay the city's debts), and another $4.25 million for community-based arts organizations and individual artists. More than $1 million went to the strengthening of Eastern Market and expansion of its economic development activity on downtown's eastern flank. More than $1.5 million in new grants continued to support economic and residential development by Midtown Detroit Inc. More millions went to efforts to stabilize teetering neighborhoods and to seed the city's community development talent pool with a cadre of up-and-coming workers, known as Detroit Revitalization Fellows. And a $1 million grant over three years supported Excellent Schools Detroit, an organization promoting reform, new schools, and new early childhood programs in the Detroit public schools — a system even more troubled, organizationally and financially, than the city itself.[30]

In that year's annual report, Rapson affirmed Kresge's commitment not just to supporting some hopeful projects and individual bright spots in Detroit's bleak economic landscape, but to "deep, integrative work" on the city's recovery, "cross-walking among disciplines, embracing risk, working in partnership with other foundations, and finding joint cause with the public and private sectors."

The following year, as lawyers for the city and its creditors battled in court over the prospects for Detroit's survival, The Kresge Foundation unveiled a $30 million-plus Woodward Corridor Investment Fund, with a $5 million loan and a $1.25 million loan guarantee from the Foundation and the remainder from an assortment of local and national foundations and lenders.[31] Another $2.8 million went for implementing Detroit Future City; nearly $1 million more to Midtown Detroit, and $750,000 went to LISC for various neighborhood development projects.

But alongside these long-term efforts at rethinking and rebuilding Detroit, The Kresge Foundation was also once again funding what would have been, in a financially healthy city, some of the most basic of municipal functions. As part of its support of Data Driven Detroit, the Foundation had helped launch Motor City Mapping, a project of the public-private Blight Removal Task Force, convened by the federal Department of Housing and Urban Development, that would verify the condition of all of Detroit's 380,000 parcels of land.

In a city where property records had until only recently been kept by hand — and where multiple, antiquated computer systems operated on separate, incompatible platforms — an easily accessible digital record showing the precise location and current state of each property was a profound step forward. But was it "deep, integrative work"? The results were both impressive and indispensable — but the effort was something most other city halls would have conducted on their own, as a matter of course.

In 2014, Kresge had provided $250,000 for the city to restructure and strengthen its grants-management office — another basic municipal function — to help improve Detroit's chances of raising and accounting for public and private grants. Even more surprising was a $1 million grant in 2013 to the Downtown Detroit Partnership, responding to a plea from Mayor Bing, toward the purchase of 100 new police cars and 23 ambulances for the bankrupt city government.

There was no questioning the need: Some two-thirds of the Police Department's vehicles were run-down, and many were unsafe or unusable. The newly appointed police chief, James Craig, had had to acknowledge that, thanks partly to the vehicle shortage, "There were times when Detroit police officers were called, and no one would ever show up."[32] Several local funders, including Kresge, consequently responded to an urgent plea for help from the city, its Police Department, and an emergency manager who had made improved public safety a personal priority. In addition to paying for the vehicles, the Foundation in 2013 also supported Detroit's adoption of a version of New York City's CompStat system, which compiles and analyzes crime statistics to guide the deployment of officers and equipment. The result of the initial rollout of CompStat was a steep reduction in crime in the areas where the system was piloted. It has now been expanded elsewhere in the city.

Here again was a boundary that traditional philanthropy had been loath to cross: Not only were these among the most fundamental of public responsibilities, well outside the normal mission of private philanthropy, but the crisis surrounding them resulted from years of neglect and mismanagement, not from some natural disaster. It is a staple of foundation management that charitable dollars must not pick up the tab for governments' bad decisions. (In fact, when first asked if the Ford Foundation would consider rescuing the Detroit Institute of Arts from the auction block, its president, Darren Walker, reportedly answered, "Foundations fund the future; they don't pay for the mistakes of the past."[33])

Detroit Grants by Focus Area, 2007 – 2017

The total amount Kresge has committed to Detroit:

$460,507,558

Neighborhood Development:

$120,331,551

Arts and Culture:

$54,956,792

Entrepreneurship and Economic Development:

$34,390,105

Woodward Corridor Development:

$33,950,000

Education (P-20):

$36,341,954

Nonprofit and Civic Capacity:

$25,157,156

Other:

$2,055,000

The Foundation has committed $100,000,000 to Detroit's Grand Bargain, to protect city pensioners and the Detroit Institute of Arts collection.

The Foundation was also the major contributor to M-1 RAIL, and has had significant involvement in working toward a regional transit system. The total amount committed to mass and regional transit is $53,325,000.

Yet Kresge had earlier agreed to fund an essentially municipal office to coordinate the city's response to foreclosures and abandonment. It had underwritten a significant portion of the cost of grants management and comprehensive land-use planning, and it was cooperating, with public and private interests, in the creation of a transit system. Purchasing city vehicles, equipment, and software was unquestionably a big step further in this direction — but the direction had already been set. These were, at least in part, emergency aid to compensate for public deficiencies and to satisfy immediate needs.

No matter; to Rapson, not everything in this period of looming catastrophe needed to aim for the fences. Instead, he saw the Foundation's multifaceted approach to Detroit — both the long-term investment and the short-term lifelines — as part of a "civic scaffolding that we believed would be necessary for Detroit's recovery over time."[34] Without taking stock of its fallow real estate, the contagion of abandonment and decay would spread. Without an equitable and rational land-use plan, the neighborhoods' strengths would wither and the city would fall ever further behind in providing them basic services. Without effective grants management, the city could lose out on hundreds of millions of dollars for which it would otherwise be eligible. And without properly equipped emergency services, population would continue to hemorrhage and a reputation for lawlessness and chaos would destroy the city's nascent appeal to new residents and businesses.

For Kresge, as Laura Trudeau, then the managing director of the Foundation's Detroit team, described it, the principle was not to set "rigid rules for what qualified for foundation support." Instead, "Kresge was looking at the longer-term trajectory for Detroit and attempting to put in place, step by step, the basic building blocks of recovery."

In that sense, rather than "scaffolding," some of Kresge's emergency support might more aptly be seen as "buttressing" — not yet a sturdy platform on which to build, but at least a prop to prevent further decay while the more strategic work slowly took effect. With resolution of Detroit's bankruptcy and a consequent modernization of its government and rationalization of its budget, the buttressing could gradually come down and more lasting, fundamental, and strategic contributions from philanthropy could then undergird a true rebuilding.

Multiple lines of intervention

By 2014, as a resolution to the bankruptcy was beginning to take shape, the contours of Re-imagining Detroit 2020 were looking more pertinent, more closely aligned with the city's prospects for recovery, than they had even when Kresge enunciated them in 2009. The bankruptcy would bring a relatively fresh start: relief from ruinous debt, the replacement of much of the city's administrative leadership with skilled technocrats, and the availability of city revenues to pay — for the first time in years — for upgraded city services and rationalized land use. With those new resources, the city had plausible grounds to hope for resurgence.

But much of that hope would depend, as Re-imagining Detroit had envisioned it five years earlier, on improved employment prospects in an environmentally sustainable economy, on rising entrepreneurship, a sensible approach to reviving neighborhoods, better transportation and education, vigorous civic and political leadership, and the nurturing of arts, culture, and the associated grace notes of urban life. These were all things in which philanthropy, prominently including The Kresge Foundation, could invest.

In November 2013, after Mayor Bing announced that he would not seek a third term, Detroit elected its 75th mayor: the former deputy county executive and Wayne County prosecutor Mike Duggan, who had left government in 2002 to spend eight years as CEO of the Detroit Medical Center. There, at the helm of one of central Detroit's anchor institutions, Duggan had engineered a dramatic turnaround, strengthening the hospital's perennially weak finances and modernizing its operations so that it could eventually be sold to Vanguard Health System, which was later acquired by Tenet Healthcare, the operator of the complex at the time this is written.

Duggan's demonstrated talent for business management recalled the fondest expectations for his predecessors Dennis Archer and Dave Bing. His experience in government, including a remarkable come-from-nowhere campaign for mayor, in which he won a place on the November ballot through a write-in campaign, suggested a level of political savvy unmatched since the rise of Coleman Young. And his experience as a prosecutor, plus a solid reputation in politics and business, seemed to promise a complete break from Detroit's recent past. Just as the bankruptcy proceeding was about to relieve the city of its debt and bureaucratic sclerosis, the election showed that voters were prepared to break with tradition as well, in hopes of a fresh start. It was becoming easier to re-imagine Detroit — financially, administratively, and politically — and, for philanthropy, easier to participate in the newly imagined city.

For Kresge, the expansive nine-part architecture of Re-imagining Detroit 2020 had not changed, but its own goals and responsibilities within that structure had clarified and focused. In four areas — **TRANSPORTATION**, the creative development of lower **WOODWARD AVENUE**, the reinvigoration of **NEIGHBORHOODS** in light of Detroit Future City, and the cultivation of a healthy environment for the **ARTS** — the Foundation had taken an especially prominent position. We explore these areas of work in more detail in the sections that follow. But Kresge also continued to invest heavily in other parts of the framework, such as economic development and education.

In promoting **ENTREPRENEURIAL DEVELOPMENT** — a mix of small business, employment, and investment growth — the Foundation invested in several organizations and funds aimed at aggregating capital for both business and real estate development. After the financial crash, Detroit's already anemic supply of capital for major development had all but dried up, and the fragmented, haphazard system for allocating what little capital was available made revitalization projects prohibitively complicated. For example, the renovation of the historic Book Cadillac hotel as a luxury property required 22 layers of financing from 17 sources — and years of planning and negotiation to line them all up. As late as 2011, according to one plaintive assessment, the city had no "predictable or replicable model for financing real estate projects." A cluster of grantmaking, advisory, and lending organizations worked on scattered, sometimes overlapping projects, though often with only limited capacity to expedite high-priority projects or to collaborate with one another. With investments drawn from both its grants budget and its core endowment, Kresge sought to strengthen the most accomplished of these sources of redevelopment lending and investment, and to draw the programs into a larger, stronger, and more streamlined source of smart, ready money.[35]

Even as the Re-imagining Detroit framework was still taking shape, Kresge and the Hudson-Webber Foundation helped transform a modest civic investment fund into Invest Detroit, now a federally certified community development financial institution (CDFI) with $225 million in managed funds and a growing share in the financing of large-scale neighborhood revitalization. Kresge's nearly $2 million in financial support, plus its sustained effort to expose the fund's managers to larger, more ambitious programs in other cities, helped transform the new institution's sense of what was possible: "We got to look outside what we're comfortable with," said Invest Detroit's CEO David Blaskiewicz, "to explore real opportunity to grow this into something substantial."

Kresge was also instrumental in recruiting Capital Impact — already a significant CDFI on the national scene and, starting in 2010, a major investor in housing, retail, and mixed-use developments in Detroit. With a substantial capital infusion from JPMorgan Chase, Capital Impact has become a central source of financing for, among other things, the burgeoning redevelopment of Midtown. Another large CDFI, Chicago-based IFF, likewise created a Detroit program with support from the Kellogg and Kresge foundations, concentrating particularly on the capital needs of organizations serving children and families.

More fundamentally, the Foundation has urged the various capital organizations into greater cooperation and consultation with one another and, through collaborative mechanisms like the Neighborhood Forum, with the rest of the revitalization universe, including city government, nonprofits, and private developers. Drawing these resources together and helping them broaden their operations in Detroit, Trudeau believes, has "augmented the ability of the city's long-standing CDFIs — LISC and Enterprise Detroit in particular — to attract enough capital to address the gigantic scale of the need."

The New Economy Initiative, begun in 2008, likewise contributed to economic growth, partly by fomenting a richer and more cohesive "ecosystem" for entrepreneurship in Detroit. It has offered information and training, and opened lines of communication, across the rapidly growing community of small and start-up businesses drawn by Detroit's research and healthcare institutions, its clusters of creative and tech-related business, and its comparatively low costs. In early 2012, the initiative launched the Detroit Regional Innovation Network, to promote coordination and harmonize services among the organizations that serve Detroit entrepreneurs. Among many other things, NEI has supported the Detroit Development Fund, a microlending program.

In **EDUCATION**, the road has been rockier, not least because of the parlous condition of the Detroit public schools — long financially insolvent, perennially near the bottom on measures of student achievement, and governed until recently by an emergency manager, with little improvement to show for it.* In September 2016, a federal class action lawsuit against the governor and Michigan education officials argued at length that many Detroit schools were not even equipping students with what it claimed was a Constitutionally required basic ability to read and write, nor "even a fighting chance" to succeed.

*DPS has been reorganized and renamed the Detroit Public School Community District, headed by an elected Board of Education that took office in January 2017.

Those schools, plaintiffs alleged, "are functionally incapable of delivering literacy access." Running throughout its 136 pages, the complaint details widespread instances of nonexistent or obsolete textbooks, classrooms without trained teachers, decrepit and unsafe buildings, extremes of heat and cold, pervasive vermin, overcrowding, and "the complete lack of any considered policy or system for the delivery of education."[36] The denial of literacy access, the complaint concluded, "creates a discrete underclass in our society." In late June 2018, Federal District Judge Stephen J. Murphy III dismissed the suit. While he agreed that learning conditions in some Detroit schools were "nothing short of devastating" and that the importance of literacy was "incalculable" he held that access to literacy was not a "fundamental right" under the Constitution and that the state was not shown to be practicing discrimination.

In 2009, the Skillman Foundation, Detroit's leading private funder for K-12 public education, convened a policy roundtable, in which Kresge participated, initially aimed at planning a coordinated public and private response to the mounting crisis in the schools. Much like the Neighborhood Forum, this education collaborative, called Excellent Schools Detroit, was meant to integrate the various school reform efforts into a coherent whole. It included the mayor and school-district leadership, public and private educators, union officials, community organizations, and funders. After a roughly yearlong planning period, the project launched as a nonprofit organization in 2010 with a goal of moonshot proportions, summarized as 90-90-90: raising the graduation rate dramatically, to 90 percent, with 90 percent of graduates going on to further education or training, and ensuring that 90 percent of those in postsecondary programs would not require remedial help to pursue their studies.

The importance of these goals is beyond dispute. But public education has been a harsh terrain for philanthropy nationwide for at least half a century, from the Ford Foundation's 1960s push for school decentralization in New York to Mark Zuckerberg's $100 million bet in 2010 on turning around public education in Newark. Through nearly all that period, even the most promising reform programs have ended up with mixed results, and known failures have outnumbered evident successes by a wide margin. Many attempts at reform, as Kresge's Managing Director Wendy Lewis Jackson puts it, "try to solve student-achievement problems through governance" — that is, they attempt to reform the leadership and decision-making structure of public education (independent school boards, mayoral control, more power for principals, community-level policymaking, etc.) as a way of changing the way teachers teach and students learn. It is a winding and unpredictable route to reform, and it often leads to disappointment.

Many efforts also focus on segments of the K-12 system, rather than on the whole bewildering continuum from early childhood through late adolescence. For example, recent efforts — particularly since the early 2000s, following a path trod by the Bill and Melinda Gates Foundation — have tended to focus on high school, with a search for better ways of keeping students enrolled and learning all the way through 12th grade and beyond. Like Gates, many funders have found this avenue frustrating, though efforts at high school reform remain popular.

Early on, Excellent Schools Detroit took both these approaches — rethinking governance and emphasizing the later grades — but it then diversified to include early childhood education and equipping parents with better information in choosing schools for their children. It also invested in human and organizational leadership, hoping to bolster education reform by supporting emerging leaders and strengthening organizations that support educational improvement. It created a handful of new initiatives, including one aimed at helping parents choose and enroll in a school, and another that helps families prepare for college testing, applications, and financial aid. Excellent Schools Detroit also established the Detroit K–12 School Scorecard, which assigns a letter grade to every school in the city, including private and charter schools.

Kresge contributed $1 million in 2012 toward the cost of establishing the organization over three years and continued to participate in its deliberations afterward, but it gradually sought other routes to improving education. Excellent Schools Detroit closed in June 2017, and several of its initiatives transferred to other organizations. However, another Skillman Foundation initiative, the Coalition for the Future of Detroit Schoolchildren, continues to function as a broad-based community voice for better schools. Kresge remains a participant in that effort, but thus far not a funder.

Even as it was supporting Excellent Schools Detroit, Kresge's analysis of where it could make the biggest difference pointed increasingly to the early years — to the time before and up to kindergarten, when children's skills and attitudes toward learning are taking shape. Although seven Detroit organizations offered Head Start programs serving nearly 7,000 children, there was no real system for ensuring that all children had equal access, or that the providers were offering consistently high-quality education. Service areas overlapped, cooperation was spotty at best, and the quality of teachers varied widely. Neither did the city have any systematic approach to the transition between Head Start and elementary school — a critical factor in determining whether the beneficial effects of Head Start continue.

With these concerns in mind, a sizable group of foundations in 2007 had banded together as the Southeast Michigan Early Childhood Funders Collaborative, mainly to compare notes and coordinate their grantmaking. But by 2013, it was clear that a larger, more focused, and more unified effort was needed, and with Kresge's encouragement the group created a Detroit Early Childhood Innovation Fund, managed by the Community Foundation for Southeast Michigan. Its main goals include improving the quality and content of early childhood programs by investing in the strongest models, promoting collaboration among them, and helping them use data more effectively to measure progress and hone their services.

Beyond an initial $1.5 million grant to launch the fund, Kresge has also hoped, in Lewis Jackson's words, "to seed the ground" by finding and supporting high-quality program models both within and outside the city, and "looking for some strategic investments, either in organizations, research, or other expertise, that could help us shape a strategy." For example, the Foundation has supported a promising project in nearby Inkster, about 20 miles downriver from Detroit, that integrates mental, physical, and emotional development with other family services. A branch has since opened in Detroit.[37]

A review of the early ground-seeding projects by the international education consultancy Parthenon-EY led to the conclusion that these embryonic initiatives formed a good basis for an expanded program. The consultants affirmed Kresge's impression that it was time to draw back from other education work and focus on birth to age 5, which is where the Foundation now concentrates. In January 2016 it announced a $20 million, five-year program, the Kresge Early Years for Success (KEYS): Detroit, that, with grants and below-market loans, invests in high-quality early childhood centers, maternal health services, and neighborhood collaborations focused on early childhood development. It also supports early childhood workers and the redesign of infrastructure that aids young children in the city. "With only 14 percent of Detroit children estimated to be kindergarten-ready and more than two-thirds living in poverty, we have a crisis that reverberates from generation to generation," Rapson said when the KEYS program was announced.[38]

In late 2016 as an extension of KEYS, Kresge and the Kellogg Foundation jointly embarked on a 10-year plan to aid the youngest of Detroit's schoolchildren. The program, called Hope Starts Here: Detroit's Early Childhood Partnership, aims to enlist parents, civic and business leaders, child health and education experts, and other interested groups to try to produce "a comprehensive early childhood development plan — a roadmap from the community for the community." The goal, Rapson said, is to "ensure children are born healthy, prepared for kindergarten, and on track for success by third grade and beyond."[39] The plan, released in November 2017, was preceded by a process that elicited ideas from some 18,000 Detroiters. With $50 million from the two foundations, it established a central coordinating body for early childhood programs citywide, aimed at boosting program quality, improving facilities, enriching teacher training, bolstering services like health screenings and parent education, and raising additional resources, among other things.

Toward the Grand Bargain

Among Kresge's larger arts grants in recent years was a multimillion-dollar commitment in 2011 to the Detroit Institute of Arts (DIA), the city's pre-eminent cultural institution, with an internationally renowned collection of more than 66,000 pieces. The grant followed a $10 million earlier commitment to help enlarge the facility, redesign the display of its art work, and sharply increase attendance. But this time, the support was intended to help the museum work its way out of a financial hole and move toward financial stability, in the run-up to an election in which voters in all three counties of the core metropolitan region would approve a temporary tax to bring the city-owned DIA back to financial health.

The 2011 grant was valuable to the museum not only as a cash infusion, but even more for the vote of confidence that it conveyed from The Kresge Foundation, other local funders, and the voters: that the museum's board and its financial recovery plan were credible and endorsed by knowledgeable and attentive backers.

Given the unimaginable wealth represented by the DIA's collection, the museum inevitably became a fixation for creditors when the city declared bankruptcy. As they scoured the parched landscape for sources to repay the city's $18 billion in aggregate debt, they found nothing to compare with the Rembrandts, Van Goghs, and Picassos lining the institute's walls. An unusual alliance of Wall Street financiers and the city's public pensioners and unions began to view liquidating the art as the only way to protect themselves from devastating losses. City retirees were being warned of 50 percent cuts to their already very modest pensions — a change that would have abruptly plunged thousands of older Detroiters into severe poverty.

Whether it was even feasible to conduct a giant art fire sale of priceless art was a matter of vigorous (ultimately unresolved) debate. But at least one conservative estimate, by Christie's, suggested that the sale of 1,700 items alone might net more than $800 million. But regardless of the economics, legal and practical issues made the prospect of an art sale dubious, and the question would probably have ended up mired in lawsuits for years, holding up the bankruptcy proceedings while the city crumbled and its creditors remained in limbo. Consequently, the court-appointed chief mediator, U.S. District Judge Gerald Rosen, set out in late 2013 to determine whether it might be possible to raise enough public and private money to place the museum's assets in trust, and use the proceeds to repay creditors while removing the DIA permanently from the city's books (and from any future municipal trouble).

"Private" support, in this case, primarily meant foundations, with additional contributions from corporations and individual donors. But the use of tax-exempt foundation dollars would mean that the only creditors to benefit from the money must be legitimate charitable beneficiaries — i.e., pensioners — not investment banks and swap insurers. Rosen's idea made excellent economic and legal sense, but it was still doubtful that foundations would contribute hundreds of millions of dollars solely to "pay for the mistakes of the past," as Darren Walker of the Ford Foundation had put it several months earlier.

Given The Kresge Foundation's prominent support for both the DIA and the city of Detroit, and its leadership in arts philanthropy nationally, one of the first people Judge Rosen consulted on the idea was Rip Rapson (they had worked and played tennis together years before in Washington). Although Rapson was skeptical that other large foundations would sign on, he was intrigued by the prospect of preserving both the DIA and the pensions — and, by extension, the city's hopes for a sustainable future — in a single stroke. He offered Rosen some tips for appealing to big out-of-town institutions like Ford, Kellogg, and Knight.

Most important, Rapson suggested, would be explaining to them how a quick end to the bankruptcy would not be a bailout. Instead, it would help launch Detroit — now equipped with vast improvements to its budget, leadership, and technology — on a realistic path to recovery. It would be, to follow Walker's maxim, a chance to "fund the future."

Local funders, Judge Rosen knew, would be easier to persuade. Mariam Noland, president of the Community Foundation for Southeast Michigan, had already expressed openness to the idea in a brief conversation with Rosen. But the larger dollars would have to come from big national endowments. In effect, although purely informally, and with no promises made, The Kresge Foundation was the first of these to entertain the prospect of large-scale support to a proposition that reporters soon christened "the Grand Bargain."

In the end, 12 foundations provided $366 million over 20 years — $100 million of that from Kresge — matched by $350 million in state aid and $100 million from the museum itself. The total came to roughly as much as Christie's had projected for a sale of hundreds of masterpieces. Though financial creditors fought the arrangement for months, it became the "cornerstone" of the city's rescue,[40] resulting in an astonishingly fast end to the bankruptcy and a real but comparatively small sacrifice by pensioners, who voted overwhelmingly to approve it.

The story of the Grand Bargain has been amply told. Its relevance here — besides the obvious significance of a $100 million Kresge grant, on top of its half-billion dollars in other support for Detroit over the preceding two decades — is that the Foundation's deep financial commitment to the museum, to the arts, and to the people of Detroit generally had made it a singular resource, and a first stop for Judge Rosen, in resolving the city's greatest crisis.

Kresge was not the largest contributor to the Grand Bargain; the Ford Foundation's share was larger, at $125 million. But relative to its asset size, Kresge's proportional commitment far outstripped that of any other national contributor. (With $3.5 billion in assets, Kresge had committed nearly 3 percent of its entire endowment to the Grand Bargain. The comparable percentage for Ford was 1 percent; for the other national participants, it was between 0.5 and 2 percent.)[41]

Because of that large commitment, bolstered by years of large-scale philanthropic "scaffolding" of the city's essential services and quality of life, Rapson was one of just three civic leaders summoned to testify in the bankruptcy trial. His testimony was intended, in part, to assure the court that philanthropic support for Detroit would not end with the Grand Bargain. "As you sit here today, is it your belief that The Kresge Foundation would continue providing funding and support as its done in the past for the City of Detroit?" Rapson was asked at the trial. "Yes," he confirmed, "although it might take very different form."[42]

All in

The Kresge Foundation was established with a broad, national mission. Despite a special regard for the city where Sebastian S. Kresge made his retail fortune and a long record of support for major projects in Detroit, the Foundation did not, until the mid-1990s, have resources exclusively earmarked for the city. Nor did it, until after 2006, insert itself into any overall civic strategy for Detroit's well-being — or, as Rapson put it in 2009, undertake to "change the trajectory of Detroit" with the limited resources at its disposal. At the time of that statement, Detroit's city government was spending more in one year than the Foundation held in its whole endowment.[43]

The decision to shift from backing discrete capital projects toward "taking on [an] entire" city, as Rapson had put it in a 2008 speech, had been nothing short of audacious — especially considering that 80 percent of the Foundation's spending continued to be devoted to national programs extending far beyond southeastern Michigan. In that light, the boldness of the Grand Bargain seems like a big step up in degree, but not profoundly different in kind, from what was already by then a six-year-long, full-bore Kresge commitment to Detroit's turnaround.

The full measure of that commitment is manifest not only in its scope, measured by the amounts of money involved, but in its granularity — the degree to which Foundation staff personally immersed themselves in the day-to-day forging of coalitions, interaction with partners, managing of special funds and initiatives, and the smoothing of roadblocks and rough patches as major programs and projects rolled out. The next four chapters illustrate both the breadth and the detail of Kresge's involvement in four aspects of its Detroit grantmaking: the lower Woodward Corridor, neighborhood development, transportation, and the arts. But the principles of expansive involvement and ground-level participation are not particular to these four lines of work. They are the soul of the Foundation's Detroit program.

And just as the dollar amounts do not fully capture the expansiveness of Kresge's effort — the largest commitment to Detroit of any foundation anywhere — they also do not describe the enormity of its risks: not just risks to the Foundation's budget, but to its reputation and its relationships with other major players in Detroit. The involvement, in a poor city, of a large foundation with hundreds of millions of dollars a year, headquartered in a tony suburb (the Foundation opened a Midtown Detroit office in 2012), known for its distinctively sleek communications and expert media relations, is bound to provoke suspicions and resentments among less-advantaged organizations and leaders.

When, in an informal conversation, one local foundation executive referred to Kresge as the "big dog" in Detroit philanthropy, the phrase seemed to convey equal portions of respect and mistrust. Serial city administrations have struggled to assert the independence of their judgment and choices, even as they sought Kresge support and cooperated in Foundation initiatives with which they couldn't help but agree. Just as inevitably, some city officials have failed to win the Foundation's confidence for one or another of their initiatives, or have dissented from some Kresge project, and ill feelings have flared as a consequence.

No foundation would welcome these tensions (much less a national headline like the one in the Wall Street Journal in 2011[44], explicitly pitting the Foundation CEO against the mayor). But, for Kresge, they are all but unavoidable. Detroit political and civic affairs have been so fractious for so long, and the fractiousness has so undermined progress, that it would arguably be irresponsible for a "big dog" not to assert a unifying vision, to rally other funders, to insert itself into struggling but necessary projects, and to make its case for overall social and economic development as forcefully and creatively as it can.

In Detroit's constantly roiling politics of downtown vs. neighborhoods, wealthy investors vs. low-income residents, suburbs vs. city, longtimers vs. newcomers, and the ever-present divisions of race and ethnicity, a philanthropic voice can be essential in building trust and alliances. But performing that role year after year takes forcefulness, tenacity, thick skin, and self-assurance, traits that are bound to strike some other local leaders as impertinent, even aggressive. Foundation officers and trustees have had to manage that risk, along with all the others that normally attach to any kind of strategic grantmaking. Along the way, they've had to ease hard feelings as much as possible when they arise.

At the end of this book, we will consider the advantages and perils of Kresge's all-in approach to Detroit's recovery. First, though, it will help to see that approach in action, in four of the Foundation's most ambitious and long-standing areas of work.

ONE WAY
SPEED LIMIT 25

Chapter 2

THE WOODWARD CORRIDOR: FROM DOWNTOWN TO MIDTOWN

"When push comes to shove, you cannot revitalize the regional economy without focusing your energies along Woodward Avenue, the region's central nervous system."

— Rip Rapson, Detroit News, June 30, 2009

Detroit's Thanksgiving Day Parade takes place down historic Woodward Avenue, a holiday tradition that dates to 1924. Photo Credit: The Parade Company/Mark Houston

Woodward Avenue — broad and history-laden, the first paved road in Michigan, a federally designated "All-American Road" — is often called "the spine of Detroit." From the Detroit River, it runs 25 miles north-northwesterly, across the city border at 8 Mile Road and deep into suburbs that were open fields when the city was an industrial powerhouse. Back then, the Woodward Corridor between downtown and New Center was a place where mansions were aplenty and Henry Ford could turn out the Model-T and Sebastian Kresge could jump-start a business empire with his first five-and-dime store.

That was then. Like the city of which it is the center cut, the Woodward Corridor began eroding decades ago. Symbolic of this "abandonment iceberg," as Wayne State University's George Galster put it, was the closing of the majestic J.L. Hudson department store in 1983 and its demolition in 1998. Mindful of where money and people were headed, Hudson's had opened another store in a pioneering suburban mall as early as 1954. Downtown Detroit, at night, Galster wrote, had acquired "an eerie quality," with "haunting shapes" passing by "a few furtive pedestrians. Indeed, as the city was preparing to host Super Bowl XL in 2006, it arranged to have lights installed behind selected windows of many vacant towers to give naïve visitors a different impression: Detroit as Potemkin Village, Detroit as façade-omy."[45]

Mike Duggan, who was a member of the Super Bowl planning committee and would become Detroit's mayor in 2013, remembered that "we painted over those empty storefronts on Woodward so visitors would think they were occupied."[46] In "acts of self-preservation," the University of Michigan urbanist June Manning Thomas recalled, the city had committed to such projects as stadiums and casinos, but these "strategies were palliative at best and could not help central cities remain viable, and surely they did not 'save' central-city Detroit."[47]

A widely circulated article by Ze'ev Chafets in the New York Times Magazine in 1990 had the headline "The Tragedy of Detroit."[48] Nineteen years later, a cover story in Time carried the same headline.[49] But for all the legitimate despair about Detroit as a whole — and despite the city's bankruptcy in

2013 — conditions in the downtown district, and north along the Woodward Corridor, changed radically in the years since the Super Bowl. And The Kresge Foundation was very much a part of that improvement, starting where the Corridor starts.

—

In the 1990s, and well into the early 2000s, the East Riverfront, facing Canada, was a postindustrial wasteland defined by empty warehouses and glass-strewn parking lots. The three small, uninviting parks facing the river were largely inaccessible: hard to find and harder to get to. The city had long eyed the area for recreation or housing and, in 1998, it rezoned 57 acres of riverfront for casinos. But the casinos went elsewhere in the city.

Kresge took on this neglect in 2002 with a $50 million grant, as the largest driver in remaking what Rip Rapson later called "Detroit's front porch."[50] The idea was to convert 5½ miles of the riverfront to public use as a promenade and parkland with prospects for residential and commercial activity, all the while improving the city's image and encouraging economic development downtown. Joining Kresge in this effort were the city and General Motors, whose towering, fortresslike Renaissance Center, its world headquarters, was both by the river and walled off from it. GM had already spent $500 million to open this area to pedestrians and redesign 3,000 feet of open space between its complex and the river.

In 2003 the nonprofit Detroit Riverfront Conservancy was set up to guide the rest of the transformation. Its first phase of work, along 3½ miles to the east of Joe Louis Arena, has been the handsomely landscaped RiverWalk, used by walkers, joggers, bikers, picnickers, and others, with year-round programs ranging from birding and readings to "Kids Fishing Fest" and sandlot volleyball. RiverWalk attracts three million visitors a year and a 2013 study, according to Kresge, found it had already catalyzed $639 million in investment.[51] It is not without issues, however, and, as often is the case in Detroit and elsewhere, some carry a whiff of race or class. One middle-aged black woman described RiverWalk as "an absolute plus for the city" but largely one for "the new Detroit" — including downtown-based professionals who are put off by "baggy-pantsed, loud-talking boys from the 'hood.' It's quite a balancing act," she said.[52]

Whether east or west, from east of the MacArthur Bridge that links to Belle Isle to the Ambassador Bridge leading to Windsor, Ontario, the five-mile riverfront is still a work in progress, with the Conservancy soliciting a team of experts to advise on future development. Orleans Landing, the riverfront's first mixed-use, mixed-income housing project, nearly 300 units, opened in 2017. The riverfront is also home to the southern end of a two-mile paved trail, the Dequindre

Above Left: Rivard Plaza, on Detroit's riverfront, before development. Photo Credit: Detroit Riverfront Conservancy

Above Right: Public space renovation of surface parking lots that once lined the Detroit riverfront in front of GM's World Headquarters, now part of the RiverWalk created and managed by the Detroit Riverfront Conservancy. Photo Credit: Detroit Riverfront Conservancy

Cut, inspired by the "rail-to-trail" movement. It is part of an evolving network of nonmotorized greenways in Detroit and its suburbs, led by the Community Foundation for Southeast Michigan and supported by Kresge. The 20-foot-wide Cut, a line of the Grand Trunk Railroad until the 1980s, sunk 25 feet below street level, is a key leg of the greenways system in the Woodward Corridor. When it opened in 2009, with separate lanes for hundreds of cyclists and pedestrians on weekdays and thousands on weekends, decades of graffiti and "urban artwork" were deliberately retained on bridge abutments.

The northern terminus of the Cut was recently extended to reach the Eastern Market district, a cluster of open-air food sheds, warehouses, businesses, and galleries abutting vacant, formerly residential land. The centerpiece of the district is the market itself, opened in 1891 and covering six blocks, the largest outdoor farmers market in the country, combining wholesale and retail sales, meatpacking, and farm-grown produce from the surrounding area and community gardens in one location. It, too, has been the beneficiary of Kresge support, critically in 2006.

Thriving until the 1960s, with devoted shoppers of all ages patronizing it on Saturdays, the city-owned market accompanied Detroit into steep decline by the 1990s. Its historic sheds, housing hundreds of open-air stalls, were in disrepair. Some customers who had left for the suburbs found it easier, or cheaper, to buy closer to home. Others questioned the freshness of fruits and vegetables at the market, where some vendors had taken to selling wilted, overripe produce brought from elsewhere, even from abroad. But the larger problem, recounted by John Gallagher in his 2013 book, "Revolution Detroit," was the inability of the financially ailing city "to give Eastern Market the attention it needed. The diminished police protection, the lack of city services, the inability or unwillingness to pay for normal upkeep at the market — all these took their toll. Bureaucracy at City Hall, where control of Eastern Market shuffled from one department to another, proved debilitating."[53]

Community leaders proposed to replace city management of the market with a professionally staffed, nonprofit public authority, as at the Riverfront Conservancy. The city would still own the market; it just wouldn't operate it. Municipal unions vigorously opposed the move, as did their allies on the City Council. The replacement agreement went through some 37 rewritings and rancorous debate. Former Council Member Sheila Cockrel later recalled the debate as "one of those, you know, 'Where do you live, who are you, this is a city jewel, we can't be giving away city jewels.' It was the wrong conversation."

But in July 2006, Kresge forced the issue by threatening to withdraw a $2 million grant in aid of a new authority. With the clock winding down, the Eastern Market Corp. was approved by a Council vote of 8 to 1. Some departing city workers demonstrated their anger by getting into the market's office and shredding vendor leases, purchasing and payroll data, and other key records.[54] Since then, the corporation has received more than $22 million in philanthropic support, from the W.K. Kellogg Foundation, the McGregor Fund, the Ford Foundation, Kresge, and others.

Kresge's contributions to the corporation have helped to renovate the sheds and establish a community kitchen for cooking demonstrations, seminars on healthful eating, and nutrition classes. Dan Carmody, who has been CEO of the market for a decade, has broadened his mission to include a resurgence of fresh food availability "for everyone" in Detroit and southeast Michigan, "top to bottom."[55]

Kresge's interest in the greening of Detroit extended also to Campus Martius Park, a popular, 2.5-acre oasis in the commercial center of downtown, at Woodward Avenue. Previously known as Kennedy Square, it was in a forlorn state in the 1990s, with a cracked concrete base and a fountain that didn't work. To transform the park, Kresge put up $3 million, or 15 percent of the funds needed for construction and maintenance. Corporations, many doing business in the area, contributed in celebration of the 300th anniversary of Detroit's founding in 2001. Again, a nonprofit organization, the Detroit 300 Conservancy, was formed to manage the site for the city in 2005. Today, this public park is promoted as the city's "gathering place," a relaxing spot for lunch on the lawns, and for events around the year, including a faux beach in summer and an ice-skating rink in winter.

The 300 Conservancy is now a subsidiary of the Downtown Detroit Partnership, a public-private entity for which Kresge supplies operating support, alongside nearly the full roster of local funders. Through a Business Improvement District and other means, the partnership underwrites clean and safe areas downtown, supports graffiti removal and power-washed streets and sidewalks, and encourages redevelopment. It is also helping to link downtown to the bike and trail network around it. Similarly, Kresge poured $12.5 million into a new Fund for Downtown Public Spaces, including $10 million for an endowment. With an additional $7 million, Kresge backed the $20 million Lower Woodward Housing Fund, providing gap financing for redevelopment and conversion of downtown buildings to residential use. The latter fund was among 17 sources of financing for redevelopment of the venerable Book Cadillac hotel, which had been shuttered for 20 years before reopening in 2008 as the high end of Detroit hotelry. Kresge also donated $7.5 million for a new building for the Downtown YMCA and, for the first time in its capital challenge program, put the money on the front end.

More illustrative of Kresge's new direction under Rapson — its determination to focus on economic and social issues rather than only on buildings — was its decision in 2007 to join nine other foundations in creating what grew to be the $130 million New Economy Initiative (NEI) for Detroit, the largest such fund in the country, according to Rapson. Kresge matched $25 million in commitments by the Ford and Kellogg foundations, with lesser amounts coming from others. The aim of the fund was to "accelerate the transition of the Detroit region's economy from its industrial past to a future based on innovation," and it helped spur new companies, patents, and jobs.[56] But NEI was also "a learning experience" for foundations trying to work in concert, and on projects throughout southeast Michigan. "The result was a portfolio of activities that stretched across a wide range of economic issues from workforce to entrepreneurship to culture change. NEI's capital was stretched thin, and competing priorities were wearing on the cohesiveness of the coalition," Kresge reported.[57]

By 2013 NEI had reoriented, emphasizing "efforts to drive entrepreneurial activity in Detroit," increasingly in neighborhoods outside the Woodward Corridor, and supporting everything from seed capital and affordable space to back-office operations and mentoring. In 2014, it established NEIdeas, awarding grants of $10,000 to $100,000 to existing city businesses wanting to scale up, from produce growers and printers to cafes and barber shops. When, to his surprise, 60-year-old Robert Long won an NEI grant, he was poised to add services at his West Side barbershop — repairing clippers, sharpening tools, cleaning athletic shoes, selling shoestrings and socks. "I'll make it like a boutique," he said.[58]

—

Kresge and other foundations clearly stimulated the post-recession transformation of the downtown core, creating what Laura Trudeau, who retired in 2016 as managing director of Kresge's Detroit team, called "building blocks" that helped make it attractive for investment. Kresge "helped create the narrative," said Olga Stella, a former executive of the Detroit Economic Growth Corp. who now leads Design Core Detroit.[59]

Yet for all the earlier philanthropic efforts, and for whatever contribution the beleaguered city could make, the revival of central downtown after 2010 was largely a result of private capital, particularly the dramatic infusion by the Quicken Loans owner Dan Gilbert. Gilbert was not first or alone: Compuware had relocated downtown, with 4,000 employees in a new building, in 2003. But in 2010, Gilbert — with his eye on cheap real estate and the urban lifestyle favored by many young, tech-oriented workers — set the pace anew when moving his online mortgage company's headquarters from Detroit's suburbs to downtown, where ubiquitous "coming soon" signs had been mocked. By 2017, with other businesses, restaurants, and shops following, he owned or controlled through leases some 100 properties in the square-mile district, making him one of the largest landowners in the city.[60]

Through his investment in Rocket Fiber, Gilbert has also brought extremely high speed internet to downtown. Some 17,000 of his employees now work there and, while many return to the suburbs at night, a growing number have chosen to rent or buy downtown or nearby. One result is to drive up housing prices to the point where they can make the numbers work for investment in new construction, thought they also spike concerns about the economic and social costs of gentrification.

Gilbert continues to be criticized by some for the private security operation he installed downtown, with surveillance monitors, to protect his buildings. But others are just as apt to say that he and fellow business and civic leaders have bolstered tax revenues, made downtown safer and brighter — "it's lit up at night!" marveled Rachel Lutz, a fourth-generation Detroiter — and everyone acknowledges that street traffic is vastly greater than only a few years ago. One enthusiast is Rip Rapson. He credited Gilbert's "single-handed revitalization of the central business district, at a level of ambition that may be unprecedented in modern America."[61]

Gilbert is hardly finished. In April 2016, he floated plans to build a billion-dollar professional soccer stadium and entertainment complex on the site of the partly built and idle Wayne County jail building on Gratiot and St. Antoine in downtown Detroit. The jail project, for which ground was broken in 2011, was halted in 2013 because of concerns over cost overruns. "Fail jail," it was popularly nicknamed. Within hours of Gilbert's proposal, county officials reiterated their determination to see the jail project to completion — with some $150 million already spent (covered by bonds), monthly expenses of $1.2 million, and no clear path forward. Only a month later, however, County Executive Warren Evans said he was open to reconsidering a "financially viable and timely" offer from Gilbert and his would-be partner, Pistons' owner Tom Gores, to purchase the site for a soccer arena, thus allowing the jail to be built elsewhere.[62] After much back and forth, a soccer team ultimately seemed to be headed to Ford Field instead of the jail site, but Gilbert's plans for a major mixed-used development on that site still appear to be moving forward. The jail will be relocated to a site near I-75 and Warren Ave.[63] A soccer franchise at Ford Field would make four professional sports teams playing in about a four-mile radius.

Gilbert has other plans in the area, including a boutique hotel in partnership with high-end retailer Shinola. Just northeast of downtown, where 98 percent of available rental units are occupied, Gilbert and other investors have begun construction on several hundred residential units[64] — 20 percent of them affordable for families with incomes of around $50,000 or less[65] — in largely decimated Brush Park. The project has been named "City Modern." Four of 70 mansions that once graced the area, home to such Detroit luminaries as David Whitney, Albert Kahn, and J.L. Hudson, would be restored.

Across the way, on the west side of Woodward Avenue, Ilitch Holdings has undertaken a so-called Detroit District of apartments, offices, entertainment venues, shops, and parks around Little Caesars Arena, the $863 million new home for the company's Red Wings hockey team, where play began in late 2017. All of this development presses against idiosyncratic, culture-rich Midtown, the two-square-mile Corridor area north of downtown — an area that, while changing with the times, seeks to retain its welcoming scale and livability. And here, as it both fortifies Midtown and searches for lessons applicable elsewhere in Detroit, Kresge has been as active as anywhere in the city. In 2012, when the Troy-based foundation opened a satellite office for its Detroit program, it was in the heart of Midtown.

If Dan Gilbert is synonymous with the turnaround of downtown, the same can be said, in Midtown, of the indefatigable Sue Mosey, the executive director of Midtown Detroit Inc. (MDI) and, in common parlance, the unofficial "mayor of Midtown." Mosey has few greater admirers than Rip Rapson, who in a 2015 interview in the Free Press cited her "skill and tenacity, honed over a quarter-century of selfless effort."[66] And she has few closer working partners than Kresge, which has given more than $10.6

million to what it called "the City's most effective nonprofit development entity."[67] Mosey, who went into community organizing in Southwest Detroit after graduating from Wayne State, returned to Midtown in 1987 as head of a small nonprofit with ambitions for community development, the University Cultural Center Association. The association, and the New Center Council, merged in 2011 into MDI.

Historically, Midtown — bounded by the Fisher, Chrysler, Lodge, and Ford freeways and including a long-derelict but now trendy strip known as the Cass Corridor — was an eclectic area, with imposing institutions like the Detroit Institute of Arts and the central branch of the Detroit Public Library on its northern edge, and SROs, drug dealing, and frequent prostitution on its south, around lower Cass Avenue. The worst conditions, if not the pockets of grittiness, are largely gone. But "even in the worst of times," Mosey said, Midtown "had a whole artist and university community, a Bohemian kind of cachet to it ... a melting pot of crazy diversity of all types."[68]

Apart from thousands of transient workers and students, that pot has gotten smaller, at least until recently. Having already suffered stark population losses, like the city generally, Midtown lost another 23 percent between 2000 and 2013, leaving it with an estimated 13,000 residents and a poverty rate of 41 percent, slightly higher than the city's at that time.[69] In 2014, in a city where some 83 percent of the residents were then African-American[70], the proportion in Midtown was estimated at 63 percent.[71]

To Kresge, Midtown was "the vital center of the region." Working with MDI, which it helped quadruple in staff and budget, the Foundation has zeroed in on Midtown since 2008, undertaking a range of investments and incentives to "upgrade the built environment" — much housing stock had withered — and to "attract residents, businesses, and visitors while improving the quality of life."[72]

"It really accelerated after Rip got here and set up this whole Detroit team," said Mosey.[73] In 2010, with the backing of Kresge and the Skillman Foundation, the urban revitalization collaborative Living Cities chose Detroit as one of five cities on which to concentrate resources in its new "Integration Initiative" to knit together policies and operating systems of various institutions contributing to urban development. In Detroit, Midtown was the focus, with Living Cities assembling some $24 million in grants, commercial loans, and program-related investments. "Woodward Creative Corridor" and "Innovation District" became bywords for a spectrum of philanthropic activity in Midtown. In 2011, Kresge and the Hudson-Webber Foundation retained U3 Ventures, now U3 Advisors, to design an "anchor strategy," bringing together such insular Midtown mainstays as Wayne State University, the Detroit Medical Center, and the Henry Ford Health System into a coordinated working relationship that would benefit all of Midtown.

One product of that strategy was a five-year Live Midtown program. Under the program, new homebuyers working for the anchor institutions could qualify for a forgivable $20,000 loan; first-time renters, $2,500; and existing renters, $1,000 toward lease renewal. Up to $5,000 was available to homeowners for exterior improvements. The program drew more than 1,000 new residents to Midtown — 40 percent of whom were black, 30 percent white, 20 percent Asian, and 10 percent Hispanic — with half the residents making less than $50,000 a year. "It was a really nice mix," said Mosey.[74] The residential program was regarded as so successful that it was replicated by employers downtown. However, a three-year pilot effort in Midtown to promote local buying of goods and hiring by the anchors was less well-defined and had mixed results.

Consistent with its new direction in 2008 and as part of that emerging "creative corridor" along Woodward and Cass, Kresge helped capitalize "at a critical early window" Midtown's Tech Town, a research, business, and technology incubator — grants significantly supplemented by NEI. Tech Town, started by Wayne State University in a vacant building on the northern edge of campus, is a major feature of a plan to convert a depleted 12-block section of Midtown into a state-of-the-art "entrepreneurial ecosystem," economically and culturally.

Across from Tech Town, Next Energy, an alternative energy developer, is another Kresge grantee. So, too, is the nearby second campus of the College for Creative Studies. In 2008, Kresge contributed $4 million to help transform a landmark GM building, the Argonaut, into a home for the college's new Master of Fine Arts program, design departments, student housing, community arts activities — and a charter school. Further down the Corridor, Kresge supported the new Detroit Center for Design + Technology, an urban unit of Southfield-based Lawrence Technological University. The center, opened in 2015, is anchor tenant of an $11.5 million mixed-use development at Woodward and Willis avenues, spearheaded by Midtown Detroit Inc.

Kresge is the lead donor to another Wayne State program, Detroit Revitalization Fellows, to seed myriad nonprofit organizations with young, midcareer professionals from around the country. The $2 million-a-year program, also funded by Ford, Hudson-Webber and other foundations, was inspired by the John S. and James L. Knight Foundation's CUREx Fellowships (Center for Urban Redevelopment Excellence), based at the University of Pennsylvania. The Rockefeller Foundation later worked with CUREx to send 25 fellows to help in redeveloping post-Katrina New Orleans. "We'll steal ideas from anywhere," said Rip Rapson. Since 2011, when the Detroit program started, 93 fellows have been chosen from some 2,055 applicants. Fellows receive a two-year salary, partly supported by the organization in which they are placed, for which they engage in "real-time, practical problem solving" while building their skills and careers. They address such issues as open data and technology, transit and mobility, homelessness assistance, neighborhood and youth development, public health, community engagement, place-making, and riverfront renewal.

"We're giving city organizations an opportunity to think about leadership in a different way," said Graig Donnelly, a WSU official who has directed the program. "Our fellows are diverse in what they do, the places they're from, their work and life experience, age, race, and culture. What they all have in common is that they could be doing this work anywhere. They choose to do it in Detroit."[75] In 2015, the program was

Above and on next page: Midtown's Tech Town, a research, business, and technology incubator. Photo Credit: Julianne Lindsey

augmented by the Kresge Mayor's Fellowship, which, through a competitive process, assigns to the mayor's office several Revitalization Fellows who have completed their two-year term. Kresge hoped that alumni of the program would remain in Detroit, providing an "exponential impact" for the city. And that has generally been the case: Of the first cohort of fellows, 80 percent stayed in Detroit; of the second, 85 percent. In each of those two cohorts, half kept to their jobs after the fellowships expired.[76]

—

In addition to its other concerns, from beautifying streets and parks to operating the nationally acclaimed Inn on Ferry Street to organizing arts festivals with Kresge's support, Midtown Detroit Inc. tries to ensure safety in the area — and that requires working with the Wayne State University police. Between 2009 and 2016, violent crime in Midtown fell 51 percent; property crime, 56 percent.[77] Erica Raleigh, executive director of Data Driven Detroit, recalled that when she lived just across from WSU a decade ago: "I wouldn't go out after 10 p.m. Now I would walk around there at midnight. It's different. You can feel it. It's the stores, the bars, the presence of people."[78] Much of the credit for the decline in crime, for the heightened sense of security by old-timers and newcomers alike, is given to the WSU force, whose officers — all with bachelor's degrees — are fully commissioned by the Detroit Police Department and have the same enforcement powers as city police. Stories abound of the WSU police's responding within minutes, if not seconds, to a call. Chief Anthony Holt likes to say that when a call comes in and an officer remains in the station, "there must be a crime here in the station."[79]

A mile south of the WSU police station, on the southeast corner of Cass and Canfield, is the Auburn Building, opened in 2013 with 9,000 square feet of locally owned bookstore, design, and other businesses, topped by 58 mixed-income rental apartments. The Auburn "activated that block" and catalyzed development around it, said Benjamin S. Kennedy, managing director of Kresge's Detroit program and head of the Foundation's American Cities Practice. On the block of Canfield to the west of the Auburn, Shinola, the luxury watch, bicycle, and leather goods maker, opened its flagship store in an abandoned Willys Overland building. It was soon joined on the block by the likes of Third Man Records and the Jolly Pumpkin brewery, where President Barack Obama inaugurated the "Obamaburger" (7 oz. patty, cheddar cheese, lettuce, tomato, Dijon mustard, hold the mushrooms) when he visited Detroit in January 2016 for the automobile show. Shinola executives have made much of the company's faith in "comeback" Detroit, and the company is routinely praised for the quality of its products and the jobs it brings. But some refrain from the hoopla, deriding Shinola's presence as a marker of unwanted gentrification, unswayed by the company's efforts at neighborhood outreach, such as its co-sponsorship of a much-used enclosed dog park on the corner.

To Kresge, the Auburn Building and its effect on Midtown embody a replicable achievement in collaborative financing, something the Foundation had been after for years. Even when helping to win the Living Cities "Integration Initiative" in 2010, Kresge recognized that Detroit lacked a robust finance system for housing and economic development, including important community development financial institutions (CDFIs). These were institutions with muscle and flexibility, relied upon by the U.S. Treasury as conduits for capital and tax credit allocations to low-income communities. In 2011, Kresge persuaded Invest Detroit to secure CDFI status.

Following page: Rip Rapson's drawing of midtown Detroit, with potential grantmaking opportunities, capitalizing on its existing assets.

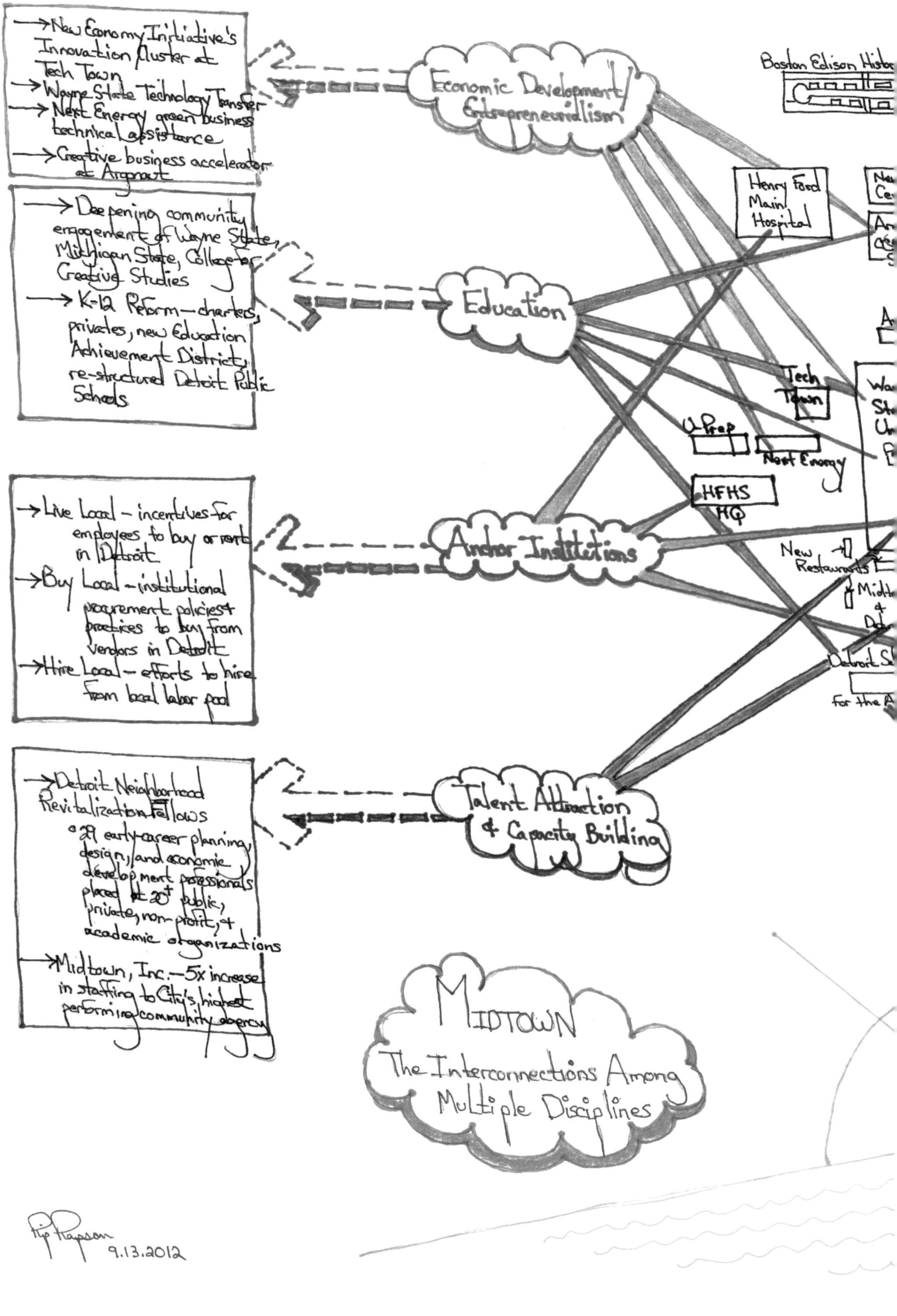
→New Economy Initiative's Innovation Cluster at Tech Town
→Wayne State Technology Transfer
→Next Energy green business technical assistance
→Creative business accelerator at Argonaut
Economic Development/ Entrepreneurialism
→Deepening community engagement of Wayne State, Michigan State, College for Creative Studies
→K-12 Reform—charters, privates, new Education Achievement District, re-structured Detroit Public Schools
Education
→Live Local - incentives for employees to buy or rent in Detroit
→Buy Local - institutional procurement policies & practices to buy from vendors in Detroit
→Hire Local - efforts to hire from local labor pool
Anchor Institutions
→Detroit Neighborhood Revitalization Fellows
29 early-career planning, design, and economic development professionals placed at 20+ public, private, non-profit, & academic organizations
→Midtown, Inc.—5x increase in staffing to City's highest performing community agency
Talent Attraction & Capacity Building
Boston Edison Histo
Henry Ford Main Hospital
Tech Town
U Prep
Next Energy
HFHS HQ
New Restaurants
for the A
MIDTOWN
The Interconnections Among Multiple Disciplines
Pip Rapson
9.13.2012

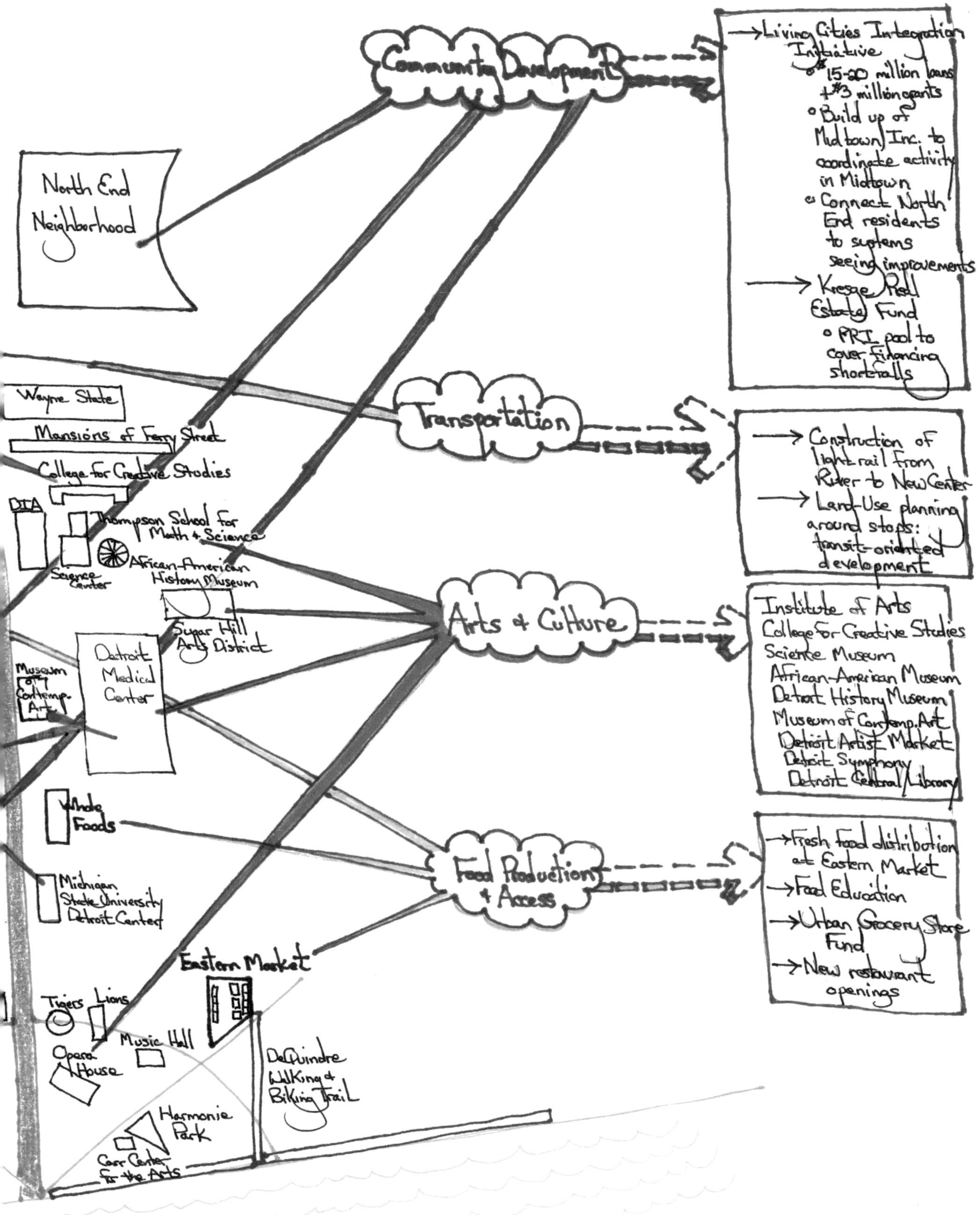

Community Development
Living Cities Integration Initiative
15-20 million loans + $3 million grants
Build up of Midtown, Inc. to coordinate activity in Midtown
Connect North End residents to systems seeing improvements
Kresge Real Estate Fund
PRI pool to cover financing shortfalls
North End Neighborhood
Transportation
Construction of light rail from River to New Center
Land-Use planning around stops: transit-oriented development
Wayne State
Mansions of Ferry Street
College for Creative Studies
DIA
Thompson School for Math & Science
Science Center
African-American History Museum
Sugar Hill Arts District
Arts & Culture
Institute of Arts
College for Creative Studies
Science Museum
African-American Museum
Detroit History Museum
Museum of Contemp. Art
Detroit Artist Market
Detroit Symphony
Detroit Central Library
Museum of Contemp. Art
Detroit Medical Center
Whole Foods
Michigan State University Detroit Center
Food Production & Access
Fresh food distribution at Eastern Market
Food Education
Urban Grocery Store Fund
New restaurant openings
Eastern Market
Tigers
Lions
Music Hall
Opera House
DeQuindre Walking & Biking Trail
Harmonie Park
Carr Center for the Arts

Capital Impact Partners, a national CDFI working with Living Cities in Detroit and focusing on the design and the volume of capital for local development, established an office in the city in 2014, with significant operating support from Kresge. The Foundation also assembled its signature investment vehicle, the Woodward Corridor Investment Fund, with more than $30 million managed by Capital Impact Partners. While protecting investors, the fund aggregates early-stage capital not available through traditional means for "mixed use, mixed income, transit-oriented" projects that "promote density, diversity, vibrancy and walkability in the city's core."[80] The two leading funders for the Auburn project were Invest Detroit and Capital Impact Partners.

For sure, amid hot new commercial successes like the Hopcat pub and Chartreuse restaurant and Peacock Room vintage apparel shop, there are still venerable local establishments like Detroit Hardware (1924), Mario's restaurant (1948), and Fred's Key Shop (1962). But the mix of patrons, including the vaunted "creative class" that is superseding a previous generation of Midtown artists, is inevitably changing — as are prices. In every direction in Midtown, including areas west of Cass that would not have been touched by developers only several years ago, residential buildings are being constructed, or restored. And many of the rehabs are remnants of Detroit's glory days. Such is the once-elegant Forest Arms, built in 1905 as the largest apartment building in the Corridor and uninhabitable for a decade. Again, Capital Impact Partners and Invest Detroit are helping bring it back, and so is Kresge, which, through MDI, contributed critical funding for a new roof. When the Rainer Court apartments opened on West Alexandrine in 2015, Mayor Mike Duggan marveled that he had long run the Detroit Medical Center "down at the other end of the street, and this area was 40 percent vacant 10 years ago. Now you look at the transformation, it's remarkable."[81]

According to Kresge, 37 percent of the thousand new or renovated apartment units that came on line in Midtown between 2010 and June 2015 were "affordable" by federal standards. Some 22 percent of the dwelling units then in the pipeline met the same criterion.[82] Affordability is a regular

Above: Opening day of the Whole Foods Market in Midtown Detroit, June 5, 2013. Photo Credit: Whole Foods Market

concern of the Foundation's Detroit team. "We see the need to preserve a strong element of affordability in Midtown and discourage the kind of exclusive residential development that pushes out longstanding residents," the team wrote in 2015.[83] Yet, as with the Shinola dissenters, some Detroiters remain uncomfortable, citing what one well-placed observer said were "episodes of displacement that have been extremely contentious and fraught with anxiety. ... To whom and for what is all this economic development happening?" Even more fundamental than displacement, he added, was whether someone would have "access within a reasonable arm's length of this place, if he or she wanted to live in this area."[84]

—

In September 2015 Kresge's Detroit team concluded that, although "we can safely wind down certain grant support" in downtown, "we feel continuing foundation investment in Midtown remains a high priority" in coming years.[85] That investment will likely extend to Sue Mosey's latest move along the Woodward Corridor, immediately north of Midtown in the New Center neighborhood, where the Fisher Building's gold dome is a Detroit landmark. In June 2015, with financing by the usual CDFIs and others, MDI purchased 11 buildings in New Center, on Woodward and West Grand Boulevard. Mosey envisions a mixed-use development of retail, multifamily residences, and perhaps a boutique hotel. Private investors have meanwhile purchased the Fisher and nearby Kahn buildings, with plans for massive renovations. "The Next Hot Detroit Neighborhood," Forbes magazine quickly labeled New Center, which is now the northern terminus of the Kresge-initiated M-1 light rail line. Prospective tenants in New Center, a Kresge official gleefully forecast, "will blow your mind."

Actually, some minds were blown four years ago in Midtown, when the "Holy Grail of urban revitalization," as historian Thomas Sugrue put it, arrived.[86] Whole Foods opened its first Detroit store in a 20,000-square-foot building at Mack and John R, in a low- to middle-income area off Woodward. The lines were out the door that day. Within a year, the store exceeded revenue projections for a decade and it is still thriving.[87] At opening, 72 percent of its employees lived in Detroit; 120 of its products were made in Detroit. "I love it," said Lauren Hood, a black woman who co-directed the "Live6 Alliance" in northwest Detroit but lives near Whole Foods. "It's full of black people, customers, and workers."[88] Brad Frost, who was white and a former Detroit Revitalization Fellow who became head of the Woodward Corridor Initiative, described the store as "one of the best successes in the city, inclusive of Detroit's demographic."[89] (Frost died of kidney cancer in 2017, at age 35, a loss to the city of immense talent, energy, and promise.)

Walter Robb, Whole Foods co-president at the time, explained that, with Detroit "at an inflection point" but losing several hundred million dollars annually from city residents who grocery shopped in the suburbs, his company was eager to confront "the disconnect between accessibility and affordability in healthy food."[90]

Among others who pushed for the store, Robb told civic leaders at the Detroit Economic Club in 2012, was "the relentless, relentless, relentless" Sue Mosey, Kresge's Midtown district steward. Robb, who later also praised Kresge for its "commitment to the re-emergence of Detroit — their focus, their passion, and their follow-through,"[91] acknowledged that Whole Foods had "benefited indirectly" from incentives to open in Detroit. Kresge, through the Detroit Economic Growth Corp.'s Green Grocer Project, had provided $750,000, with no payback provision, to the developer, Ram Real Estate, to defray rent at the store site, given a more down-market location than usual for Whole Foods.

It was "a huge leap of faith," according to Rapson. "I suspect some of you may ask why in the world we would do that, when they were perfectly capable of paying their own way," Rapson reflected in a speech in 2015. "But they completely retooled their model. They recreated their price points. They created different products. They downsized and, actually, it has become a model that Whole Foods has now taken to Chicago and a couple of other places."[92]

HOTEL EDDYSTONE

Chapter 3

NEIGHBORHOODS: BEYOND THE CORE

"[It] is a mistake to draw bright-line distinctions between downtowns and neighborhoods. But that is exactly what has emerged over the last six years in Detroit, as downtown began its transformation while neighborhoods slipped into even deeper decline. We found ourselves too frequently trapped in a polarizing narrative — the corrosive poverty, disinvestment, and blight of the neighborhoods landscape measured against the substantial real estate, commercial, transit, and recreational investment in the central business district and the Woodward Corridor. That divide is simply unacceptable — morally, economically, politically."

— Rip Rapson, June 25, 2015[93]

View of downtown Detroit from Midtown. Photo Credit: Detroit Future City

Few issues so fire the concerns and emotions of Detroiters as the condition and fate of their diverse and sprawling neighborhoods. Many residents would recognize the truth in the headline of a New York Times article of Aug. 13, 2016: "In Detroit's 2-Speed Recovery, Downtown Roars and Neighborhoods Sputter." Kresge's considerable efforts to revive downtown and the Woodward Corridor, especially in the past decade, were driven in part by the Foundation's belief that absent a thriving and attractive downtown there could not be a renewed city. But, as Rip Rapson noted in 2015, the balance between Detroit's downtown and neighborhoods had become grimly askew.

Detroit's neighborhoods outside the city core — neighborhoods where 95 percent of the city's nearly 700,000 residents live — have been on Kresge's radar since at least the beginning of its Detroit Initiative in 1993, and even more markedly when that initiative was renewed in 1999 "as a more flexible, bold and visible initiative" addressing "large, systemic issues and needs."[94] This commitment was a recognition by the Foundation that decades-old problems afflicting Detroit, including its neighborhoods, required greater philanthropic focus. Kresge was then allocating about 10 percent of its grantmaking to Michigan, much of it in Detroit. And while the initiative's objective to "revitalize Detroit" was aimed at "especially the downtown core," grants under the program also went for public school reform and arts education, renovation of school health clinics, youth recreation facilities and community engagement, planning for private investment in neighborhoods, and parks renewal and maintenance. But in the scope of its ambition; in the depth of its assessment of Detroit's condition; in its use of research, observation, and outreach; and in terms of scale — in dollars and otherwise — the program was materially narrower than the calibrated neighborhood effort later developed by Rapson's Detroit Team, especially after its remodeling in 2013-15.

The team issued its first reports to Kresge's trustees soon after Rapson took over the Foundation in 2006. For neighborhoods, the team's objective was to "expand economic and social opportunity for all Detroit residents, with an emphasis on strengthening neighborhoods as safe, supportive places for children and families." Both realistic and hopeful, the team wrote: "Family life occurs, when all is said and done, in the region's neighborhoods. And perhaps no perception has contributed more powerfully to the City of Detroit's negative image than the sense that our neighborhoods are bombed out, unsafe, and unsuitable for young children. And yet, there is enormous energy beyond the riverfront, Woodward Avenue, and Midtown."[95]

As would be expected, the initial reports in late 2006 offered more insight into the team's intent than details on its programs. They noted Kresge's support of the Local Initiatives Support Corp. for "safe, viable housing in mixed-income neighborhoods" and said this could be supplemented by "work to increase access to good schools, early education, and high-quality health care." They mentioned that, on the city's Far East Side, former HUD Secretary Henry Cisneros and others were planning housing on 1,200 largely vacant acres (for lack of funding, that development did not pan out), and that in southwest Detroit, "Mexicantown is pulsing with the energy of small businesses and Hispanic culture."[96]

—

In this spirit, Kresge approved $600,000 in 2007 to facilitate Mayor Kwame Kilpatrick's five-year, $125 million NEXT Detroit Neighborhood Initiative to promote community development in six targeted neighborhoods, home to more than 15 percent of the city's then 800,000 to 850,000 residents. In some neighborhoods, like Brightmoor in the far northwest and the central neighborhood known as North End, the accent would be on demolition of abandoned buildings and redesigning land use; in others, like Osborn in the northeast and Grand River-Greenfield in the northwest, on reducing crime and unemployment while increasing youth activities. In other parts of town, like East English Village to the southeast and 7 Mile-Livernois to the northwest, the emphasis would be on retaining and expanding city services and retail availability.

In a March 2007 memo, Kresge's Detroit team described this concept of rehabilitating a network of neighborhoods as "Priority Area #1": "We anticipate investing in three to five Detroit neighborhoods where the City" and private partners "are focusing their energy and resources," the team wrote. "This will permit us to identify and accelerate the work of others, provide important 'glue' money to tie various efforts together, or furnish 'gap' money to fill in important cracks. It will also require that we take the lead to convene various actors for a series of hardheaded conversations about ... our respective efforts."[97] The emphasis on "gap" and "glue" opportunities was to become a hallmark of Kresge grantmaking in Detroit — a search for cases where a Foundation grant could help otherwise separate projects link up for greater effect ("glue") or could supply a form or amount of capital without which projects would not be able to proceed ("gap").

Mayor Kilpatrick's initiative fell apart a year later, when he was indicted for perjury and pressured to resign. (He was later convicted of perjury and separately of corrupt practices.) By then, Kresge had concluded that the NEXT Detroit Initiative, as well as several other attempts to upgrade the neighborhoods, suffered from "unclear objectives and area boundaries. There was little alignment or rationale for their selection."[98] But the idea of addressing the needs of multiple neighborhoods together — "especially in areas that connect to existing physical, institutional, employment and natural assets," Kresge wrote in late 2008 — would re-emerge in new forms driven by the Foundation.[99]

In 2007 the NEXT Detroit plan had been a topic of the first meetings of a significant and novel assembly convened by Kresge that year and still going strong. The Detroit Neighborhood Forum (DNF), meeting monthly, brings together foundation leaders, financial institutions, corporate funders, and government officials to discuss means of stabilizing and revitalizing the city's neighborhoods. The forum, according to Edward Egnatios of the Kellogg Foundation, was "a brilliant move" and "the beginning of a new era" of collaboration, particularly among foundation executives who had tended to circle one another warily.[100] Laura Trudeau of Kresge's Detroit team described the DNF "as the city's primary philanthropic vehicle to learn about and respond to the critical physical, social, and economic challenges facing Detroit's neighborhoods."[101]

Wendy Lewis Jackson, one of Trudeau's successors as managing director of the Detroit program, noted that in April 2008 DNF hosted a consultative session with the board of Living Cities — a meeting, she said in a study for the Federal Reserve Bank, that provided the "underpinnings" for what became the Woodward Corridor Initiative, Detroit Future City, and Excellent Schools Detroit.[102] Another idea, honed at DNF, resulted in Kresge's multimillion-dollar support for what became Data Driven Detroit, or D3, a technologically sophisticated research service that could provide much-needed data to help direct investment and measure outcomes as funders looked for opportunities to combine or synchronize their efforts. Data Driven Detroit, also supported by the Kellogg and Skillman foundations, was the brainchild of Kurt Metzger, who, as United Way's research director, lobbied for it. Metzger, a former Census Bureau demographer in Detroit who was later elected mayor of suburban Pleasant Ridge, became the first director of D3 in 2008.

But even as the DNF was getting started, trying to align various funders' interests in the North End, it was confronted with a crisis that overwhelmed Detroit as much if not more than any urban area in the nation. As Laura Trudeau later wrote, "the 2008 economic crisis exacerbated the effects of Detroit's chronic decline" and "flattened our hopes of rebounding, despite some promising signs. ... [M]ortgage foreclosures reached epidemic proportions, creating hollowed-out neighborhoods with many boarded-up homes." Detroit's public schools, where students' results on national standardized tests ranked at the bottom, "struggled to remain fiscally solvent as tens of thousands of children moved to schools outside the system." Even "our long-dominant auto industry" — which had largely decamped from Detroit for the suburbs and beyond — "seemed on the brink of collapse."[103]

Trudeau's recollections were echoed by those of Wendy Lewis Jackson, who had joined Kresge in January 2008. In her study for the Federal Reserve, she recalled that no Detroit neighborhood was "immune to the effects of the economic downturn" and the impact was prolonged as well as pervasive. "By late 2007, the telltale signs of blight and vacancy were evident in a handful of Detroit neighborhoods but by 2011, mortgage foreclosure had touched one in every four habitable houses in the city — more than 63,000 of them." Tens of thousands of tax foreclosures by Wayne County between 2011 and 2015 further compounded this problem. Even in Detroit's strongest neighborhoods, she wrote, "the economic shock waves from structural unemployment and the crash of the housing market have left blocks riddled with blight and burdened with a persistent public safety crisis," rife in places with arson, home stripping, and scrapping. The devastation "is almost unfathomable."[104] "Dresden-like," observed Rip Rapson.[105]

With the city in free fall, some residents in southwest Detroit and elsewhere took matters into their own hands, uniting in a sort of "bootstrap urbanism" to ward off scavengers and drug dealers from abandoned houses.[106] In the city's northwest, John George, founder of Motor City Blight Busters, said of his organization's efforts: "We're just looking for a way to bridge the difference between complete madness and some normalcy."[107]

As a first shot at remediation, Kresge, joined by others at the DNF in 2008, funded an Office of Foreclosure Intervention and Response, to be housed at the Detroit Economic Growth Corp., a quasi-governmental entity with "a strong and independent Director and staff who will coordinate a high-level of interventions."[108] The office was charged with a multitude of specific tasks, from developing a "comprehensive" plan of attack to protecting "against predatory or fraudulent practice," to keeping Detroiters informed. But the task was Herculean, requiring the far-reaching effort that only a fully funded city agency could have provided. It was a bold philanthropic move, but with just a three-person staff, it was pitifully overmatched by

Opposite: Volunteers located, logged and photographed every structure and parcel in the city of Detroit as part of the Motor City Mapping process. Photo Credit: Manda Moran

the sheer magnitude of the crisis. In the end, Trudeau pronounced it "ineffective."[109] It was closed in 2012.

In 2009, to overcome city departments' chronic failure to share data even among themselves, and to get a realistic grip on blight and other conditions, Data Driven Detroit embarked on an unprecedented survey of residential parcels across the entire city, at first using the instruments it had most readily available: paper and pencils. The handwritten data was hard to collate — "it was a mess," remembered Erica Raleigh, who joined D3 in 2009 and succeeded Kurt Metzger as its chief in 2013.[110] But the results supplied at least some rudimentary information on residential conditions citywide, when national interest in Detroit was surging, yet current data (even when it existed in isolated file cabinets and individual computers scattered around the bureaucracy) was all but irretrievable.

In September 2013 the Obama administration announced that it would allocate $300 million to Detroit for, among other things, foreclosure mitigation. Repurposing some funds earmarked for "Hardest Hit" areas in the federal government's Troubled Asset Relief Program, and with investment by Kresge and the Skillman Foundation, a Blight Removal Task Force took shape late in the year. At the request of HUD Secretary Shaun Donovan, Rapson, Trudeau, and Jackson served as unofficial members. Quicken Loans owner Dan Gilbert played a forceful role. Like others, Gilbert was interested in a fuller, more state-of-the-art survey than the one done in 2009 — a survey of all 380,000 Detroit parcels, taking advantage of an app designed by Loveland Technologies. Nothing like it had been done before in Detroit. Raleigh was already putting together a proposal, with the aid of Diana Flora, a Detroit Revitalization Fellow assigned to D3, and Gilbert wanted no time wasted: "Start Monday," Raleigh recalled him urging, typically.[111]

More than 150 surveyors, all Detroit residents, were hired for the job, trained in what to look for and gather, and supplied with cellphones to photograph the outside of parcels, almost 85,000 of which turned out to be blighted

Above: Detroit residents were hired by the Blight Task Force to digitally document every property and parcel in the city of Detroit. Photo Credit: The Kresge Foundation

or presumed vacant — about one orphaned property for every eight Detroiters. Gilbert provided drivers for the survey, which became known as Motor City Mapping. Feedback included data points on occupancy, lot vacancy, fire damage, presence of dumping, and the nature and use of each property. All this information was instantaneously uploaded via a livestream feed to survey control, where it was reviewed for quality. Eventually, this data and 24 additional subsets were used in a 325-page task force report and action plan published in 2014.[112]

The information was invaluable to the Detroit Land Bank, a nonprofit authority established by the Michigan Legislature in 2009. With state and federal aid, and later, $1.1 million from Kresge, the land bank was charged with holding, managing, and developing tax-foreclosed property. It can clear title and buy, sell, demolish, or rehabilitate derelict properties. Laura Trudeau remembered the survey as a remarkable achievement of both logistics and technology — sophisticated enough to satisfy modern needs, but simple enough to be accomplished in a matter of months: "The fact that the entire Gilbert organization brought its technical skills to bear meant that the system developed in Detroit was light years ahead of what any other municipal entity in the country could muster."

Even as the Blight Removal Task Force report was being issued, D3 was using the data to help such organizations as Community Development Advocates Detroit (CDAD), a citywide collective of neighborhood improvement associations, pursue block-by-block mapping and neighborhood quality of life. CDAD, another Kresge grantee, is headed by Sarida Scott, who had been a Detroit Revitalization Fellow. Her fellowship experience, she said, was "an amazing thing," giving her leadership development, mentoring, and "exposure to a network that was extremely valuable."[113] CDAD worked closely with yet another Kresge grantee, the Project for Public Spaces (PPS), an urban planning organization that had advised Kresge on such Woodward Corridor projects as the transformation of Campus Martius Park and renovation of the Eastern Market sheds. PPS helped identify "lighter, quicker, cheaper" common neighborhood needs that could be acted upon with small grants. Minigrants were part, too, of Kresge's SAFE (Security, Alternative Funding, and Empowerment) program — which targeted public safety, maintenance, and beautification efforts for vacant property.

All the while, Kresge was building on a parallel commitment to draw more and better fresh food into residential markets. In 2008, well before Whole Foods opened in Midtown Detroit, Kresge provided first funding for a Green Grocer Project that, through incentives for better refrigeration and lighting, promoted the availability of fruits and vegetables in neighborhood grocery stores that had offered little beyond processed foods. One successful and popular result was the opening of the Peaches & Greens produce market by the Central Detroit Christian Community Development Corp. Kresge later supported a Fair Food Network to bolster the purchasing power of participants in the federal food-stamp program, to establish a Detroit Food Law Clinic, and to update the city's Food Policy Council.

—

Among the nine modules of Re-imagining Detroit 2020, the one officially designated "Neighborhoods of Choice" was sometimes also called "complete neighborhoods," referring to the Foundation's desire to invest not just in physical improvements to houses and shops, but in all the essentials of a decent quality of life. The initiative eventually evolved into the place-based strategy "Green, Healthy, Active Neighborhoods." Its original goals included "comprehensive support systems" for residents, stabilization of the city's tax base and property values, and "increased economic opportunity" for Detroiters. Getting there, the strategy statement said, required reframed neighborhood initiatives; improved deployment of funding, data, and foreclosure mitigation; stronger neighborhood schools, health centers, and youth development systems; greater investment in specific neighborhoods; and a revised vision for population density and land use.

Two neighborhoods that Kresge took an early interest in helping to sustain were southwest Detroit — including the immigrant hub known as Mexicantown that Kresge had described in 2006 as "pulsing" — and the Grandmont-Rosedale area in northwest Detroit. Both were relatively stable areas, with strong community organizations, when the recession took hold. Kresge poured millions of dollars into southwest Detroit, for everything from counseling and foreclosure reduction to health centers, small business, and affordable housing development, from rehab and streetscape infrastructure to conversion of a dormant police station into an arts and culture center. Kresge funds helped renovate a historic church, establish a "family financial fitness" program, and organize a neighborhood-based, problem-solving court modeled after one in New York.

Tim Thorland, executive director of Southwest Housing Solutions, recalled how it all started when he got a surprise call around 2007 from Laura Trudeau. "She said she had just gotten out of a meeting, and Kresge wanted to do something about the foreclosure crisis. 'If we gave you $500,000, could you make something out of it?'" Trudeau had asked. Thorland, whose organization received little philanthropic support at the time, allowed that he could. But not knowing Trudeau and not having had a previous relationship with Kresge, he "didn't know what to think" of the offer. He would later realize, he said, "that that's how Kresge does business in Detroit, looking to be out front, to thwart issues before they become issues."[114]

Some 12 to 15 miles northwest of Mexicantown, Grandmont-Rosedale is a cluster of five neighborhoods, with mostly single-family homes developed for many of Detroit's business executives and professional people, though not on the grander scale of areas like Boston-Edison or Indian Village. Tom Goddeeris, who was director of the Grandmont-Rosedale Community Development Corp. for 26 years, estimates that, if there were a dozen vacant properties in the community in 1990, the number had swelled by hundreds with the recession and foreclosures. Kresge made its first grant to the corporation around 2010, supporting its purchase, renovation, and resale of homes that might have become unmarketable. Kresge helped "fill a gap" where traditional home financing was absent, Goddeeris said, and that was "not something most foundations would do. Kresge was willing to break the mold."[115]

To Rip Rapson, the Foundation was just trying to "keep foreclosed properties out of the hands of irresponsible landlords and turn those properties over to first-time Detroit homeowners who'll bring stability to one of Detroit's premier neighborhoods."[116] He also noted that Kresge was supporting the renovation of a North Rosedale Community House and park for meetings and such activities as youth sports, Zumba classes, and productions of the Park Players, the city's oldest community theater. Goddeeris' organization also benefited from the contribution of a Detroit Revitalization Fellow, Martha Potere, a former Peace Corps volunteer, who worked on improving the commercial corridor in the area. The fellowship, said Potere, who has now moved on to the Detroit Economic Growth Corp., was her "dream come true."[117]

—

In none of this, of course, was Kresge operating in a void. The Foundation's neighborhood, and larger, agenda was inevitably influenced by Detroit's volatile political situation, as well as by the varying perceptions and desires of residents. Two reports in 2010 captured the climate. In one, for Living Cities, professor Karl Seidman of MIT concluded there was "no consensus for Detroit's future," "no predictable or replicable model for financing real estate projects," a "frozen pipeline of deals, with severely limited availability of bank" or other financing, and, perhaps most important, "a dysfunctional public sector, with outdated regulations, unpredictable processes and poor use of HUD funds."[118]

The other report, by Grassroots Solutions, was a "community engagement audit" and was commissioned by Kresge itself.[119] Trudeau summarized the findings of the consultant's 71 varied interviews, omitting gnawing depictions of Kresge as a "white," "ivory-tower," "suburban" "outsider" to Detroit. To the good, Trudeau wrote, the report found "a number

Opposite: Grandmont-Rosedale neighborhood on the city's northwest side. The Foundation provided funding to its community development corporation to "fill a gap" where traditional home financing was absent. Photo Credit: The Kresge Foundation

of assets conducive to community engagement: resilient, loyal residents; a vibrant faith community; the opportunity created by the current crisis; and improved data for resident discussion and decision-making." On the downside, it found "a sense of immobilization" based on the magnitude of the problems and doubt about solutions; frustrations with philanthropy, government, and community leaders; relatively few organizations capable of undertaking organizing; "planning fatigue"; and "turf protection issues." Racial divisions also "infect attempts to organize across lines of difference."

Drawing lessons from the report, Trudeau underscored the importance of communications — of an early and continuing "relationship approach" with communities. "Because Kresge lacks a history of direct engagement with residents," she wrote, "some of the interviewees were skeptical of our more active role in the Re-imagining Detroit framework," while "others, understandably, weren't familiar with the effort. Despite both of these considerations, however, interviewees frequently applauded the Foundation's willingness to assert leadership at a critical time."[120]

Dave Bing, who had been elected mayor in May 2009, wasn't always applauding Kresge's leadership. Bing had turned to Kresge to help create, guide, and fund his signature planning and visioning initiative, the Detroit Works Project, which was meant to chart "a new course" for Detroit. That project eventually morphed into the Detroit Future City plan, or Strategic Framework.[121] But the process of forging the plan virtually collapsed within a year, according to a later account by Kresge officials. Cooperation "reached a nadir in the fall of 2010, after a series of well-intentioned, but poorly executed community meetings, growing tension over roles and responsibilities, and political maneuvering over credit and control."[122] Though the project clearly needed an emergency rescue, attempts by the Foundation to intercede tended to rile a city administration that was wary of "outsiders," struggling to assert its authority, and prickly about its image.

"Everyone talks about Kresge, Kresge, Kresge," an exasperated Bing complained in a Wall Street Journal interview in mid-2011. "We're pleased with the support we're getting from them, but ... Kresge is not doing this in a vacuum by themselves."[123] Nowhere was the acrimony more evident than in public discussions of the fate of neighborhoods, which Kresge acknowledged drew more "passion" than any other Detroit issue.[124] Bing's widely publicized inference that there would be "winners and losers" among the neighborhoods, and his suggestion that some residents would have to be removed from parts of the city, only inflamed community anxieties.[125] They also distressed the participating planners, who had actually envisioned, as Trudeau put it, "alternative neighborhood forms" that "would allow long-time residents to remain in less populated areas if they choose to do so, but in a greener, safer environment that has been reformed to embrace lower density."[126]

Under any circumstances, land-use planning is sensitive, all around. Community participation — especially on a large scale — is fiendishly hard to do properly. Among other things, it demands a bedrock of trust, and trust was sorely lacking in Detroit. Nor has Detroit ever been an easy client for "outside" consultants, even ones like Toni Griffin, a black urban planning star who had proved her chops in Chicago, Newark, and southeast Washington, D.C. At an inaugural town-hall session in September 2010, where Griffin and a group of consultants were preparing to start a discussion in a large church packed with residents, Sommer Woods, then a City Hall staffer sitting in the crowd, spotted immediate signs of trouble: "I'm looking around and I see some of the known agitators in the community, and I'm thinking, 'They're getting ready to hand it to these people.' You could just see it was getting ready to take place. It was these architects and urban planners," leading the discussion, "and it wasn't resonating with the people who were there. And that's when it starts: 'Where are you from?' 'Where do you live?' And it was 'I'm from Philadelphia,' and 'I'm from Ann Arbor.' And that was It — 'How are you going to tell me about my neighborhood?' It never recovered from there."[127]

The problem on that occasion was not simply that some of the experts were from outside Detroit, but that the venue was too small, the preparation for the meeting had been faulty (for example, audiovisual equipment wasn't adequate, and many participants couldn't hear the consultants), and community leaders hadn't been sufficiently enlisted in the preparation and execution. Later meetings were more carefully organized and focused on concrete issues; they were smaller and better equipped, thanks in part to some additional Foundation funding; and local interests and leaders were more front and center. The Detroit Economic Growth Corp. and its 14-member steering committee of civic, community, and business leaders moved the responsibility for participatory planning to the Detroit Collaborative Design Center, which took substantial control of the process and created multiple channels for resident participation. These included social media, hundreds of meetings and gatherings, surveys that drew some 70,000 total responses and comments, and a Civic Engagement Team charged with reaching out to organizations, leaders, and institutions of multiple kinds across the city.[128]

The 354-page Detroit Future City plan for neighborhood and business districts was two years in the making and was released on Jan. 9, 2013. Regarding neighborhoods, and looking out across 50 years, the plan foresaw varied living and housing options chosen by residents, and recommended strategies to achieve dense, walkable, mixed-use areas; regeneration through "fusion of art and industry"; repurposing of vacant land into green areas; utilization of "productive landscapes"; and renewal of "traditional" neighborhoods.

Neighborhood Resuscitation was only one of five components of the plan, alongside Economic Growth, Land Use, Land and Buildings Assets, and City Systems and Environment.[129] However "complex and interrelated," Kresge's Detroit team wrote, all these elements were "grounded in economic renewal." That was the plan's "touchstone" and "imperative." Though it might be seen as a "classic, academic" exercise, the plan was far more than that, the team argued. "In setting out innovative strategies to improve the quality of life and business environment in Detroit, it is a decision-making guide for multiple community stakeholders. In its combination of long-term aspirations and short-term pragmatism, it is both a vision for Detroit's future and a blueprint for investment."[130]

Districts throughout Detroit were classified broadly as residential neighborhoods (some including only scattered dwellings interspersed with sizable green space), industrial areas, or "landscape." This last designation included major parks, but also many thinly populated neighborhoods that would, over time, become farms and gardens, tree nurseries, forests, meadows, stormwater-management sites (known informally as "blue fields"), or some combination. Classifying once-populous areas as "landscape" was a political powder keg, which the mayor's reference to "depopulating" neighborhoods had not made any safer. So the plan was careful to explain what the designation of "landscape" areas did — and did not — entail:

> Not all areas of the city that were historically traditional residential neighborhoods can remain as such. In areas with high levels of vacancy, eroding physical condition, diminished quality of life, and virtually nonexistent market demand, new investment in residential uses cannot be recommended. *No resident should be forced to move, however.* The Detroit Strategic Framework recommends a range of approaches to serving residents in these areas, while preparing for the transformation of these areas as residential population declines. [Emphasis added][131]

Laura Trudeau, the Kresge program director who negotiated much of the process with the other key players, described one critical challenge as the need to find the right blend of local, resident knowledge with technical expertise that listens and hears the realities on the ground. Residents have a solid grasp of their neighborhoods' strengths and weaknesses, the patterns and networks that define the life of each community. Experts have tools and concepts that can help conjure new

possibilities and clarify options. "It's hard," she said, "for either group separately to reach the level of understanding that they can in dialogue together."

Kresge had committed $150 million toward fulfillment of the Detroit Future City plan, through a new DFC Implementation Office that got off to as slow and rough a start as the project itself.[132] The office's beginnings were not helped by the controversial appointment of two white co-directors (later replaced by a black director).

In its first two years, DFC produced a "Field Guide to Working with Lots," offering detailed guidance — and, in some cases, "minigrants" — to neighborhood groups wanting to transform vacant lots into a variety of landscapes. It also offered technical services for other activities across the city. By 2016, however, half the DFC staff, and many board members, had left. Anika Goss-Foster — an experienced nonprofit leader whose mother, Carol Goss, had led the Skillman Foundation — became executive director in January 2016. Goss-Foster began a "rebuilding" process that is ongoing and focused on land-use sustainability, community and economic development, and the kind of analytical, issue-oriented publications that could also position DFC as a "think tank" for Detroit. In March 2017, DFC produced a special report on renting in Detroit. In August 2017, it released "139 Square Miles," a 77-page statistical portrait of the city.[133]

Kresge had vowed that all its future investments in Detroit would align with the full DFC Strategic Framework.[134] But the Foundation also had to confront other realities at play: the appointment by Gov. Rick Snyder of a powerful emergency manager, Kevyn Orr, to oversee Detroit; the city's 2013-14 bankruptcy upheaval and resolution via the "Grand Bargain"; and the election in November 2013 of a strong-minded mayor, Mike Duggan, who, with a new City Council — now elected from individual districts and thus presumably more accountable to neighborhoods — re-acquired authority over Detroit. Duggan, the first white mayor of Detroit in more than 40 years, had campaigned on the slogan "Every

Neighborhood Has a Future," borrowed from Sarida Scott's community advocates organization. All these changes introduced new players and perspectives on neighborhoods, among many other alterations in Detroit's political arena, with which the implementers of Detroit Future City — and by extension The Kresge Foundation itself — would now have to contend.

With release of the DFC plan in 2013, and owing to it, Kresge greatly ramped up its attention to neighborhoods, declaring that the Foundation "must now become more intentional about transforming neighborhoods outside the city core."[135] Among its first moves, in 2014, was a $5 million, three-year pilot program to fund "ground-up" neighborhood projects devised by nonprofits and residents across the city. The program, called KIP:D (for Kresge Innovative Projects: Detroit), was meant to build confidence and "organizational muscle" in areas "where little concentrated investment has taken place of late."

In the program's three rounds, Kresge approved 56 projects. They ranged widely, from education to infrastructure to the arts: reworked curriculum at a high school; flower farming on vacant lots; renovation of a 14,000-square-foot commercial building; rehabilitation of athletic fields and outdoor fitness equipment; a youth boxing program; transformation of shipping containers into retail space for entrepreneurs; and job training for "at risk" youth. The projects generally adhere to the DFC plan, and include rehabilitating a two-family apartment building into the city's first LEED Platinum home, redesigning a derelict home into a passive solar subterranean greenhouse, and converting a building into a free medical clinic and community food hub.[136] In the diverse northeast Banglatown neighborhood, Kresge aided Power House Productions, which integrates artists' projects and live-work spaces, and Global Detroit, which seeks to strengthen the local economy and attract job opportunities.[137] Encouraged by the results of the pilot program, Kresge is now planning to expand these kinds of neighborhood-generated investments in 2018.

Above: The Alley Project is one of the Foundation's Kresge Innovative Projects: Detroit grantees in Southwest Detroit. This effort encourages community members to participate in art projects throughout the neighborhood. Photo Credit: Erik Howard

Among the KIP:D grantees in southwest Detroit was Young Nation, whose history with Kresge is illustrative of the Foundation's aspirations. Founded in 2008, Young Nation is a nonprofit, grassroots organization educating and mentoring youth through arts projects. Its best-known effort is The Alley Project (TAP), in which participants have created vivid, inspired murals on garages along an underutilized alleyway, as well as spaces for residents of all ages to gather and engage in mutual community activity, often for the first time — "a sort of block club on steroids," said Erik Howard, Young Nation's executive director and co-founder.[138]

In 2012, when one of its members' works was chosen for exhibition at the Venice Biennale, Howard wanted to take the artist, Freddy Diaz, then 19, to the exhibition and to four other cities where he could display his talents. Young Nation needed $7,500, in a hurry. Several foundations turned down their request, until someone — "probably to get me off their back," Howard said — suggested a call to George Jacobsen at Kresge. Jacobsen, the senior program officer who led the Foundation's Detroit arts portfolio, took the call from this 34-year-old stranger and decided to put up the money for the trip, though the Foundation didn't ordinarily support travel. Howard recalled Jacobsen's saying, "I get you. This is exactly the kind of thing we ought to be doing more of if we're looking to be real as a foundation." Jacobsen "saw us for what we are," Howard said, and when the pair returned from Europe, Jacobsen asked about their vision for the future, which included an all-weather performance studio. Kresge contributed another $40,000, matched by the New York-based Surdna Foundation. The organization was on its way to significant funding.

Like other area foundations, Kresge has long supported such major cultural institutions as the Detroit Institute of Arts, Detroit Symphony, and Michigan Opera Theatre. But in recent years, and as a strong component of the Foundation's "Re-imagining Detroit 2020" program, it has become a virtual arts council for Detroit, spending millions on heavily attended Midtown festivals like Dlectricity and Art X Detroit, and on an array of fellowships and awards for musicians, dancers, actors, filmmakers, writers, and other artists throughout the city. In a Kresge Arts in Detroit (KAID) program alone, carried out with the College for Creative Studies, the Foundation by the end of 2017 had awarded more than $4.5 million to more than 170 artists, aiding professional development and other opportunities.[139] "Ready for a Renaissance: Anything Goes Now on Detroit's Arts Scene and That's By Design," the New York Times reported in July 2015.[140] That September, Kresge's Detroit team wrote that, just as the Foundation is looking ever more to supporting activities in the neighborhoods, it is seeing "positive impacts" on awardees.[141]

One such, surely, is Marsha Music. A writer who has lived in Detroit all her 60-plus years and whose father was a legendary pre-Motown record producer, Music said that all she knew about Kresge before 2012 was that "it had something to do with shopping, five-and-dimes and Kmart, and sometimes I'd hear its name on PBS."[142] (Kmart is the successor to the S.S. Kresge department store chain.) On the suggestion of an artist friend who had been a Kresge Fellow, she applied for a $25,000, no-strings-attached,

Opposite: One of many vivid murals painted on a garage in the Southwest neighborhood where The Ally Project concentrates its efforts. Photo Credit: Erik Howard

Kresge literary fellowship. "If he could win, maybe they were giving money to black people," she recalled thinking. "I was shocked when I won. For me personally, Kresge changed my life, because I was laboring as a writer. Many people didn't know I was a writer. This changed my trajectory."[143] Music, whose works include a cogent essay titled "The Kidnapped Children of Detroit,"[144] later joined the selection committee for Kresge's annual $50,000 Eminent Artist award, appeared in a spoken role with the Detroit Symphony, and won a Knight Foundation award to host what she hopes to be a salon in her Lafayette Park home.

—

Kresge's encompassing neighborhood strategy, consistent with its position even before it adopted the Re-imagining Detroit program in 2009, was to invest primarily in what Wendy Lewis Jackson called "middle-market neighborhoods that have traditionally competed exceptionally well to hold and attract population, but whose future was threatened by the economic damage of the 2000s."[145] By the end of 2015, Kresge had committed new or expanded support to five "catalytic investment districts," including the North End, southwest Detroit, the East Jefferson corridor due east of downtown, and the Eastern Market district a mile or so north of that corridor.[146] A special focus was put on the Livernois-McNichols neighborhood and commercial corridor on the city's northwest side.

This second area of "eds and meds" (urban planning shorthand for universities and health institutions), was where Kresge and partners hoped to replicate the accomplishments clustering around the eds-and-meds anchors of Midtown, albeit with local input and character. The area is home to the University of Detroit Mercy and Sinai-Grace Hospital, and to a rich cultural history, handsome brick houses on tree-lined streets, and a once-thriving commercial zone — the "Avenue of Fashion" along Livernois Avenue. But it had deteriorated markedly, with a rash of boarded-up buildings and perhaps three-fourths of the stores along McNichols Road (6 Mile Road) vacant.

Above: {The Amazing!} House of Fog: il Cinema Nebbioso by DMet, a Detroit-based architectural practice, for 2017 Dlectricity. Photo Credit: David Lewinski, courtesy of Midtown Detroit Inc.

Trying to turn this around, in concert with the Duggan administration, Kresge contributed $200,000 in 2014 to beautification of the Livernois median and committed $400,000 to the creation of a "Live6 Alliance," a community development corporation to coordinate revitalization strategies.[147] Lauren Hood, the former co-director of the alliance, sees it as essential to enlist neighborhood involvement in development plans, and is adamant about protecting residents from being priced out of the neighborhood. To reinforce that involvement, a new "HomeBase" facility, supported by Kresge, will give Live6 and urban planners from the University of Detroit-Mercy a welcoming space for working directly with residents. It broke ground in 2017.

Looking ahead, said Hood, "I see people on the street. I see green alleys. I see people riding bikes. I hear music. I smell different kinds of food. It's just a culturally rich and vibrant place."[148] Hood knows the area well, having grown up in its Bagley section at a time when, she recalled, she could ride her bike until dark, without her parents worrying. As times worsened, Hood saw many of her friends' families depart for the suburbs. Her own parents, who had bought their comfortable home in 1969, wanted to stay and did so until 2013. That's when they were held up at gunpoint in their dining room.[149]

In December 2015, Kresge's Detroit team observed that, while Detroit was recovering from its bankruptcy, "the impact is just beginning to be felt in the city's neighborhoods."[150]

One new tool to drive the neighborhood impact is the Detroit Home Mortgage program, which Mayor Duggan called "a game changer."[151] The innovative program, a partnership among Kresge, the Duggan administration, the State of Michigan, and a half-dozen banks, aims to close the "appraisal gap" that often stymied potential homebuyers and renovators as Detroit's real estate values sank, by allowing them to borrow more than a home's currently

Above Top: Dlectricity 2017: in::Sequence is an audiovisual participatory installation created by husband and wife team of Annica Cuppetelli and Cristobal Mendoza, in collaboration with Detroit-based musician Shigeto. Photo Credit: David Lewinski, courtesy of Midtown Detroit Inc.

Above: King of Arms Procession, choreographed by Rashaad Newsome for Dlectricity 2017. Photo Credit: David Lewinski, courtesy of Midtown Detroit Inc.

depressed appraised value. Kresge committed $475,000 for start-up operations of this program (the Ford Foundation gave another $400,000) and intends to provide a $6 million guarantee to protect borrowers who, in extreme hardship, would otherwise have to sell their mortgaged home.

More broadly, Kresge views its evolving neighborhood efforts as a key factor in whether "Detroit's comeback has staying power."[152] Aided by the consulting firm FSG, the Foundation recently undertook a rigorous "developmental evaluation" of its neighborhood activities and concluded anew that the years-old Re-imagining Detroit program had reached "an inflection point, one that impels our energies and resources more squarely toward the challenges Detroit neighborhoods face."[153]

In a memorandum to the Kresge trustees in June 2016,[154] a veritable *cri de coeur*, the Foundation's staff noted significant gains under Mayor Duggan in many municipal functions, from blight removal (since 2014, some 12,000 structures have been demolished) and restoration of streetlights to improved fire and police department response times. Still, high crime rates are a feature of Detroit's life.*

The Kresge team lauded the "transformational talent" hired by Duggan, who was re-elected overwhelmingly in 2017. Yet, the team observed, Detroit's overall poverty rate, 39.3 percent in 2015, was the highest among the nation's big cities. And while jobs were being created, especially along the Woodward Corridor, "there remains a significant skillset and education gap for residents" wanting to work in the city, where 73.5 percent of jobs are held by people living outside Detroit. One in three African-American and Hispanic/Latino males in Detroit, the memorandum said, fail to graduate from high school and nearly half of young African-American males (age 20 to 24) are unemployed. (Only half of all working-age Detroiters, many of whom lack internet access when searching or applying for jobs,[155] are thought to be participating in the city's work force.)[156] Nearly half of the city's residents are said to be functionally illiterate and according to Stephen Henderson, then the editorial page editor of the Detroit Free Press, adult literacy programs are woefully underfunded by government, business, and philanthropy.[157]

In sum, "Detroit won't be whole again until our neighborhoods thrive and our youngest succeed," the staff wrote in June 2016. "People have to want to live in the city. They have to want to establish roots, work, raise their families, and seek greater opportunity in Detroit. While there may be a symbiotic relationship between downtown economic development and improvements to nearby neighborhoods, we must now become more sophisticated in our understanding of what strategies and investments are likely to transform neighborhoods outside the city core."

In September 2016, the Kresge board authorized a major "pivot" toward the challenges posed by the neighborhoods — a "big bet," the staff called it.

*According to FBI data released in September 2017, Detroit had the highest violent crime rate (murder, robbery, and aggravated assault) among the 30 largest cities in 2015 and 2016. And while the violent crime rate rose 1.9 percent among the 30 largest cities between 2014 and 2015, it went down in Detroit by 11.9 percent. In 2016 however, it rose again by 16.6 percent, while in the 30 largest cities, the violent crime rate rose an average of 5.2 percent. As to murder alone, Detroit's rate rose by 3.3 percent in 2016 obtaining the third highest rate among cities with over 250,000 inhabitants—behind St. Louis and Baltimore. Source: Email to authors, Sept. 26, 2017, from Ames C. Grawert, Brennan Center for Justice at NYU School of Law, citing FBI statistics.

KALES
QLINE
DETROIT
287
QLINE
DETROIT
M-1RAIL

Chapter 4

ON THE RAILS:

CREATING THE M-1 RAIL STREETCAR

"Kresge has really been willing to take risks and use their resources in ways other foundations aren't willing to — and here I'm talking [about] the light rail down Woodward."

— Tonya Allen, vice president for programs, later CEO, the Skillman Foundation, 2009[158]

The QLINE – a 3.3 mile streetcar running down Detroit's main artery, Woodward Avenue – began passenger service on May 12, 2017. Photo Credit: Ryan Southen

On April 8, 1956, Detroit's last streetcar rolled off the rails — the end of what had been, at its World War II zenith, the largest municipally owned street rail network in the country, with more than 500 miles of track and feeder buses and a peak of some 490 million rides a year. Detroit's streetcars died from a combination of deferred maintenance, labor conflict, postwar competition from the automobile, and the judgment of city planners that buses would be more modern, flexible, and affordable. Over the next 60 years and more, as the frequency, reliability, and quality of bus service declined, Detroit increasingly came to be known, at least among transit aficionados, as a public transportation desert.

To make matters worse, when a regional system was formed to accommodate the growth of Detroit's suburbs — driven partly by a flight of white households, jobs, and capital that made the region one of the most segregated in the nation[160] — Detroit opted out, largely because the city bus system provided better and more frequent service than the regional plans would offer. A result was two separate transportation networks — one for the city and one for the surrounding ring of suburbs. The suburban buses that entered the city were primarily for suburban commuters, and they could not stop for passengers along the routes within the city limits. Although planners and many users considered the arrangement bizarre, it made sense to people who had moved to the suburbs precisely to avoid mixing with Detroit's mostly black population.

The search for a more rational, equitable system never disappeared. But advocates for a true metropolitan transportation network floated proposal after proposal and failed every time. The most shocking failure — one still described in tones of astonishment half a century later — was when President Gerald Ford in 1976 offered the region a $600 million federal grant — the equivalent of more than $2.5 billion today — for a public transit system built around a central rail line up Woodward Avenue from the RenCen to Pontiac, with ancillary spokes running northeast and northwest out of downtown. The one condition: creation of a single regional transit authority to

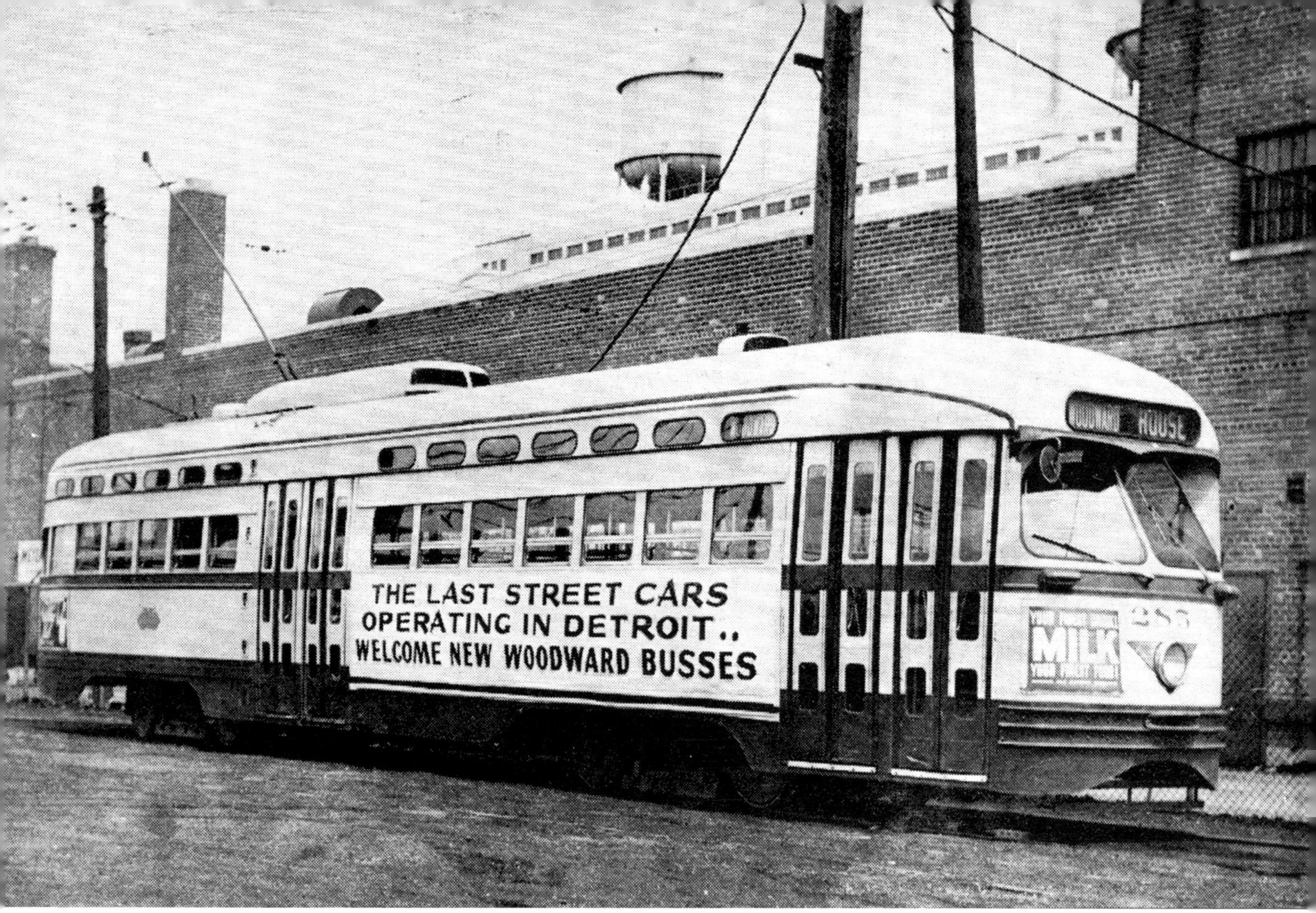

manage it all. Haggling between City Hall and suburban jurisdictions over how to satisfy this condition dragged on fruitlessly across two more presidential administrations, until President Ronald Reagan finally rescinded the offer.[161]

Over the years, state legislation to create a unified regional system failed some two dozen times. The closest the idea ever came to reality was in 2002, when an interlocal agreement created something called DARTA, the Detroit Area Regional Transportation Authority. But before it could have any real power or raise tax levies to fund operations, the authority needed state approval. Remarkably, the Legislature approved the plan at the end of its 2002 session — only to see the bill vetoed by departing Gov. John Engler. A regional transportation system would remain a dream for another decade and more.

In February 2006 Detroit hosted Super Bowl XL at Ford Field, then a 4-year-old stadium at the northern edge of downtown. The event, with its nationwide publicity, partying crowds numbering in the tens of thousands, and a parade of celebrities (including several famous Detroiters), pumped a shot of adrenaline into the city's beleaguered mood and image. Years of planning, driven by a civic coalition adroitly led by Roger Penske, made it "a tipping point for changing the conversation about Detroit," as Susan Sherer, staff director of the Super Bowl Host Committee, put it a decade later.[162] Although the vast majority of Detroit remained economically and physically troubled — conditions that would soon worsen in the Great Recession of 2008 — the ability of its factious civic and government establishment to pull together and produce so much visible improvement was energizing. Civic collaborations of the recent past — particularly those to organize the celebration of the city's 300th birthday and to create the Riverfront Conservancy — had already signaled a growing cohesiveness among Detroit's public and private leadership. The Super Bowl dramatically confirmed the trend.

Above: Detroit's last streetcar, April 9, 1956.
Photo Credit: Detroit Historical Society

The preparations and immediate aftermath included extensive improvements to Woodward, Washington Boulevard, and Broadway, the conversion of several office buildings to apartments, street-level facade improvements, and the opening of new shops in long-vacant storefronts. What it did not provide, as became clear amid the massive burst of street traffic, was a convenient way of traveling beyond the vicinity of Ford Field and downtown, whether to visit Detroit's cultural, educational, and medical institutions farther north in Midtown, or to connect with the wider region. It appeared that the momentum that had been developing downtown was more than ready to extend northward, but the distances between the most popular destinations needed to be bridged — safely, conveniently, and attractively — if they were ever to become more than separate nodes of activity.

To Roger Penske and Matt Cullen, both key players on the Host Committee and in the spreading redevelopment, linking the various growth spots seemed like a natural way of combining their respective strengths, spurring redevelopment in the gaps between them, and fusing their economic energies into a single, rebounding Woodward Corridor. The same idea had occurred to Rip Rapson, who, in a seminal conversation with Penske soon after the Super Bowl, recommended that philanthropy and the downtown civic leadership join forces in what Rapson later called a "grand adventure" to bring rail transit back to Detroit. Newly arrived at Kresge after six years as president of the McKnight Foundation in Minneapolis, Rapson had seen firsthand the economic and community development benefits of well-designed transit. McKnight had, in fact, supported exercises in transportation planning that had forged a previously elusive relationship between grassroots interests and citywide transportation planners.

Rapson was baffled that transportation had thus far played little or no role in Detroit's redevelopment planning. Laura Trudeau, who would soon be appointed to lead Kresge's Detroit Program, tried to explain to him why the idea of transit had long been considered a poor fit for the city's history and economic demography: "We had all these disparate job centers," she told him, "and very dispersed, single-family housing — not really an amenable physical layout to be connected by a transit system. But he said, 'No, you've got it backward. You have to build the transit, and then over time the development will happen where the transit is.' He said, 'You just have to get started and build it. Build something that people can see and feel, and they'll want more of it.'"

Where Penske and Cullen saw a chance to galvanize and accelerate economic growth in the city's core, Rapson also saw a means of using that growth to benefit at least the immediately surrounding neighborhoods with a combination of physical improvements, ease of access, and opportunities to cultivate local businesses and jobs. By linking a lower Woodward rail line to hubs of wider transit, particularly the Amtrak lines to Ann Arbor and Chicago and the downtown People Mover, Rapson also saw the potential to encourage further transit beyond the core — and to achieve, at long last, a regionwide transit system befitting a large and reviving city. But for any of that to happen, it was necessary to start *somewhere* — and the somewhere was unquestionably lower Woodward.

Penske fleshed out the idea, consulting with other civic figures and transportation experts, and arrived at a rough estimated cost of $100 million. With a global financial implosion underway, and given the straitened condition of the city's finances even in stronger times, it at first seemed likely that this would have to be an entirely private undertaking. Eventually, a fully functioning, economically sound system could then be turned over to a public authority for permanent operation. But raising $100 million for an unprecedented project of this kind, in an environment with little or no appetite for rail transit, would be a tall order, even for Roger Penske.

As Rapson told the story some years later, "Roger looked at me and said that if Kresge would be willing to invest the first $35 million, he would enlist others to secure the rest. At one level, it was a crazy idea — municipal governments, not foundations, build streetcars. But the audacity of the

Opposite page: Detroit's People Mover, an elevated rail line that circles downtown Detroit. Photo Credit: Ryan Southen

aspiration justified the risk, or so it seemed to me. I agreed, and we moved forward."[163]

The next eager participant was John Hertel, then head of the Regional Transit Coordinating Council, a body with little formal power but with a mission of encouraging coordination of transportation policy across Wayne, Oakland, and Macomb counties and the City of Detroit. Like Rapson, Hertel believed that true regional transit would require some initial project around which to build momentum, and he had been alert for any signs of movement in that direction. At the invitation of Dave Egner, then president of Hudson-Webber, Hertel attended an early planning meeting and provided a crucial voice for regional government in the midst of discussions that were otherwise almost entirely private-sector — essentially foundations and business leaders, with Rapson and Trudeau, Penske, Cullen, and soon Dan Gilbert at the fore. Because Woodward Avenue is a state roadway north of downtown (its official state designation is M-1), Hertel approached the director of Michigan's Department of Transportation, Kirk T. Steudle, who assigned a senior official with experience in rail transportation, Tim Hoeffner, to devote significant time to the project. With a leadership team in place, Kresge proceeded with a pair of planning grants in 2007 and 2008 to develop the idea into a feasible proposal.

The initial concept called for a streetcar line just over three miles long, with 12 stops running from the waterfront to Grand Boulevard. Although participants loosely referred to the project as "light rail," that phrase technically describes a more express form of commuter train, typically running a longer distance with a dedicated lane separate from traffic. The Woodward rail plan, by contrast, was meant to run along the curb, blend in with traffic, and encourage passengers to step on and off at relatively short intervals. It would, in essence, make the entire three-mile span a single shopping/business/educational/entertainment/residential complex, by removing the need to drive from one point to another. Still, planners at first believed that the multistop circulator line they were envisioning could later be extended or attached to a true light rail that would someday carry passengers at higher speeds to the city limits and into the suburbs.

But to raise the money for the first stage, and to sustain the coalition of supporters through all the challenges that lay ahead, it was first essential to create a consensus about what the project would be — what it would represent for the city and, eventually, the region, and what it would contribute to the economic development of central Detroit. To start creating that kind of understanding and enthusiasm, and to see comparable systems in operation, in March 2008 Penske invited a team of participants — business and civic leaders, foundation executives, and government officials whose support would be essential — on a marathon tour of urban rail projects that had been catalytic for economic development.

The group began with Minneapolis-St. Paul and Portland, Ore. The Twin Cities' first rail lines opened in 2004 and have been expanding ever since; Portland's system started in 2001, running as a loop comparable in length to the one envisioned for Detroit. It, too, has been extended several times in the ensuing years. Significantly, Portland's initial streetcar system was built primarily with local money; less than 5 percent of the initial development cost came from federal transportation subsidies.[164]

The group set out on Penske's private plane from Oakland County Airport in Pontiac, toured transit lines and met with transportation leaders in both cities, and returned home, exhausted but inspired, nearly 18 hours later. Soon after, another group visited Denver's light rail system, which opened in 1994 and has since expanded considerably. As Hoeffner remembered it, "what we got to see was the traditional way of doing [rail transit] in Minneapolis," under the Federal Transit Administration and using federal funding. "And then we compared that with Portland, where it was more private-sector led, less conventional." The Portland experience particularly impressed the civic and corporate participants, who, as Hoeffner puts it, "felt that they could deliver [the project] under a private-sector model faster and cheaper, without the bureaucratic processes" that burden most publicly sponsored transportation projects. Before long, a chance to win some federal support, without sacrificing the project's independence as a private venture, made the idea even more appealing. But even before that, the possibility of a privately led development made a strong impression.

So did the economic effects of rail transit on surrounding neighborhoods — a distinguishing feature of all three cities' systems, and a critical factor for Kresge. In all three cities, the growth of what's called "transit-oriented development" along the rail lines — clusters of new shops, restaurants, markets, mixed-income housing, public attractions, and amenities — tended to peak in places that drew transit traffic. The two tours not only showed that urban rail systems were feasible and popular, but that they more than repay their cost by enriching the surrounding economy.

Encouraged by the tour, and persuaded by the completed feasibility study and business plan, in March 2009 Trudeau presented to the Kresge Board a proposal for $34.6 million to back the project. Some Foundation trustees, blanching at the huge price tag, asked whether it might be better to commit just to the first phase of work, totaling some $1.6 million, and then consider additional support later. But as Trudeau pointed out, transportation developments are essentially an either-or proposition: You can't win the requisite political and regulatory support unless you have a clear financial path to completing the job.

In that context, a limited and tentative grant would only encourage public officials and possible funders to say, "Come back to us when you have the means to do this." What the rail project needed most of all was a large, solid commitment to show that the work would not merely begin, but would continue until everything was finished. The Kresge Foundation, with its financial and philanthropic credibility as an independent actor, with no business or profit motive, had unique standing to give the project that seal of approval. But for that to happen, the commitment would have to be large and unequivocal.

In the end, the Board agreed. It was the second-largest grant approval in the Foundation's history, after the RiverWalk. It was also, according to Trudeau, the first time an American foundation had ever underwritten the capital costs of a transit project. The dramatic gesture paid off: Hospitals, universities, and Detroit businesses soon pledged some $39 million in exchange for naming rights at the stations.[165] Further private commitments followed. A nonprofit organization called M-1 RAIL, incorporated a year earlier, set out to raise and manage additional money, undertake the required environmental assessment, and begin developing the project.

At about the same time, in an attempt to recover from the financial crisis and recession, Congress passed the Obama administration's economic stimulus bill, which put a heavy emphasis on funding "shovel-ready" infrastructure projects. A portion of the money was earmarked specifically for transportation. In July 2009, at the opening of a new bus terminal in downtown Detroit, Rip Rapson found himself sitting next to Transportation Secretary Ray LaHood — a prime opportunity to describe the M-1 venture to the person who would have the ultimate say over stimulus funding for transit. Rapson later told Laura Trudeau, as she recalled it, that LaHood "was excited, because the department was looking for more private-sector investment in transportation, as a way of filling some of the gaps in transit funding." A Woodward Avenue streetcar seemed ideally suited to the goals of the stimulus, and LaHood's response was encouraging. So among M-1 RAIL's first goals was to make the system "shovel-ready," posthaste.

However, unbeknownst to the early M-1 organizers, planners in City Hall had quietly embarked on a light rail plan of their own, this one conceived as a more genuine form of commuter transit, making infrequent stops all the way to 8 Mile Road, with much longer distances between stations. The city's plan would, of course, be vastly more expensive — around half a billion dollars — and it would rely mainly on public funding that, frustratingly, would be more likely to be granted if it were attached to a pre-existing transit segment, which did not exist. Worse, the commuter line would do little to fuel the awakening economic energies in Midtown and downtown, where the long-haul train envisioned by city officials would likely make only one or two stops.

No matter. The city had won the crucial endorsement of Congresswoman Carolyn Cheeks Kilpatrick (the then-mayor's mother, a member of the House Transportation Appropriations Subcommittee, and a powerful supporter of Detroit on Capitol Hill), who had secured a planning grant to get it moving. The news of a competing plan came as a dispiriting surprise to the M-1 coalition, which had little choice but to try to splice the two plans into one.

It would not be easy. To begin with, at the most fundamental level the city plan and M-1 were a terrible match. The commuter line was designed for a speedy shot: 8 Mile to downtown in 20 minutes, running in the middle of Woodward, stopping only once per mile. The streetcar was designed for multiple stops no more than a quarter-mile apart; it was meant to encourage people to linger and explore the area, not whiz through it. A speedy express line that suddenly turned into a leisurely local service just as it neared its destination would be a jarring experience for commuters and a significant dent in their time-to-destination.

Eventually, the two ideas were awkwardly welded together, and the project limped ahead. "For the better part of two years," Rapson recalled in a 2014 speech, "M-1 and the city mud-wrestled to clarify which of the two visions should be pursued. We finally forged a compromise: The portion from the river to the New Center would be designed according to the M-1 objectives of maximizing land use along 12 stops; the portion from New Center to the city limits would be shaped by the city to maximize the number of commuters."[166] When Secretary LaHood announced a $25 million stimulus grant for Detroit, the recipient was the city government, with M-1 as a component and a crucial source of private capital. But the purpose was a hybrid circulator/commuter line running all the way to the city limits.

"It looked as if we had steered around the potentially fatal political and engineering shoals," Rapson continued. "We had little idea that we would almost run to ground because of Obstacle 2: the federal Department of Transportation."[167] The department was at this point an ally, not a hostile force. Yet its rules and restrictions are notoriously intricate and demanding, and for M-1, they were about to become a mortal threat.

To help navigate the arcane world of U.S. transportation policy, and more generally to help with the complex integration of private and public resources, Rapson in 2010 recruited Jared Fleisher, an authority on transportation policy and an attorney with the powerful legal and lobbying firm Patton Boggs, to serve as a consultant to M-1, paid with Kresge funds. What started as mainly a technical consultancy — helping the project meet FTA requirements and sorting out the legal and financial responsibilities of the various partners — soon became a much deeper involvement for Fleisher. "I basically fell in love with the project," he said, "and what it meant for the city." In a matter of months, the love affair would prove crucial to M-1's survival.

By 2011, with the mortgage-foreclosure crisis tearing through Detroit neighborhoods like a wildfire, it had become clear that City Hall could not afford the ambitious rail plan it had been promoting to the FTA. As property values and city tax revenues collapsed, and municipal services all but ceased to function — including transportation, but also police, fire, sanitation, ambulances, and other indispensables of urban life — it was nearly impossible to make a case for spending $500 million of mostly public money on light rail. "Boondoggle in the Motor City" was the title of a YouTube video about the rail project that went viral at the time, starring the Pulitzer Prize-winning Detroit News journalist Charlie LeDuff, howling in outrage at the prospect of spending government money on rail transit when elemental city obligations were going unmet.

Federal transportation officials recognized the financial impossibility of the commuter-rail plan, but were reluctant to give up the idea of a broad-scale commuter system. So instead of reverting to the original three-mile streetcar, Secretary LaHood swung his support toward an idea favored by Michigan Gov. Rick Snyder: three lines of Bus Rapid Transit, or BRT, running along Woodward, Gratiot, and Michigan Avenues. The $25 million in federal money originally earmarked for rail would be repurposed for BRT, which would create dedicated lanes (known as "busways") and mass-transit-like stations for express buses running out to the city limits. Snyder, a proponent of regional transportation planning, envisioned BRT as an affordable, readily expandable asset that could appeal to suburban jurisdictions and usher in the long-delayed dawn of metropolitan transit. It was a reasonable view, at least in the long run. But it would take years to get off the ground and, again, it offered little or no stimulus to the lower Woodward Corridor, the one segment of the Detroit economy visibly primed for accelerated growth.

"Our initial reaction," Rapson remembered, "was that after five years of work, we probably had to throw in the towel. The transportation secretary, governor, and mayor were all moving in another direction."[168]

But Fleisher and Paul Childs, the engineer at the helm of the M-1 project, believed that the streetcar had not yet died, even if it was just barely clinging to life. Among other things, M-1 had been carefully planned, whereas no plans had yet been made for Bus Rapid Transit. Private funding of $100 million stood behind the rail project; all of that would have to be renegotiated, and much of it would disappear, if the plan switched to buses. M-1 had a feasibility study and an environmental assessment nearly complete; none of that had even been started for BRT. The bus project was nowhere near "shovel-ready." Did the Transportation Department really want to freeze tens of millions of dollars for an idea that would still have to run a yearslong obstacle course, while the city's transportation system continued to crumble and development potential in central Detroit languished?

With a draft letter prepared by Fleisher, the M-1 organizers lofted what Rapson later described as a "Hail Mary pass": a written appeal to LaHood and FTA Administrator Peter Rogoff asking for a chance to present, in person, the merits of returning to the original design of M-1 as a "rail circulator" — a downtown-to-New Center streetcar integrated into regular traffic on Woodward Avenue. Parallel letters went to Gov. Snyder and Mayor Dave Bing; copies went to the region's entire congressional delegation, including Michigan Sens. Carl Levin and Debbie Stabenow, and the county executives of Wayne, Oakland, and Macomb. All were signed by Roger Penske as chair of M-1, Matt Cullen as its CEO, plus board members Dan Gilbert and Rip Rapson.

The letters began by asserting that there need be no either-or choice between M-1 and bus-transit — as long as the rail project was completed first, after which a larger bus network could follow:

> We ... fully share the commitment to regional transit and believe that regional Bus Rapid Transit (BRT) is an important mobility solution and a predicate for a regional transit authority.
>
> We believe, however, that it remains possible to achieve a rail circulator project that can have incredibly significant economic development and mobility impacts in Downtown Detroit as well as the regional Bus Rapid Transit project. We believe that we can have a win-win — and avoid the reality and perception of loss that would follow the cancellation of the Woodward Avenue rail project. [Italics in the original]

Following page: Photo Caption: Rip Rapson's 2012 drawing depicting the challenges and benefits of establishing a streetcar system along Woodward Avenue in Detroit, and a regional transit authority in Southeastern Michigan.

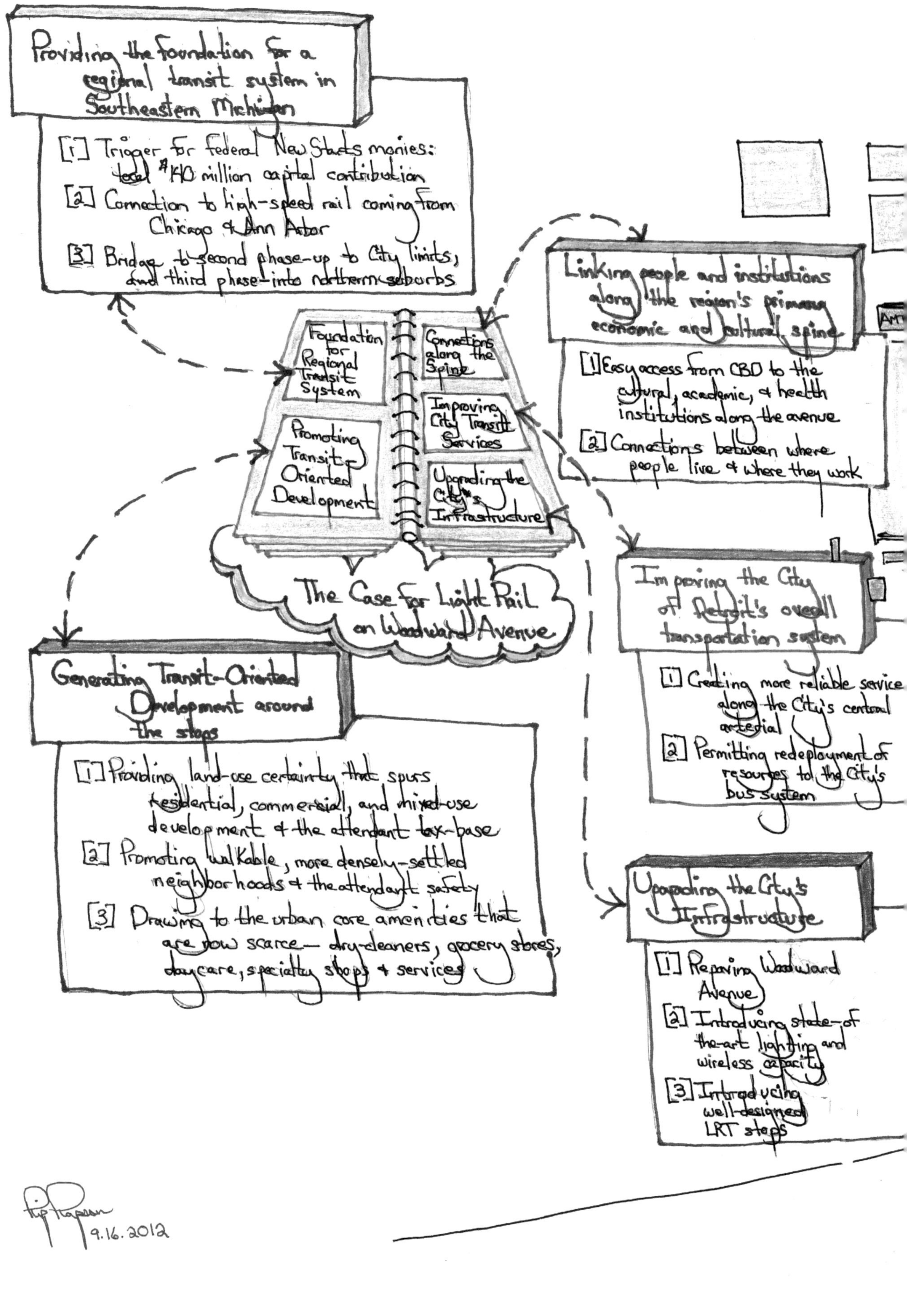

Providing the foundation for a regional transit system in Southeastern Michigan
[1] Trigger for federal New Starts monies: total $140 million capital contribution
[2] Connection to high-speed rail coming from Chicago & Ann Arbor
[3] Bridge to second phase-up to City limits, and third phase-into northern suburbs
Foundation for Regional Transit System
Connections along the Spine
Improving City Transit Services
Promoting Transit-Oriented Development
Upgrading the City's Infrastructure
The Case for Light Rail on Woodward Avenue
Linking people and institutions along the region's primary economic and cultural spine
[1] Easy access from CBD to the cultural, academic, & health institutions along the avenue
[2] Connections between where people live & where they work
Improving the City of Detroit's overall transportation system
[1] Creating more reliable service along the City's central arterial
[2] Permitting redeployment of resources to the City's bus system
Generating Transit-Oriented Development around the stops
[1] Providing land-use certainty that spurs residential, commercial, and mixed-use development & the attendant tax-base
[2] Promoting walkable, more densely-settled neighborhoods & the attendant safety
[3] Drawing to the urban core amenities that are now scarce — dry-cleaners, grocery stores, daycare, specialty shops & services
Upgrading the City's Infrastructure
[1] Repaving Woodward Avenue
[2] Introducing state-of the-art lighting and wireless capacity
[3] Introducing well-designed LRT stops
9.16.2012

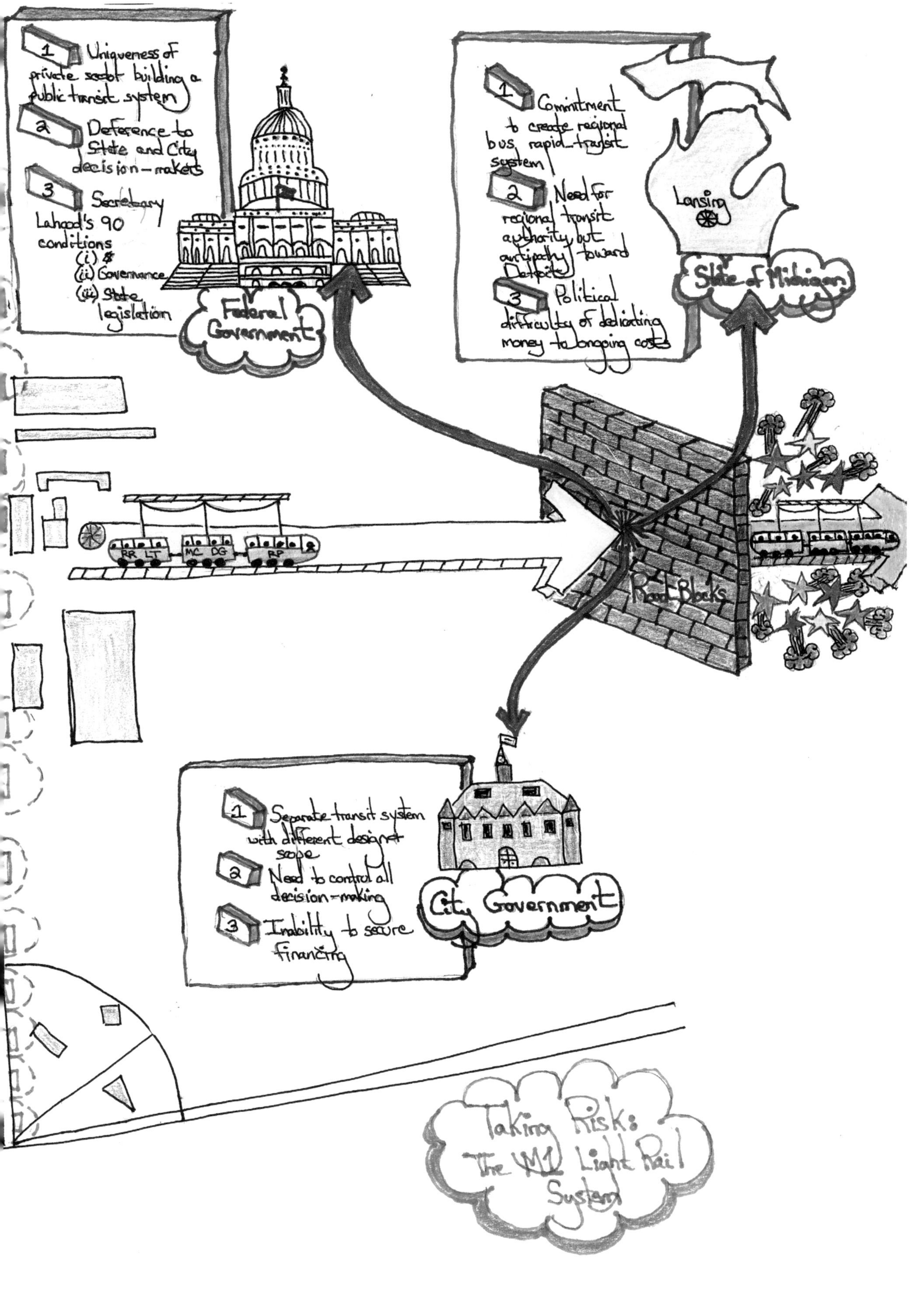
1 Uniqueness of private sector building a public transit system
2 Deference to State and City decision-makers
3 Secretary Lahood's 90 conditions
(i) $
(ii) Governance
(iii) State legislation
Federal Government
1 Commitment to create regional bus rapid transit system
2 Need for regional transit authority, but antipathy toward Detroit
3 Political difficulty of dedicating money to ongoing costs
Lansing
State of Michigan
RR LT
MC DG
RP
Road Blocks
1 Separate transit system with different design + scope
2 Need to control all decision-making
3 Inability to secure financing
City Government
Taking Risk: The M1 Light Rail System

The letter left no ambiguity about what would be lost if the achievable, near-term prospect of M-1 were sacrificed to the longer-term vision of BRT. Such a choice, Fleisher wrote, "would leave unfulfilled the promise of light rail on Woodward Avenue that we have all stood behind, leave unused all the work that has come to date, leave on the table $100 million in private and philanthropic investment, and leave to the next generation the prospect of rail transit on Woodward Avenue."

Recognizing that LaHood, Rogoff, and Snyder were all committed in principle to regionwide transit — as, indeed, was Kresge — Rapson urged that the letter end by weaving the streetcar into a broader vision for eventually achieving Bus Rapid Transit and a consolidated Regional Transit Authority. Fleisher accordingly married the two goals:

> We see every reason [the streetcar] would be a complement to a regional BRT network — not in that riders would transfer from a BRT to the rail line for the final 3.4 miles into Downtown, but in that it would spur and support a revitalized, livable, walkable, vibrant Downtown where businesses want to invest, people want to live, and retail wants to locate. ...
>
> As significantly, it appears that moving forward with the 3.4-mile rail project would be complementary to the BRT from a timing perspective. Despite an assured intention to expedite the BRT project, the fact remains it is but a concept, and that it must begin at stage one of a long and multi-stage process.[169]

With no small assist from the congressional delegation, some of whom were irked at not having been informed sooner that the Woodward rail plan was in jeopardy, LaHood and Rogoff promptly accepted the invitation and flew to Detroit on Jan. 6, 2012, for what Rapson described as a "mega-meeting."

Nearly every recipient of the letter attended, along with, in Rapson's words, "more staff members than you could count."

After elaborating on all the arguments in the letter, the M-1 team made a last-ditch appeal: Give us 90 days, they pleaded, to prove that this project, as originally conceived, can reliably be delivered on schedule, within the available resources. As they spoke, the outcome was impossible to guess. At least one participant in the meeting suspects that the M-1 officials, by themselves, would probably not have carried the day, despite the strength of their arguments. It was the enthusiasm of both the state's senators and the two longest-serving members of the House of Representatives, Reps. John Dingell and John Conyers of Detroit, that proved hard for the Transportation executives to ignore. By the end of the meeting, the M-1 team had its 90 days.

But the bar was set high. As Rapson put it years later, with still-lingering irritation, Secretary LaHood "committed that if M-1 could meet every engineering, financial, environmental, and political requirement the FTA could identify, he would give us a chance." They would now have to prove their case to a skeptical government agency or surrender $25 million of federal support.

Besides Fleisher's consulting fee, Kresge had also provided Laura Trudeau as all-but-full-time loaned staff to help prepare the response. The team submitted its new plan in April, but as FTA officials raised more and more questions, 90 days turned into 180 and the list of technical issues continued to lengthen. Research, analysis, and presentations stretched from weeks into months, filling thousands of pages. But by June 2012 the planners believed they had assembled the best case they could to demonstrate that the project was, in every relevant way, "shovel-ready."

And that, as Fleisher put it, "was the end of Chapter One."

In June, in a deflating turn of events that opened Chapter Two, the Transportation Department announced that it still wasn't convinced. Among other reservations, the department wanted to see the pot at the end of the rainbow: Show us, they said in effect, that southeast Michigan *will* have a functioning regional transit authority, or RTA, that can sponsor tax levies, eventually take control of the rail line, operate it sustainably, and integrate it into the region's wider network of transit options. For now, a Bus Rapid Transit system would not be a condition of federal support, but an authority capable of building such a system would.

Federal officials were also concerned about other things: how M-1 would deal with cost overruns, where it would get operating subsidies (no transit system is fully self-supporting), and other questions related to running a privately owned and operated transit system on a public thoroughfare. "But we had answers to all those," Fleisher recalled, "even if not to their initial satisfaction in June. We could deal with all of that" — and in fact did deal with it in the ensuing weeks.

But the first, big concern was the tough one. A private team, no matter how public-spirited and well connected, cannot create an RTA. Only the Legislature can do that, and it had already failed. Repeatedly. To make matters worse, at that moment in mid-2012, the Legislature was gridlocked over unrelated legislation that would make Michigan a right-to-work state (and ultimately did). Democrats, who disproportionately come from metro Detroit and would be more likely to support regional transit there, were refusing to vote for anything sponsored by Republicans, including the Republican governor. Republicans, many of whom represent districts far outside Detroit, and some of whom are disdainful of what they regard as a profligate city, were not exactly a ripe constituency for Detroit-area transit. Gov. Snyder, who favored the regional transit plan, thus faced slender prospects for winning his own party's support and, at that moment, zero prospect of winning the other party's.

When the team presented its report, it had thought the federal requirement for an RTA was somewhat flexible — perhaps it would be enough to show legislative progress, rather than a final, signed law authorizing the new agency. On the contrary, the FTA ruling was adamant: no regional authority, no federal support, financial or regulatory, for M-1. LaHood did offer a bit of a sweetener: He would authorize funding for an expedited environmental impact study that would be needed to accommodate the latest proposed changes in the project. But the clock was ticking on creation of an RTA, without which the major grant for M-1 would likely be reallocated elsewhere.

In that case, the team would have to wait for the next budget cycle (if there was one — the stimulus funding was only temporary) and then restart its application for federal support virtually from scratch. That, in Fleisher's view, "would have killed the project. With the Secretary of Transportation saying, 'Come back in a year, and maybe then ...,' the donors who had been holding millions of dollars in this were going to start drifting away." Investors eyeing development opportunities along the route stops would lose confidence that their efforts would pay off. Legislators would likewise have lost the main reason for taking immediate action. They would instead most likely conclude that there was no need to move now, amid the roiling politics of the moment and with their session drawing to a close, if the federal government had no intention of responding promptly.

Thus began another high-level effort, which Fleisher described as Chapter Three, to persuade the department to keep its $25 million commitment open a while longer. Once again, senators and representatives were enlisted to express support, and state and city eminences made phone calls and wrote letters, all pleading, as Fleisher puts it, "to just hold the $25 million. Hold it and say, 'We're giving you an extension of time to satisfy these conditions, but meantime, the money is there.' Because if you hold the money, we can hold our coalition."

Secretary LaHood agreed to keep the offer open so long as the RTA legislation was still alive. The corporate leaders of M-1 RAIL used that opening to raise pressure on legislators

in both houses and both parties to pass the full legislative package. Steudle, Hoeffner, and their colleagues at the Michigan Department of Transportation likewise lent support, as did Gov. Snyder. Business executives spent days in Lansing meeting with lawmakers and demonstrating that the project was a top priority for the state's corporate establishment. A veteran of the Michigan Legislature led the front-line push in the capitol, while M-1 staff and volunteers answered questions and briefed legislative staff.

The one entity that could not push for the legislation, or even fund others to push for it, was Kresge. As a private foundation, it is forbidden to lobby or to directly fund lobbying. Having labored, literally and figuratively, on virtually every stage and aspect of the streetcar project for close to five years, the Foundation was for once relegated to the sidelines — just at the moment when the project's survival was about to be decided.

It was able, however, to keep up the effort to resolve all the other questions and concerns federal officials had raised. Trudeau, Fleisher, and other M-1 team members systematically responded to question after question, offering to raise additional money as a reserve for operating subsidies, firming up cost projections, verifying sources of capital, defending ridership projections, and creating the labyrinth of interlocking legal and financial entities required for blending the multiple sources of money. By this stage, as Fleisher remembered it, "the concerns weren't really about, 'Is this a good transportation project?' By now, I think they knew it was going to be a great transportation project. I think the failure they were really worried about" — apart from the fate of the RTA legislation — "was, 'Can this group of philanthropists, this nonprofit consortium, really pull this off?'"

On Dec. 19, 2012, in the small hours of the legislative session's final day, with the holidays approaching and temperatures in Lansing near freezing, the Legislature approved Public Act 387 creating the Regional Transit Authority of Southeast

Above: U.S. Transportation Secretary Ray LaHood announced $25 million in federal funding for the M-1 Rail Project on Jan. 18, 2013. Photo Credit: John T. Greilick / Detroit News

Michigan. The governor promptly signed it. A separate bill also authorized state funding to support streetcar operations. A month later, on Jan. 18, 2013, Secretary LaHood traveled to Detroit to announce, with the governor, mayor, and much of the congressional delegation in attendance, that all conditions had now been satisfied, and that a $25 million federal grant would support the creation of the M-1 rail line.

Next came the dizzying work of implementation, such as completing the final engineering on which to base firm costs; letting of contracts; allocation of risks; creation of the necessary legal entities; and collecting on the various financial pledges. These occupied most of 2013, as the M-1 team dealt with one technical challenge after another.

For example, because the federal money could be awarded only to a government agency, not a private nonprofit, and because the City of Detroit was now in bankruptcy, the Michigan Department of Transportation (MDOT) had to step in as the official grantee. Separate organizations then had to be created to build the rail system and "lease" it to MDOT, which would in turn contract with M-1 RAIL to operate it.

The other major federal subsidy in the project, the New Markets Tax Credits, introduced a different set of complications. In that program, the federal subsidy flows through the tax system to *private* equity investors, not public agencies. The project must be a private enterprise and remain private for seven years — meaning that the new Regional Transit Authority could not assume ownership of the streetcar line until that period had elapsed. Cameron Piggott, an attorney for the project and a veteran of many of the region's more difficult, high-level business deals, concluded: "It's an amazingly complicated transaction." *

Yet as Rip Rapson sees it, the complexity was a feature, not a bug. Admittedly, the blending of so many kinds of private and public dollars was difficult to pull off. But in Rapson's view, such combinations are only going to become more

*Besides being complicated, these arrangements broke novel administrative and legal ground. For example, MDOT's role as recipient of funds for a project that it was not directly undertaking was altogether new. Similarly, the New Markets Tax Credits had never been used to develop public transportation or to finance a project that was ultimately intended to be owned by a public entity. Simply navigating the legal requirements of so many administrative agencies and sources of funds, with no precedents for guidance, demanded months of research and negotiation.

necessary and more common, and they have economic and social advantages. Designing structures to make them succeed is worth the trouble. "As federal sources of transit funding become more difficult to come by," he said in 2014, "and as we continue to defer expenditures, capital innovation becomes essential. The first dimension of this innovation is expanding the range of who pays."[170]

Apart from the financial and legal complexities, there was also the challenge of laying track along Detroit's central artery — the state's oldest paved road — portions of which were scheduled for "heavy resurfacing" in the near future. But now, with a rail line about to be installed, state transportation officials saw no point in tearing up part of the road for the track work only to resurface the rest of it later. In any case, the whole point of the project was to create an inviting setting for economic development. From that perspective, as Tim Hoeffner of MDOT explained it, "The best solution would be the total reconstruction of Woodward" from curb to curb, in conjunction with the laying of track, and adding new drainage and street lighting. "But we had a project that was budgeted for a lot less than that. And we were also in a funding crisis at this point, so we had very limited resources. Still, we made the decision that if the private sector was going to build the light rail system, we should put our best foot forward and reconstruct Woodward Avenue." The state made a similar decision about the two bridges on which Woodward crosses I-94 and I-75: They had been scheduled for an upgrade; instead, they would be replaced.

A completely transformed roadway would unquestionably be the best possible outcome for the street, the rail line, and the neighborhood. But it would mean integrating several strains of road and bridge work into a single mega-project on a tight deadline. MDOT agreed to let M-1 RAIL take the lead in coordinating the redevelopment of Woodward with construction of the rail. A single engineering firm would serve as project manager for the whole undertaking. Although that meant a far more complicated mission for M-1, the result seemed likely to be worth the effort.

Above: September 2015 M-1 RAIL construction celebration. From left: U.S. Rep. John Dingell, U.S. Rep. Sander Levin, U.S. Sen. Carl Levin, U.S. Sen. Debbie Stabenow, Rip Rapson, Matt Cullen, U.S. Secretary of Transportation Anthony Foxx. Photo Credit: Eric Hobson

But that was just the beginning. Beneath Woodward Avenue runs a thicket of pipes and wires for utilities such as water, sewers, gas, and electricity. Hoeffner pointed out that "One of the things you obviously don't want to do on infrastructure is put down a new road surface and then have to come back in and replace the utilities. You end up with all kinds of patches. So generally, when we do a total reconstruct, we want to make the underground utilities new, too. Remember, here we're dealing with sometimes 100-year-old water lines. Whenever you open old infrastructure in an urban environment like this, you don't know what you're going to find. Sometimes, nobody knows exactly where the utilities are. If they're supposed to be here, sometimes they're not here; you find them over there." Replacing all the infrastructure as part of the reconstruction of the road and the laying of rail thus seemed the best solution. "It would ensure that nothing under the rail system was going to become a problem later." The project plan would thus play out on multiple levels: the track, the road surface, and four layers of utilities below.

By the start of 2014, the project budget was also posing unexpected difficulties. As usually happens in construction projects, some costs had come in higher than expected. Proceeds from the New Markets Tax Credit investments now seemed likely to be some $7 million less than originally forecast. The various changes in scope and character of the project had required additional planning, engineering, legal work, and other costs.

Laura Trudeau, who was once again serving as loaned staff to M-1, remembered the fiscal concerns arising in the midst of a feverish pace of work aimed at bringing the project to the starting line: "All through 2013, we were planning the system, redoing the environmental impact statement ... staffing up. We were continuing the design of the plan, looking for a company that could supply the cars, which was a huge process by itself. And as the figures all started coming together and we started penciling them in, there was another funding shortage — partly from the passage of time, partly because the [economic] downturn had eased and there was

Above: Many Detroit-based, minority- and women-owned engineering, construction and technical services businesses were engaged in the 3-year M-1 RAIL construction project. Photo Credit: M-1 RAIL.

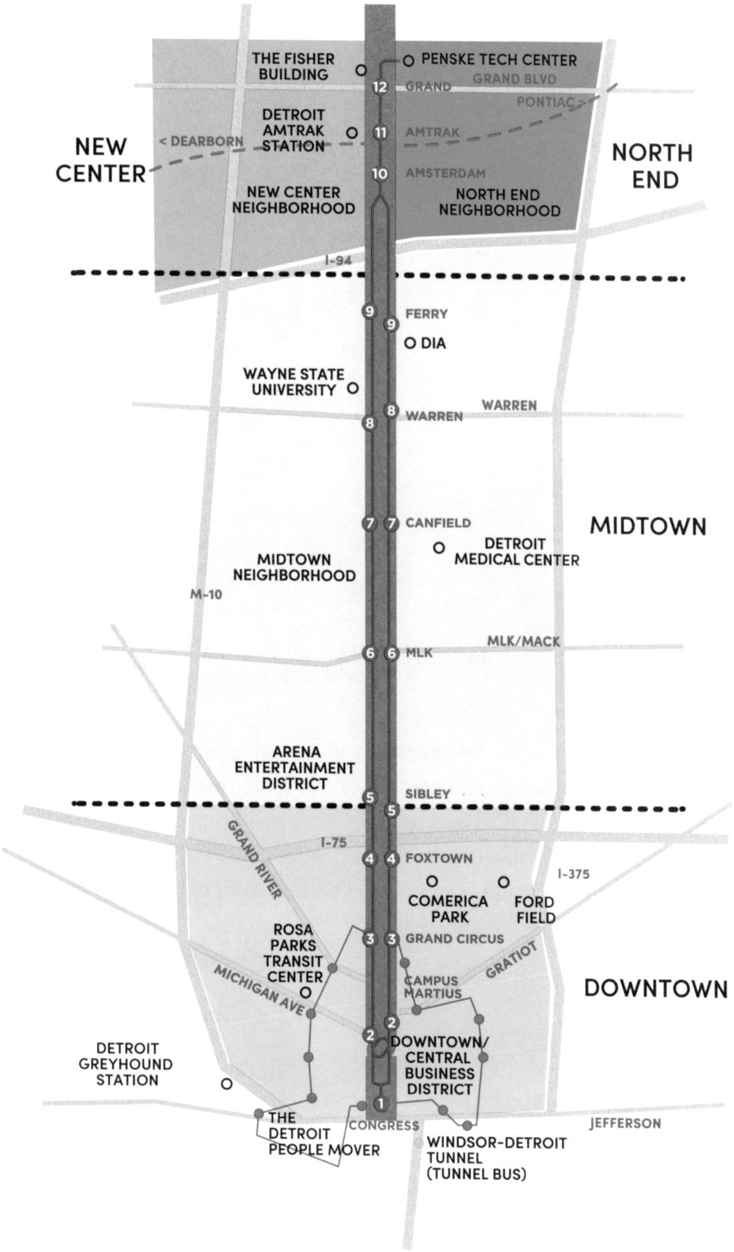

more building going on, so steel was really hard to get. Steel is a huge cost in a rail project, obviously. And we had spent a lot of money doing that business plan and securing all those consultant teams. We had spent a ton on legal expenses. So we found ourselves with another shortfall."

The M-1 team would now have to carry out a delicate balancing act: passing the hat for more money while projecting unruffled confidence that the project was not only viable but charging ahead. Once again, Kresge lent its credibility to the project by anteing up an additional $15 million. Roger Penske and Dan Gilbert likewise stepped up to help fill the gap, as did the Ford Motor Co., DTE Energy, and others. Most remarkable of all, in late 2014 the project won an unprecedented second grant from the same pot of federal transportation funding, an additional $12.2 million on top of the original $25 million.

Meanwhile, though, the news media had inevitably sniffed out some of the financial concerns. To stave off a perception of mounting trouble, M-1's communications team, led by Laura Trudeau, had to reassure reporters, investors, and government officials that the project remained firmly on track (the pun was becoming common). But the time for communications and spin was growing short. As Fleisher put it, "We kept saying Yes! This is real! We're getting into the ground this year! So we had this absolute imperative: to be in the ground by summer 2014."

And so they were. Construction commenced on July 30, 2014, though with some nail-biting behind the scenes, given that the second federal grant had not yet been confirmed. That announcement came in September, more or less completing the project's major funding. Two years later, new tracks ran the length of the 3.4-mile streetcar route, a maintenance and administrative facility was built and operating, and long stretches of Woodward Avenue shone with new blacktop, concealing a stack of new, up-to-date utility lines.

The first red-and-white streetcar was delivered in September 2016, and road work ended in November on those portions of

Above: M-1 RAIL Streetcar Map. Courtesy, M-1 RAIL

the avenue that were still under construction. Each station platform displayed a plaque bearing the name of the company that contributed to its creation. Crucially, many pockets of new enterprise and housing investment were becoming visible along the route even before the work was done, and Kresge and other funders offered support to help existing businesses weather the disruption and lost business caused by construction. A report in 2017 estimated that "more than $7 billion in new investment has poured into or is planned for 211 development projects on either side of the streetcar's path," since the federal funding was approved four years earlier.[171]

The streetcar line itself is now officially known as the QLINE, for Dan Gilbert's Quicken Loans, which paid for the naming rights and has supported the line to the tune of $11.4 million.[172] The first new car made its maiden test run down Woodward Avenue on Dec. 13, 2016, just a bit more than 60 years after the last Detroit streetcar went into mothballs.

Five months of testing and tweaking followed, before the line opened for preliminary business on May 12, 2017. Some 50,000 passengers climbed aboard in the first week.[173] Yet despite the long test period, technical problems became apparent almost immediately. For example, the automated system for telling riders when the next train was coming was often wildly inaccurate. Traffic congestion and other roadway complications held up some trains and disrupted what was supposed to be an even rhythm of arrivals and departures. As a result, wait times were sometimes long and often unpredictable.

All of this was fixable (although the system for forecasting the next arrival proved fiendishly hard to get right). But meanwhile, passengers were naturally frustrated. Stories of long, chaotic commutes appeared in the local news. Complaints ricocheted around social media. Managers believed they needed a goodwill gesture to avoid alienating a public that was only beginning to form an opinion of rail transit.

Rides during the first 10 days had always been intended to be free, so in light of the complications, it seemed logical to extend the no-fare period into June. But that was about all the free service the QLINE budget could afford. Engineering and repairs were certain to take weeks, probably months, longer than that — meaning that passengers would soon have to pay the full $1.50 fare for service that the line's operators acknowledged was sub-par.

An emergency grant from The Kresge Foundation resolved the crisis, covering the cost of everyone's ride for the remainder of the summer. That gave managers and contractors time to grapple with each problem and produce a system that, by Labor Day, was providing consistently acceptable service. (A few kinks remained even then, but they were relatively minor.) The total capital cost had come to $144 million, less than 5 percent above the initial estimate.[174]

At 6 a.m. on Tuesday, Sept. 6, 2017, the first paying passenger stepped aboard. Once the free rides ended, the passenger count dropped some, from a daily average of 5,000 riders in the no-fare days to an average of 3,000 per day in the first two weeks of paid service, where, as of the late months of 2017, it appeared to be holding steady.[175]

But the story doesn't end there. Construction of a successful streetcar line on lower Woodward was supposed to be the *beginning* of the transit revolution in metro Detroit, not its culmination. At the time of the groundbreaking, the broader goal remained distant and still hard to envision: the creation of a genuine regionwide network of modern public transportation. Thanks to the last-minute act of the Legislature, southeast Michigan officially had a Regional Transit Authority. But that new agency had only a minimal budget, nowhere near enough to create transit lines or do much else of lasting consequence unless it could persuade taxpayers to provide a revenue stream.

The authority is governed by a 10-person board, two each from Wayne, Oakland, Macomb, and Washtenaw counties, and one each appointed by the governor and the mayor of Detroit. In order to fund a transit system, at least seven members (not counting the governor's appointee, who is the nonvoting chair) must agree to place a property tax levy on the ballot. The vote must then take place in a general-election year.

In May 2016 the board released a comprehensive plan for regional transit, essentially a blueprint of what voters would be funding if they agreed to a tax increase. The new plan incorporated Bus Rapid Transit along Woodward, Gratiot, and Michigan avenues linking downtown Detroit with Oakland and Macomb counties and Metro Airport in southwestern Wayne. A separate BRT line would connect Ann Arbor with Ypsilanti in Washtenaw County. These spokes would be linked by an array of "Cross-County Connectors," essentially express buses, mostly running east-west, operated by the current city and suburban bus systems. A commuter train would link central Detroit with Ypsilanti and Ann Arbor — providing, among other unprecedented conveniences, a door-to-door rail connection between the University of Michigan and Wayne State University. Passengers could transfer among any combination of these services with a single fare card.

The plan bore all the hallmarks of a sales proposition to southeast Michigan voters: For a small tax increment (the plan prominently mentions a 1.2 mil increase, "equal to about $8 a month for the average home"), you could transform the way people move around the region and substantially improve the prospects for investment and jobs across the four counties. "The fundamental challenge," the plan's brochure said, "is that transit in Southeast Michigan is underfunded and uncoordinated." As a result, it concluded, "We don't have the rapid, reliable, and regional transit we need to connect people to jobs and opportunity, provide independence for seniors and individuals with disabilities, and strengthen our economy."

On Aug. 4, 2016, the board formally placed the tax proposition on the November ballot.[176] But in the anti-establishment wave that year, the measure fell short by just 18,000 votes out of more than 1.8 million cast. It prevailed in Wayne and Washtenaw counties, with strong support from Detroit and Ann Arbor. But it failed narrowly in suburban Oakland County and much more decisively in Macomb, where overall voter discontent was especially pronounced.[177] (Macomb County was often cited in national reporting as the epicenter of Michigan's shift from Democratic to Republican in the presidential election.) The proposition cannot legally be presented to voters again until at least 2018.

Though The Kresge Foundation remains a prime supporter of the Woodward streetcar line, and Rapson continues to serve on the M-1 board, in the months before the election the Foundation's focus in transportation had increasingly shifted toward the RTA. Here again, the Foundation was not legally permitted to lobby public bodies, much less fund a direct appeal to voters on a ballot question. But it could be, and was, deeply involved in the development and publication of the regional transit plan and the effort to create a broader movement for regional transit. A $300,000 grant in 2014 contributed to the RTA's administrative expenditures for three years, and the Foundation provided another $2.3 million for public information and education about regional transit. Laura Trudeau devoted a significant portion of her time in 2016 to helping with the RTA's planning, communications, and outreach. The Election Day loss was therefore an especially stinging blow to Kresge, which had backed the RTA not only with money, but with its institutional credibility.

The Foundation had gone out of its way to bolster the new authority with a kind of civic Seal of Approval, relying on its charitable bona fides and its above-the-fray status, unsullied by profit motive, to reassure skeptical players during the long years of deliberation over transportation. That backing continues, though the timeline for complete success has now grown much longer. "We are going to consider options for trying again," Trudeau wrote after the defeat. If the QLINE performs as hoped, that may well lend additional credibility and appeal to a regional plan when the time comes to present it to voters once again.

The regional transit referendum illustrates the stakes that Kresge accepted as it placed its bets, both on rail and on regional transit. As Tim Hoeffner of MDOT put it: "It's not just about money. Sometimes, there are investors who are willing to be in one aspect or another aspect, or a donor might want his name on something, and all those things bring in money. But first, people have to believe in the idea, in the whole strategy. And having an entity like The Kresge Foundation being able to package all that, to create something that makes sense and draws people in — there's tremendous value in that. A few people — Roger Penske, Dan Gilbert, Matt Cullen, and The Kresge Foundation — really put their brand on the line for this." For a project so unprecedented, with so many unknown factors and roadblocks (literal and figurative), he noted, "that's a huge risk, and it's worth a lot."

With Penske, Gilbert, and Cullen, he adds, Kresge provided a vision and purpose to the undertaking that transcended transportation alone. Where transportation officials saw a road-and-rail project, and elected officials saw a way of moving people between home and work, "it was the private sector that looked at this as an economic development opportunity, not from a transportation perspective." And MDOT "respected their decisions on that." As Rapson put it, "One of the biggest shifts in transportation policy over the last decade has been balancing efficiency and mobility with attention to how transit can enhance the identity and quality of a place." The Kresge Foundation, said Hoeffner, "stood behind that idea and put their credibility behind it."[178]

Foundations can afford to lose money, within reason. In fact, they are compelled by tax law to give it away year after year. But if their money is to have any consequence beyond the goods or services it can buy directly, the one thing they cannot afford to lose is their credibility as agents of the public interest, and as backers of genuine social advancement. At several stages in the story of M-1, the project was not only near death, but in danger of seeming foolhardy, farfetched, naïve, overweening, quixotic. The RTA referendum was only the latest of these. By risking, to borrow Hoeffner's word, the Foundation's "brand" on these initiatives, Rapson, Trudeau, and the Kresge Board were venturing their most irreplaceable asset. They had solid confidence in the soundness of their approach, but no ability to guarantee that the many other necessary partners would eventually sign up, stay on, and deliver. Their willingness to take that risk was a direct expression of the Kresge belief that, as Rapson put it in the Foundation's 2014 annual report, "Philanthropy has to be prepared to cut from its safe and secure moorings to embrace a level of risk commensurate with the magnitude of the challenge at hand."[179] With the setback on regional transit, the risk and the challenge will continue a little longer — as will the Foundation's commitment. "We can't lose sight of how long we've fought, how far we've come, or how close we came," Rapson promised. "We know transportation is fundamental to regions that are competitive in a 21st Century world. We at The Kresge Foundation stand ready to do what we can to spur conversations on what can be done next to achieve a more unified region."

Jared Fleisher, whose work for M-1 traces directly to Kresge's recruitment and funding, noted that in addition to venturing its money and its credibility, the Foundation also contributed its labor. "It's not even just leadership," he said in a 2015 interview. "This project would not have happened without Laura Trudeau's sweat equity. At these critical moments, on key questions of strategy, on interfacing with the donors we needed to step forward, in working with the city, presenting the economic argument and quantifying the case, Laura was in the mix on all these things. There wasn't an element of it where Laura's guidance, wisdom, and effort weren't critical. This Foundation has tremendous relationships, institutional credibility, and the respect and gravitas to win people's attention and hold their trust. Kresge wasn't alone in this; it was a tremendous coalition. But building partnerships and coalitions takes leadership, and leadership means long, hard work."

35

Chapter 5

ARTS AND CULTURE: THE CITY AS CANVAS

"The arts and culture have been on the front line of reinventing the city. Long before Dan Gilbert, long before the New York Times took any interest, culture was here, doing the spade work."

— Mark Stryker, former arts writer, Detroit Free Press

One of several performances staged over seven months by artist and Cranbrook Academy of Art alum Nick Cave. Pictured here is the kickoff of this ambitious project, entitled Here Hear, at The Artist Village Detroit. Showcasing Cave's Soundsuits, this performance featured an impromptu flash mob. The event was a collaborative effort with the Sidewalk Arts Festival and engaged the Brightmoor, Old Redford, and Northwest Detroit communities.
Photo Credit: Sam Deitch/BFAnyc.com

Near the end of 2015, Artsy, a popular website for artists and collectors, published a list of that year's "15 Most Influential Art World Cities." At No. 15 on the list, just below Istanbul, Beijing, and Brussels, was Detroit, "lauded as America's Berlin." (The actual Berlin registered considerably higher, at No. 6). The only American cities higher on the list than Detroit were New York, Miami, and Los Angeles.[180]

Rankings of this sort are more sport than science, but one thing that most of these cities have in common — and something especially striking for Detroit — is that art and culture are an integral part of the cities' economies, near the core of their appeal to incoming residents and businesses. In such places as New York (No. 1) and London (No. 2) — and even more in smaller places like Miami (No. 3), Venice (No. 4), and Basel (No. 8) — the arts are more than a feature, an ornament on the overall quality of life. The arts are part of the brand, a key reason to want to live and work there. Detroit's appearance on such a list signaled a remarkable change in its profile — both in its self-image and in the face it presents to the world.

To be sure, people who value a rich arts environment have long found Detroit a satisfying place to be. Its venerable downtown and Midtown arts institutions — the Detroit Institute of Arts, the Detroit Symphony Orchestra, the Michigan Opera Theatre, and the newer Charles H. Wright Museum of African American History, among others — are all of national stature. Some 400 other venues, including music clubs, performance spaces, and galleries around the metropolitan area, have made for a vigorous and lively cultural scene.[181] Among many other musical distinctions, Detroit is the ancestral home of Motown; a longtime hotbed of jazz, soul, and R&B; an early laboratory of funk in the 1970s; and later, in the 1980s, the birthplace of techno. Even in its hardest times, Detroit's wealth of culture, writ large and small, helped to soften the rougher edges of its image. Still, for most of its history, it was an industrial capital rich in arts and culture. It was not an arts capital.

For nearly all its 90-plus years, The Kresge Foundation has been a leading national supporter of the arts, including in Detroit, but not, until recently, a champion of the Detroit arts scene in particular. Until 2007, the Foundation supported arts organizations in much the same way that it supported other major nonprofits: by contributing to capital campaigns that created important new facilities and helped strengthen the organizations that developed them. By the turn of the 21st century, all of Detroit's large cultural institutions had benefited from this kind of Kresge largesse at some point or other, often in impressive sums. Smaller arts organizations were much scarcer on the Foundation's list of grantees.

In mid-2006, Rip Rapson arrived at The Kresge Foundation from Minneapolis, a city similar to Detroit in at least one respect: It is an international business hub with a vibrant arts scene. He therefore found Detroit's cultural energy and variety familiar, despite the city's far worse economic conditions. As was true in Minneapolis, he found cultural institutions playing a noteworthy part in Detroit's economic development, particularly in downtown and Midtown. A cultural district had been emerging in Midtown since at least the late 1980s, when the Detroit Symphony Orchestra moved back to its historic home in the neighborhood, after more than three decades at an acoustically inferior location on the riverfront. The orchestra's commitment to Midtown — including its later partnership with the nearby Detroit Medical Center on the blocklong office development known as Orchestra Place — was one of the first signs that the budding cultural revival downtown might spread northward.

What Rapson did not find in Detroit, at that point, was a cohesive system of leadership, support, and funding for arts and artists — he calls it an "ecosystem" — in which larger institutions support smaller ones; cutting-edge organizations incubate new talent and forms of expression for wider consumption; funders, government, and civic leaders collaborate on providing financial and moral support to the creative environment; longtime artists and presenters mentor newer ones; and individual artists and cultural organizations play an influential role in most aspects of the city's common life, including economic and community development. That kind of integration and self-reinforcement had been fundamental in Minneapolis, and a key reason for its thriving arts scene. Rapson described this integrated system metaphorically as a kind of cultivated wetland, where "eddies of ideas & activities push into other parts of the ecology, down to individual artists and up to more formal institutions, a dynamic, calibrated ecology in which, though each component part has a distinct identity and purpose, there's a porousness to talent, funding, audience development — all just pushing around and through the environment constantly."

In Detroit, by contrast, it seemed as if artists and the organizations in which they worked were essentially left to their own devices — sometimes celebrated, not usually obstructed, but largely fending for themselves. The largest institutions enjoyed a measure of corporate support and gifts from wealthy individuals, and some well-established smaller organizations had loyal sponsors and patrons — though even then, their income barely reached subsistence levels in a struggling economy whose dominant industry was in free fall. As for the newer, less well-known, and more remote cultural establishments, and most of the city's individual artists, survival was a year-to-year affair, consisting mostly of competing for scraps.

In 2000 and again in 2002, metro Detroit voters had defeated ballot measures that would have created a regional fund for culture through a small increase in the property tax. While the 2002 defeat was heartbreakingly narrow — suggesting a bedrock of support for the arts that was larger than many had imagined, even if not a majority — supporters were despondent over the back-to-back defeats.[182] Later, in a round of severe budget cuts in 2005, the city's once-influential Department of Arts and Cultural Affairs was abolished, thus silencing City Hall's official voice for Detroit's creative sector. For all its seeming vitality in creativity and culture, Detroit would continue (as it still does, at the time this is written) to have no government body to defend and promote the arts in government, and no dependable

Following page: This Rapson drawing, created in 2012, depicts a cohesive system of leadership, support, and funding for arts and artists. It provided a template for Kresge's more focused grantmaking in Detroit.

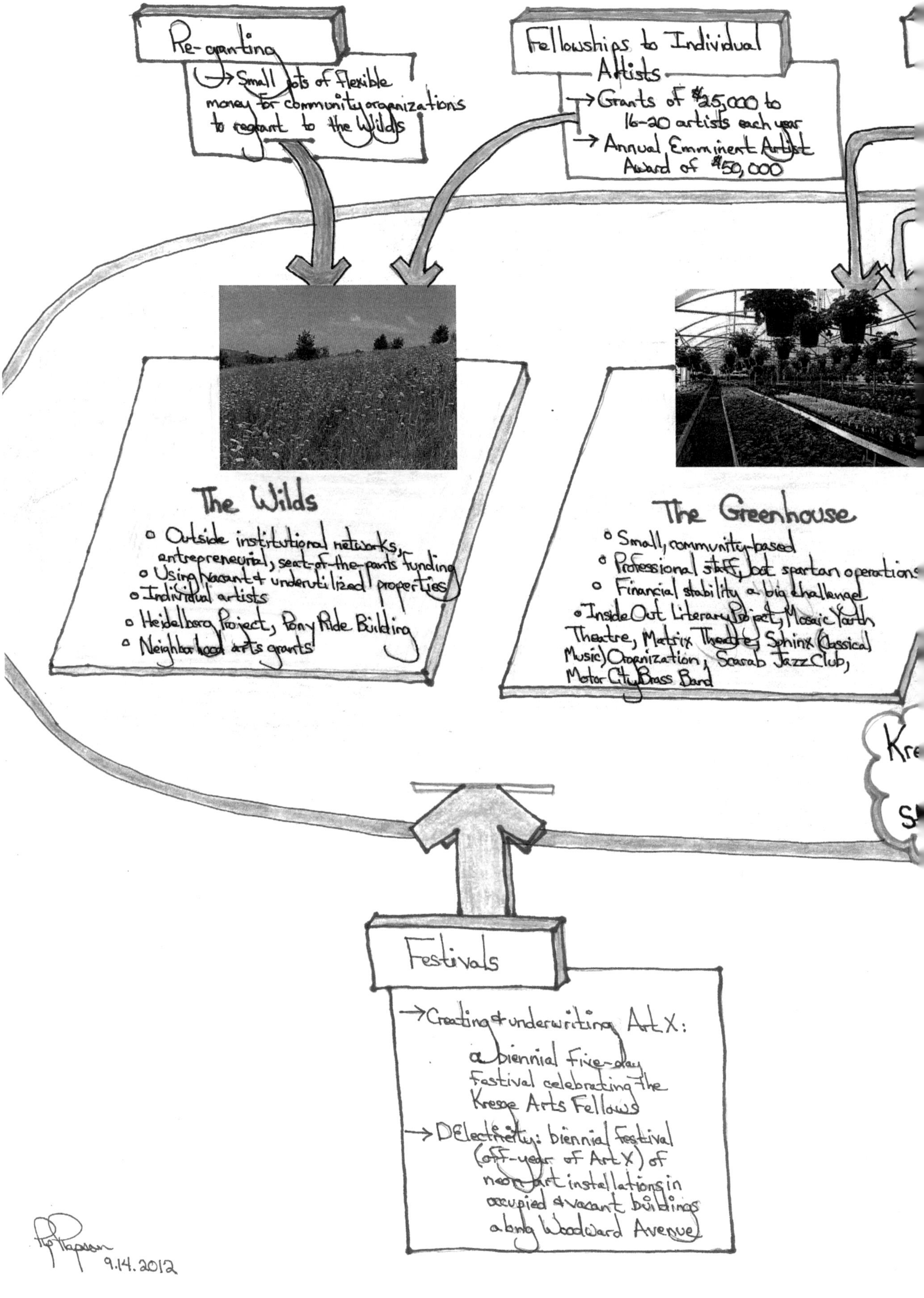
Re-granting
→ Small pots of flexible money for community organizations to regrant to the Wilds
Fellowships to Individual Artists
→ Grants of $25,000 to 16-20 artists each year
→ Annual Emminent Artist Award of $50,000
The Wilds
Outside institutional networks, entrepreneurial, seat-of-the-pants funding
Using vacant + underutilized properties
Individual artists
Heidelberg Project, Pony Ride Building
Neighborhood arts grants
The Greenhouse
Small, community-based
Professional staff, but spartan operations
Financial stability a big challenge
InsideOut Literary Project, Mosaic Youth Theatre, Matrix Theatre, Sphinx (Classical Music) Organization, Scarab Jazz Club, Motor City Brass Band
Festivals
→ Creating + underwriting Art X: a biennial five-day festival celebrating the Kresge Arts Fellows
→ DElectricity: biennial festival (off-year of Art X) of neon art installations in occupied + vacant buildings along Woodward Avenue
9.14.2012

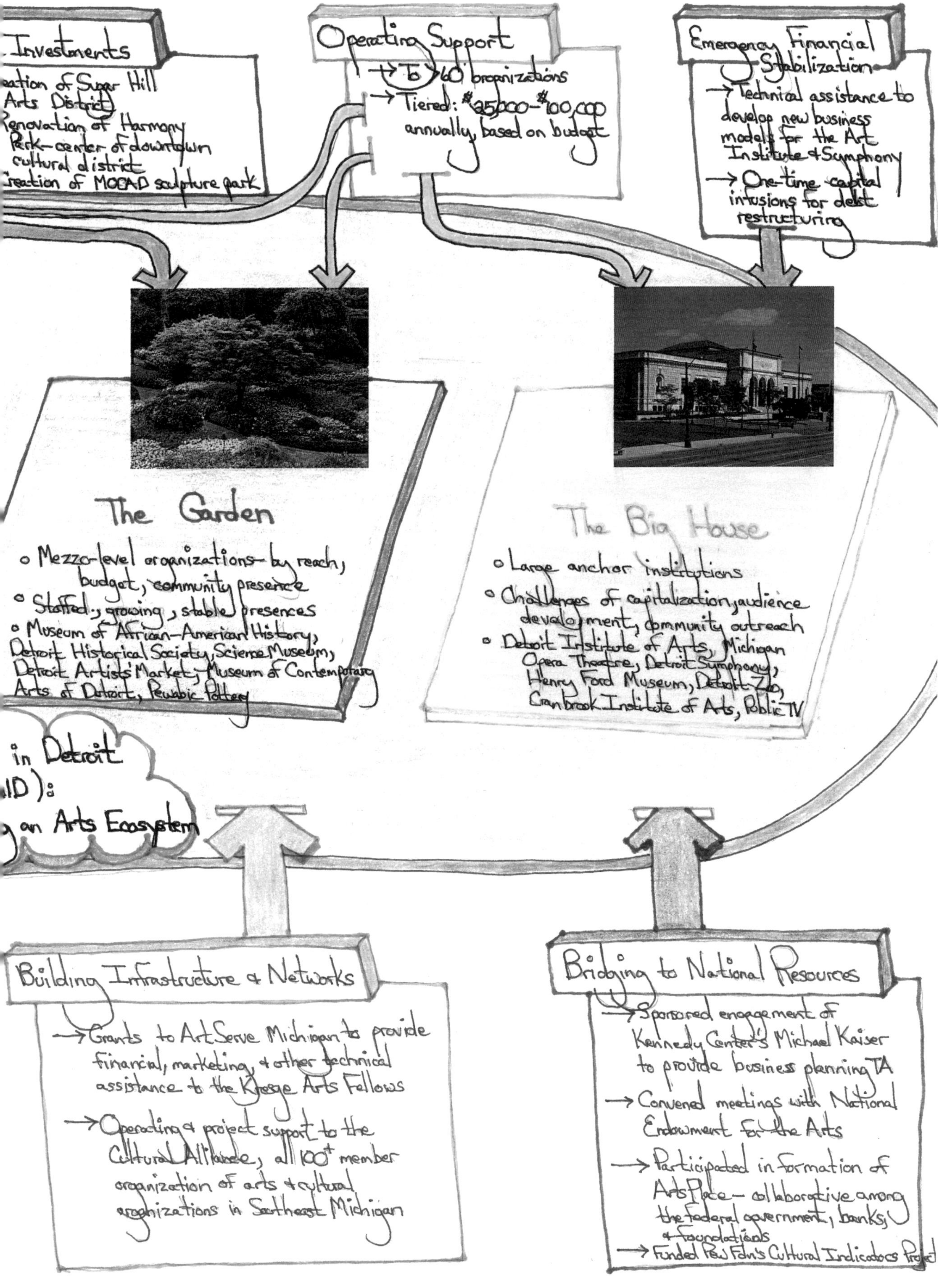

Investments
reation of Sugar Hill Arts District
Renovation of Harmony Park – center of downtown cultural district
Creation of MOCAD sculpture park
Operating Support
→ To 60 organizations
→ Tiered: $25,000–$100,000 annually, based on budget
Emergency Financial Stabilization
→ Technical assistance to develop new business models for the Art Institute & Symphony
→ One-time capital infusions for debt restructuring
The Garden
o Mezzo-level organizations – by reach, budget, community presence
o Staffed, growing, stable presences
o Museum of African-American History, Detroit Historical Society, Science Museum, Detroit Artists' Market, Museum of Contemporary Arts of Detroit, Pewabic Pottery
The Big House
o Large anchor institutions
o Challenges of capitalization, audience development, community outreach
o Detroit Institute of Arts, Michigan Opera Theatre, Detroit Symphony, Henry Ford Museum, Detroit Zoo, Cranbrook Institute of Arts, Public TV
in Detroit
ID):
an Arts Ecosystem
Building Infrastructure & Networks
→ Grants to ArtServe Michigan to provide financial, marketing, & other technical assistance to the Kresge Arts Fellows
→ Operating & project support to the Cultural Alliance, a 100+ member organization of arts & cultural organizations in Southeast Michigan
Bridging to National Resources
→ Sponsored engagement of Kennedy Center's Michael Kaiser to provide business planning TA
→ Convened meetings with National Endowment for the Arts
→ Participated in formation of ArtsPlace – collaborative among the federal government, banks, & foundations
→ Funded Pew Fdn's Cultural Indicators Project

source of local public funding to undergird the whole field. The vacuum exists even as this is being written.

Amid the despondency, Rapson's plea for a richer cultural "ecosystem" struck even some of the city's more ardent arts supporters as fanciful. "He introduced that term to Detroit," Michael Hodges, fine arts writer for the Detroit News, remembered several years later. "I'd never heard it before. It was certainly true that something artistic was happening in Detroit, and it wasn't limited to downtown or Midtown. It was happening in all kinds of unlikely places, out in neighborhoods, in largely abandoned areas. And it was happening without any real glue or support system to hold it together." Call it a system or an ecology or a creative network — pick your metaphor — Hodges remembered Rapson's plea for coherence resonating with people in creative Detroit, even in the midst of a prevailing doubt that anything could be accomplished on a large scale.

Roughly six months after Rapson arrived at The Kresge Foundation, he was scheduled to address the inaugural meeting of the Cultural Alliance of Southeastern Michigan, a new membership association of 32 organizations that made up the regional creative economy. (Renamed CultureSource in 2013, the collective now has more than 100 members.) The occasion, at the newly opened Arab American National Museum in Dearborn, called for a few ceremonial remarks, commending the formation of the Cultural Alliance and celebrating the new museum, which Kresge had supported with one of its traditional capital challenge grants. Instead, with no prepared remarks and no notice to the group, Rapson set off a rhetorical roman candle. He announced that The Kresge Foundation would soon launch a program of general operating support for cultural organizations of all sorts and, more remarkable still, annual grant awards to individual artists. Detroit had never seen anything remotely comparable to either idea.

"That just electrified the arts community," one person at the meeting said years later. "Everyone's jaw dropped. General support? Individual artists? Did we just hear what we thought we heard?"

The operating grants for organizations, although unprecedented, would be modest in size, compared with what might have flowed from the defeated tax millage for the arts. (The largest regional institutions stood to draw up to $4 million a year from the millage; Kresge's largest operating support grant would be $100,000.) But the prospect of an unrestricted grant for general operations — flexible working capital that organizations could spend on their own needs and unexpected opportunities, rather than accommodating the priorities of a funder — made them many times more valuable than the raw numbers might imply, especially for the smaller, less-famous venues.

Making grants to individual artists was an even more radical idea, according to Mark Stryker, longtime arts writer and critic at the Free Press. "No one had ever done that here in Detroit before," he said, "or even talked about doing it. And you cannot overstate how important that has been, and how much it changed the whole landscape." At $25,000 each, the fellowships Rapson was promising would hardly make anyone financially independent. But, with no strings attached, the grants could make it possible for up to 20 artists a year to quit a second job or retire debt, to take some months off for full-time creative work, to buy equipment and supplies, to travel, or to renovate and modify a workspace — luxuries beyond the reach of most of the city's artists, writers, and performers.

Rapson's announcement was not only unprecedented in Detroit, it was unprecedented at The Kresge Foundation, which at that point had no arts specialists on its staff, nor even anyone with much experience in arts philanthropy. Rapson had by then handed responsibility for the Foundation's national arts grants to Alice Carle, who had proven herself as an astute manager of Kresge's traditional capital challenge grants, including many that were awarded to arts organizations. But she is not an artist or an arts

administrator, nor had her capital grants experience given her any particular exposure to Detroit's smaller arts organizations, much less its individual practitioners.

To complicate matters further, Carle's arts experience, such as it was, extended across the whole country, with only the occasional project in Detroit. Her knowledge of the local scene derived as much from living and working in the region as it did from any professional cultural network. Meanwhile, the staffer at Kresge with the deepest expertise in Detroit per se, Laura Trudeau, was highly regarded for her knowledge of policy, development, and economics — but not for deep expertise on the arts. Yet carrying out the kind of expansive program Rapson had just outlined would mean weighing the needs and financial conditions of multiple kinds and sizes of arts organizations and — trickier still — somehow selecting 20 individual grantees a year from among the region's hundreds of practicing painters, sculptors, writers, musicians, theater and opera directors, performance artists, and on and on.

Returning to the office after Rapson's announcement, Trudeau went to tell Carle the news and start formulating a plan. "This is fantastic," Carle remembered thinking. "But what were we going to *do*? I didn't know how to do any of the things he had just promised. But we had to figure out something fast, because he had just told the whole world."

Luckily, both women had worked at various times with someone who did have experience in managing successful arts awards and who knew the regional cultural scene intimately. Barbara Kratchman had been executive director of the Michigan Council for the Arts in the 1980s and later founded ArtServe, an advocacy organization for the state's cultural community. (Since renamed Creative Many Michigan, the organization is now a major Kresge grantee.) In both positions, she had made grants to artists and arts organizations. By 2007, she was about to move on yet again and become an independent consultant — an ideal position from which to serve as a kind of adjunct operative and adviser for Kresge, as it designed and launched the new program.

The first and most basic problem would be the awards to individual artists. While it's legally possible for private foundations to make grants to individuals, the practice carries added legal and administrative responsibilities that are burdensome for both the foundation and the grantees. Both for the sake of running a fair, professionally astute competition and to avoid the difficulties of making grants directly to individuals, Kresge would need to find a nonprofit arts organization that could manage the competition on the Foundation's behalf, select the winners, and disburse the money.

Support for organizations would be only slightly less of a challenge. As Trudeau pointed out, "the idea of operational support was a huge departure" for The Kresge Foundation. "We'd never provided *anybody* with general operating support — not in Detroit, not nationally. There was zero experience to draw on. Plus, we wanted to weight [the grants] toward small organizations"— many of them too small to have qualified for any kind of Kresge support in the past. For Kratchman, this meant not only designing a new program, but participating in the creation of a "whole new mindset" at the Foundation, where, for the first time, small, struggling, grassroots arts groups would join mid-size organizations and large institutions on the grantee roster.

Still, it made sense for the organizational support portion of Rapson's plan to launch first, not only because of the added complexity of grants to individuals, but mostly because economic weakness was hitting Michigan slightly ahead of the rest of the country, and state support for arts organizations had largely dried up. The need for survival funding would therefore be especially urgent, especially for smaller recipients. With the help of another contractor, Maud Lyon, who had worked at the Detroit Historical Society and other cultural organizations, Kratchman, Carle, and Trudeau set to work on a basic structure. The organizational support program was ready by mid-April 2007, and the first grants were awarded just over three months later.

The program they designed started with an initial budget of $2 million a year for three years, to be distributed in Wayne, Oakland, and Macomb counties. (It then switched to two-year cycles, with yearly outlays declining slightly over time, to about $1.7 million in 2016.) The first tier of applicants, consisting of the largest organizations, with budgets of $3 million or more, would be invited to submit by mid-June; the winners would receive three-year grants of up to $100,000 each, and the checks would be issued by the end of July. These were all organizations familiar to the Foundation, and virtually all of them had already been grantees. But the next two tiers — mid-size organizations with annual budgets between $500,000 and $3 million, and small organizations under $500,000 a year — were newer terrain for Kresge and presented more varied and complex issues.

With Kratchman's help, the Foundation convened a panel of advisers to review these applications and advise on the final selection. Organizations were invited to apply in August, with winners announced in November. Mid-tier grantees received between $20,000 and $50,000 a year; the smallest organizations received between $5,000 and $20,000. Final amounts were based on "the size of the organization, the strength of the application, the review rankings, and the recommendations of the panel reviewers."[183] The whole process, from initial, perplexed conversations ("What are we going to do?") through actual grants to 53 first-round grantees, took less than a year.

Assembling the selection panels was tricky. "We wanted a broad range of disciplines," Kratchman explained, "plus a knowledge of organizational management. We wanted to make sure that the different populations were represented, with a mix of races and ethnicities, artistic disciplines, different frames of reference. That was a pretty good start. And, at the very least, everyone had to come from an organization that was outside the tier they were reviewing."

Although every selection process is bound to have its critics, the structure and integrity of Kresge's organizational support program have generally drawn praise in philanthropic circles. They have also attracted at least one significant local partner, the Fred A. and Barbara M. Erb Family Foundation, which now also makes similar grants to Detroit arts organizations. The Erb grantees are not necessarily the same ones that Kresge chooses (Kresge makes some grants in the suburbs; Erb does not), nor does Erb follow the same process of final selection. But the two foundations share a single due-diligence process in reviewing organizational applicants. This includes financial assessments of prospective grantees produced for both foundations by the nonprofit management consultancy TDC. A result is that each funder informs and learns from the other, and applicants to both foundations need to undergo only one application and review process. Over time, the two institutions have convened a wider circle of funders to exchange information on trends and dynamics in the Detroit arts, with the hope of stimulating more and better-informed support for the whole field.

Once the organizational support grants were launched, next came the Kresge fellowships for individual artists — a far broader, more varied universe of possible grantees, with many more imponderables. Among them: Which disciplines should apply? All of them? Certain disciplines in certain years? What form should the application take, and how should they be judged? And who should manage it all? Kratchman surveyed more than 20 arts funders nationwide and held three focus groups with artists and leaders of cultural organizations to settle on answers.

In the end, Kresge decided on 18 fellowships a year, with disciplines alternating between one year for the literary and performing arts (including music, theater, dance, prose, and poetry) and the next for visual arts (a long list including painting, sculpture, installations, photography, film and video, metalsmithing, and many other forms). Each year's awards also made provision for traditional and ethnic arts and for multidisciplinary work involving that year's categories. Applicants must have lived and worked in the Detroit area for at least two years to be eligible, and they must agree to continue living there for two years after receiving the award.

Applications are five to seven pages long, plus supporting documents and work samples. "Peer panels made up of experienced and well-respected artists and arts professionals,"[184] blending local and national artists, have been established to review each year's submissions. To administer the complex machinery of submissions, work samples, review panels, awards, and record-keeping, the Foundation chose the College for Creative Studies, a more than century-old fine arts college (and a previous Kresge grantee) in the heart of the Midtown creative corridor.

The first round of applications was in 2008, with fellows announced in early 2009. Since then, each round has drawn hundreds of applicants for the 18 annual prizes.

By the end of 2017, the program had awarded more than $4.5 million to more than 170 artists. In 2016, as the Foundation set about evaluating and updating its priorities in Detroit, the staff team took note of the beneficial effects the arts fellowships were having both on the image of the city as a creative hub and on the professional boost to the individual fellows, their careers, and the networks of support and collaboration forming among them.

The ultimate design of the Detroit arts program added three elements that Rapson hadn't mentioned in his original announcement. These grew from the national consultations and focus groups, and from weeks of deliberations over the final program design. The first is a suite of professional development opportunities for the winners of each year's fellowships — a combination of mentoring, business workshops, and networking aimed at helping artists hone their business skills and personal management, improve their prospects for income, gain exposure for their work, explore possible collaborations, and prevent burnout. To design and lead these sessions, Kresge turned to the organization Barbara Kratchman had founded in the 1990s, now known as Creative Many Michigan. One of the training modules, an intensive professional development retreat, is presented by the national artist-service organization Creative Capital.

A second additional feature started as a weeklong expo every two years to showcase the fellows' work, known as Art X Detroit. It was later extended to 10 days of programming spread over three weekends, for which the participating artists receive additional financial support for their effort and production costs. The hub of the festival was the relatively new Museum of Contemporary Art Detroit, or MOCAD, a 22,000-square-foot exhibition space in a former auto dealership, created in 2006 with major support from Kresge. From there, the festival fills Midtown with installations, screenings, performances, exhibitions, and artist-led workshops in more than a dozen venues.

Another addition was a single $50,000 grant each year to recognize an outstanding artist with long roots in Greater Detroit — a figure who blends national stature with at least 25 years of living and working locally, and who has "contributed generously to the growth, uniqueness, and vibrancy of Detroit's cultural environment."[185] In 2008, the inaugural recipient of the lifetime achievement prize, known as the Kresge Eminent Artist Award, was the internationally known painter and sculptor Charles McGee, who is revered in Detroit as much for mentoring and promoting young artists as for his own extensive body of work.

The following year, the choice was the trumpeter Marcus Belgrave, a jazz master who influenced five decades of music as both performer and teacher. Literary titans Bill Harris and Naomi Long Madgett followed in 2011 and 2012, and then the Michigan Opera impresario David DiChiera, who, more than anyone, enshrined opera and musical theater in Detroit's cultural firmament. Two legendary Detroit photographers followed: Bill Rauhauser — known for his moody, often ironic black-and-white photos that epitomized Detroit street life — in 2014 and Leni Sinclair, a photojournalist and activist whose work conveys a fiery social conscience, in 2016. Between them came Ruth Adler Schnee, among the most influential names in modern design and, more locally, a formidable advocate of historic preservation. The 2017 recipient was Patricia Terry-Ross, virtuoso harpist and beloved educator who has been a principal at the Michigan Opera Theatre for more than 40 years. Taken together, the group "is a microcosm of the diversity and depth" of Detroit's cultural heritage, as Rip Rapson described it — a living record of Detroit's distinctive brand of creativity, expressed in myriad forms.

Each year's award is memorialized in an elegant, full-color publication detailing the artist's life and work, released with considerable fanfare. The publications are themselves part of the living record — each is a miniature manifesto depicting not only the recipients' achievements and their intimate connection to Detroit, but the influence each artist has had on the wider world, whether as a practitioner, an educator, an inspiration to younger artists, or, in most cases, all three.

The Eminent Artist Award stands out from the rest of the arts portfolio in Detroit, in that it honors someone whose commitment to Detroit and much of whose creative output are already faits accomplis. At least on the surface, it seems to be less an effort to fortify the arts environment in Detroit than to recognize what is already there. But Kratchman disagrees: "Yes, it's a form of reverence. It elevates and honors whoever the artist is. But it's more than that. It's meaningful to artists. It says to the community that Kresge understands the importance of your artistic life and the kind of contribution artists make not just to the arts, but to all of Detroit, and how important it is to have creative people around. We're not New York; it's not always obvious to people how important it is to this community that we have so many artists of this caliber here. The award says: Yes, it's critically important; it's one of the most important and distinctive things about us."

As these various initiatives have matured over the years, the portfolio of Kresge arts support in Detroit has crystallized into three main parts. The first, known as Kresge Arts in Detroit (KAID), is the program based at CCS, encompassing the annual cadre of Kresge Artist Fellows and the Eminent Artist Award, along with the professional development program. A new component of KAID, added in 2015, is the Gilda Awards: $5,000 grants to artists early in their career who are "gaining momentum and who demonstrate exceptional potential."[186] The award is named for the Detroit painter and arts educator Gilda Snowden, who was a 2009 Kresge Arts Fellow and a well-known educator and mentor to young artists. She died in 2014.

The operating support grants to organizations make up a second element of Kresge's arts program in Detroit, operated for now directly from the Foundation, and still supported nearly as broadly and enthusiastically as on the day Rapson announced it. In recent years, however, the focus of the initiative has tipped somewhat toward smaller organizations, particularly the Tier 3 applicants with budgets under $500,000 a year. George Jacobsen, who was Kresge's manager of the Detroit arts program from 2010 to 2016, explained that the available dollars were much more significant for this category of grantees, and the effects on both their bottom lines and their ability to manage and grow have been impressive. These are also organizations, he noted, that might not normally come to the attention of major arts funders. But "with our vote of confidence, and with capacity-building support we've provided, they've been a little more likely to be noticed" alongside the larger, more famous institutions. In the intervening years, several of these grantees have grown enough to graduate outside the Tier 3 category altogether. Meanwhile, Kresge's support for Detroit's largest arts organizations has more often flowed through a separate "Anchor Stabilization" initiative begun in 2011, with grants more tailored to the particular needs of large, diverse institutions.

The Art X festival is a third element of Kresge's Detroit arts support, though one that has not lived up to all the hopes that the Foundation and the participating artists have had for it. On one hand, artists told a Kresge evaluator in 2016 that they highly valued the experience of participating, in which they work through "the process associated with presenting a concept for the Art X curatorial committee (including the need to develop a project budget), negotiate their programming logistics with the chosen venue, produce their work, and get paid beyond their Kresge grant award" as well as enjoying "the opportunity to create new work for a large audience."[187] On the other hand, some feel the event has not jelled into the kind of intensive arts phenomenon that organizers had envisioned, despite considerable expense. Limiting participation only to the most recent fellows and Eminent Artists has also meant that eligible presenters may not be ready with suitable work to display, while those who are ready may not be currently eligible. At the time this is written, the Foundation decided not to hold the planned 2017 festival and is considering ways of overcoming these concerns.

But besides these core elements of the Foundation's Detroit arts portfolio, another body of work has come almost to make up a fourth component. Kresge's program of small neighborhood grants, called Kresge Innovative Projects: Detroit, or KIP:D (described in Chapter 3), is not officially an arts program: All sorts of revitalization and economic development projects win support under KIP:D, and the competition is billed as supporting "projects or planning efforts to revitalize Detroit neighborhoods," with no specific mention of the arts. Yet George Jacobsen noted that a high percentage of the applicants — and of the winners — tend to submit projects in which the arts constitute much or all of the vision. Jacobsen pointed out that neighborhood organizations in Detroit tend to form either around issues of necessity and survival — cleaning up blighted lots, for example, or cultivating urban farms — or else around an urge to hold the community together, to prevent despair or disintegration, in the midst of harsh conditions. In the latter camp — and often even in the former — creative people have taken leading roles and creative enterprises have formed a kind of backbone for community organizing.

This nexus of art and neighborhood development in Kresge's urban strategy is not just a side effect of the types of organizations that happen to be seeking its support. On the contrary, it reveals a fundamental point of view about the future of Detroit that lies close to the heart of Kresge's vision of a creative ecosystem. Among the Foundation's top three goals for supporting the arts in Detroit is the "integration of arts ... into a broad spectrum of community revitalization and improvement strategies."[188] As Rapson explained in a 2011 speech at the conclusion of that year's Art X, artists "are often the first people to see opportunity in older and neglected neighborhoods. They are often the people willing to tackle seemingly intractable social issues through the verve and insight of the creative act. ... Arts organizations can imaginatively repurpose abandoned or underutilized land and property as a canvas for the ingenious and viral creation of art."[189]

The point is not that the arts should be — or even can be — simply conscripted into a campaign of redevelopment. But redevelopment tends to be stronger and more imaginative when cultural forces are invited into its ambit. Creative people and organizations can draw people together in troubled places, summon order out of chaotic circumstances, and conjure inspiration and excitement in desolate landscapes. Detroit has plenty of these kinds of raw materials to offer, and as a result, artists had already started coming there well before The Kresge Foundation made any strategic moves to support them. But their role in the city's recovery and in its gradual process of self-redefinition was still largely unexplored — if anyone was exploring it at all.

"There was a Wild West quality to Detroit," said Michael Hodges of the Detroit News. "You could do anything in Detroit. That was very appealing to some artists, long before the city started to develop a bigger reputation as the sort of sexy, oddball place to be. For a long time, this was one of the least governed cities in the country, until fairly recently. You could erect a piece of public art in a field near the Russell Industrial Center — and it would stay there! At least the authorities wouldn't take it down. They weren't even aware it was there, because there were so few official eyes on the street."

One of the earlier, and by now among the best known, examples of spontaneous public art sprouting from Detroit's derelict property has been the Heidelberg Project, a festooning of abandoned buildings on Heidelberg Street, in the East Side neighborhood known as McDougall-Hunt. The installation artist Tyree Guyton created the project in 1986, originally with a series of empty houses painted in brightly colored polka-dots and decked out in a gallimaufry of found objects. As the visual pandemonium spread to additional buildings and blocks, the city government twice stepped in to demolish portions of the project (even in the "least governed city in the country," the audacious Heidelberg Project was bound to draw official indignation). Unknown people set fire to some of its other buildings. Even so, parts of it survive, drawing tourists from around the world, although Guyton announced that much of what remains will soon be dismantled or rearranged. Guyton was in the inaugural class of Kresge Artist Fellows in the Visual Arts in 2009, and the project celebrated its 30th anniversary in 2016.

In their own way, other community leaders and their neighbors likewise were beginning to see the abandoned property around them as at worst a malleable evil and maybe, in the best possible light, as a palette on which to assert a common spirit. Murals of "street art" (city officials are still prone to branding it all as "graffiti") sprang up not only as an expression of individual painters, but as community projects. Performances, festivals, music, and art projects for youth also followed. Empty and hollowed-out places were turning into hothouses of creative growth.

Sometimes literal hothouses: Amid the gradual emergence of agriculture on several of Detroit's more windswept blocks, a few urban farmers have come to see their mission as partly environmental, partly nutritional, and also partly expressive — an art of food, cultivation, and community, in a sense.*

*This is only one of many intersections of food and art in contemporary Detroit. Many artists share the view of several chefs and restaurateurs that the culinary arts are a key part of the blossoming local arts scene as well — a phenomenon that has led to, among other things, a nod from National Geographic, which named Detroit the "top unexpected food destination in North America" for 2017. One of the early successes in the city's restaurant renaissance, Slows Bar BQ in the resurging Corktown district, is partly owned by Phillip Cooley, who has separately renovated a nearby industrial building, now named Ponyride, as a workspace and incubator for "artists, creative entrepreneurs, and makers."

Perhaps the quintessential blending of farm and art center is the artist Kate Daughdrill's Burnside Farm on the near East Side just north of Hamtramck, "a place where art, gardening, and learning alongside neighbors come together." Alongside six lots "that are gardened for sustenance and beauty,"[190] the farm includes a greenhouse as well as a gallery building and a garage transformed into an art space for neighborhood girls. In the warmer months, the center hosts community dinners with farm-to-table food, some hosted by local artists, along with workshops on art, farming, or both, and occasional concerts or other performances. Daughdrill was named a Kresge Artist Fellow in the Visual Arts in 2013.

The blurring of lines among art, community development, and property reclamation is one of the most distinctive features of Detroit's arts environment — where some practitioners use the portmanteau word "artivist" (artist + activist) to describe themselves. One striking example

of how difficult it can be to pry apart the different strains of work is the creative community nonprofit known as Power House Productions. Gina Reichert, who founded Power House in 2007 with her husband, Mitch Cope, still struggles with the question of whether it is a community development organization with a substantial arts program or an arts organization with a community development component. Power House has purchased and renovated several vacant properties in the East Davison neighborhood informally known as Banglatown, because of its high percentage of families with roots in Bangladesh. One of the properties, called Play House, incubates new performance work. Another, called Jar House, is a community gathering space, neighborhood library, and exhibition space, in addition to housing the organization's offices. Sound House is an experimental sound studio where artists use the facility and equipment gratis in exchange for presenting public performances. Squash House is a "sculptural sports arena and greenhouse."

The houses host a mélange of arts and family events, exhibits, performances, and resources for learning and creating. They are a center of local identity, community-building, and cultural expression, but they are also attractively reclaimed properties in an area with many vacant homes and pockets of blight. Any neighborhood redevelopment organization would recognize the value, and the quality, of the renovated real estate. An arts organization would notice the creation of a diverse, vibrant cultural center in a physically and economically improbable location. But neither point of view fully captures what Power House actually is.

One project, begun in 2012, helps draw the complex picture into sharper focus. Ride It Sculpture Park is a public art installation on East Davison just west of Conant, designed and built by two teams working with Power House Productions. Reichert and Cope raised some of the earliest money for the project by auctioning off skate decks (the wooden part of the skateboard) painted by artists from as far away as New York and California, who donated their work for the auction.

One of those who donated a deck was the multimedia artist Matthew Barney, who had created a specially designed skateboard with a chunk of graphite mounted to the underside of its tip. As part of his celebrated "Drawing Restraint" series, which blends physical discipline, athleticism, and artistic expression, Barney suggested inviting a professional skater to ride this board on the Sculpture Park's newly completed first phase. The graphite would then create a drawing, tracing a pattern as it moved across the surface of the ramps. Working with the photographer Joe Brook, himself a lifelong skateboarder, and the arts publication Juxtapoz Magazine, Cope and Reichert recruited the skateboarding legend Lance Mountain to pilot the graphite around the park.

As the event was being filmed and photographed for what would become "Drawing Restraint 19," youngsters from the neighborhood were gathering around the park's periphery. They were not there to gawk at an unfolding art project, or even to watch a nationally known skateboarder perform. They were carrying their boards and simply waiting to use the park. For them, it was the only well-designed skateboarding venue for many miles.

"We were hitting all these levels," Gina Reichert recalled. The park was clearly a success as a safe and appealing space for young people to enjoy what can be, in less well-suited places, a dangerous sport. But (whether the young skaters knew or cared) it was also an installation of public sculpture that had piqued more than one nationally known artist's imagination. And there was room on the site for further expansion, as the budget permits. "We felt like, Yes! This is working!" she said. "These things are coming together, we're sharing this space, it's a public experience and everyone is happy with it."

It was another case of the bane of Detroit's neighborhoods — sprawling patches of grim-looking vacant land — providing the basic material for both art and community cohesion. For Reichert and Cope, the question of which element predominates, community development or art, is only modestly interesting. "We're artists," Reichert said. "Our key partners and most of the board members are in some capacity artists. So we put the arts first, because that's what we know. But sometimes the work we do is social activism, even social work, in a sense, and sometimes social art, I'm not sure what you'd call it. But when we feel we're going too far in those directions we pull back, because it's not what we know and do best." The organization willingly collaborates with other local groups, some of which are more social activist and some more focused on human services or preserving the physical environment — though even those are sometimes led or heavily influenced by artists.

Reichert and Cope originally founded a design firm called Design 99, through which they won a Kresge Artist Fellowship in the Visual Arts in 2011. Power House Productions has received two rounds of general operating support grants to date, in 2012 and 2016, as well as a separate grant of $75,000 in 2013 to support its neighborhood revitalization efforts.

Across town in the Vernor-Springwells neighborhood of Southwest Detroit, The Alley Project is another example of a community youth effort so heavily infused with artistic expression and so focused on the community's physical surroundings that it is impossible to classify under any of the traditional headings: youth, neighborhood preservation, or arts. The photographer Erik Howard, founder of the youth organization Young Nation, which sponsors The Alley Project, described a time around 2004 when neighbors on the block between Avis and Falcon streets, just east of Woodmere Cemetery, were increasingly alarmed by "gang graffiti or other vandalism" on their garages or back fences, along the alleyway that divides the block.

"There were groups of youth who wanted to paint but didn't have a place to do it, so we facilitated introductions" to neighbors disturbed by the gang tags or just tired of the unsightly markings on their property. Better to have deliberate, creative painting on their garage doors and fences, the homeowners reasoned, than to have advertisements for gangs that many considered dangerous. The young people replaced the tags with full murals of design, color, and whimsy — and suddenly the alley had both personality and a proud group of young defenders. As more neighbors started to admire the results and ask for similar treatment, "relationships started to be formed, and more people gave permission to paint on their garages for free. It was free both ways: The youth didn't have to pay for it; the adults didn't have to pay for it. It started to become something that people celebrated."

More than a dozen years later, work on the alley has expanded, and Young Nation has converted a vacant lot into a park with four large walls for free use by anyone with an urge to paint. The celebrations have expanded as well: Tour buses sometimes roll through the neighborhood, with visitors from all over the world taking selfies against the walls and garages. The organization has also acquired a corner commercial property, which it is converting into a center for art and community. Young Nation received $80,000 in total support from The Kresge Foundation between 2012 and 2016, including two grants through the neighborhood-focused KIP:D program. In 2014, the project won a $75,000 grant from the Knight Foundation, under its multicity Knight Arts Challenge program, which "funds the best ideas for engaging and enriching communities through the arts."[191] Other national grants, from the national funding collaborative known as ArtPlace and from the Surdna Foundation, soon followed.

Still, like Gina Reichert, Howard isn't much intrigued by the question of how to classify The Alley Project — under "youth," "neighborhood," or "arts." "The artistic products are fantastic," Howard said, "and they kind of become a tangible representation or a monument to what's happening" in the neighborhood and among the young people who put their creativity into improving it. "But we really consider each mural a monument to a small set of unlikely relationships that were created as a result of the process" of drawing young artists, neighbors, and vulnerable property into an alliance for a strengthened community. "People who otherwise wouldn't talk to each other, and were afraid of each other, are now communicating on a regular basis, sharing their lives with each other, and creating together. And that's our mission."[192]

A slightly purer version of an arts project — though still one with significant overtones of neighborhood- and community-building — is the Sidewalk Arts Festival, an annual event on Lahser Road in the Old Redford neighborhood of far northwest Detroit. The festival is anchored in a cluster of formerly abandoned industrial buildings, which were rescued by a community cleanup and preservation organization called Motor City Blight Busters, as part of a development now known as Artist Village. After stripping the walls nearly bare, removing the roofs, and creating interconnecting pathways among the structures, Blight Busters had transformed part of the area into a warren of courtyards perfect for performance, film, exhibitions, or virtually any creative exercise that can fit into the space.

Ryan Myers-Johnson, a dancer and performance artist who had left Detroit for a period to work in New York, was struck, when she returned home, by how much of the city's blossoming arts scene was either concentrated in the urban core or tucked away where only the cognoscenti knew how to find it. "I thought I would like to create something close to where I grew up," she said, "in a place that's beautiful but overlooked." She spent part of her childhood in the Grandmont-Rosedale neighborhood, no more than three miles from Artist Village. For her, Old Redford was familiar turf, and a place with a strong sense of community, despite a lot of beleaguered real estate. It was a perfect place, she thought, for a come-all, boundary-breaking festival that would draw residents and visitors into "performance art, site-specific art, experimental performance — and open it all up to a broader audience."

The result, in 2012, was the first Sidewalk Festival, a ground-level profusion of performance, installations, and video in and around Artist Village but spilling ebulliently into the surrounding streets, parking lots, community gardens, storefronts, and alleyways. Participating artists include a heavy percentage of Detroiters — including a number of Kresge Artist Fellows — along with others from all over the country. Around 5,000 people attend each year. To manage and expand on the festival, Myers-Johnson organized Sidewalk Detroit, a nonprofit organization that later sponsored an artists' residency program in nearby Eliza Howell Park, where participants present "nature-based performance and installation works."[193] The organization also curates other "site-responsive" performances elsewhere in the city. In 2016, it inaugurated a bus tour, called Progressive Art Jam, escorting people to three prominent artists' collectives in other neighborhoods.

To make all of that happen, Myers-Johnson — who, by her own admission, had little or no idea of how to start a new venture or draw up a business plan — needed to persuade someone to provide seed capital. Although her idea was still barely half-formed, George Jacobsen at Kresge saw the potential and found it intriguing. He agreed to provide an initial $8,000 to get her started, and she negotiated additional grants from the Community Foundation of Southeast Michigan and PNC Bank. An $8,000 check was tiny by Kresge standards, yet it imposed far more administrative complexity than a typical six- or seven-figure award. Among other problems, the money was destined for an organization that didn't yet even exist, much less have the federally recognized tax exemption Kresge normally requires (the College for Creative Studies stepped in to act as Sidewalk's fiscal sponsor for this grant). But Jacobsen believed the effort could make an important contribution to the image and spirit of the neighborhood, which was a bet he considered well worth the stakes.

That bet has more than paid off. In the year after the first Sidewalk festival, the newly minted organization won a $30,000 Knight Arts Challenge grant, which was matched by local foundation and corporate support. Separately, ArtPlace has granted a total of $425,000 over two years, and another $72,000 has come from the Erb Foundation. The Kresge Foundation has provided additional support through KIP:D, but the festival is now raising much larger sums from elsewhere.

Although Sidewalk is not yet famous outside Detroit, it typifies the gritty, spontaneous, interactive aesthetic for which the city is becoming known. "We've had people contact us from all over to come" and perform at Sidewalk, Myers-Johnson said. "They came from Massachusetts, a lot of people from New York and Chicago, Ohio, Florida. People contact us because they want to come and do this unusual thing in this community, for this audience. But so far it's usually because they heard about it from a friend in Detroit. It's not like there's a big buzz. But the word is out there."

In the cultural ecology of Detroit's arts world, the small, upstart, community-based programs like Burnside Farm, Power House, The Alley Project, and Sidewalk (among many others) thrive in a fertile wilderness, largely free of external rules, that harbors biodiversity and pulses with continual cycles of creation and destruction. These organizations lie at one far end of a spectrum of size and wealth whose other extreme is marked by the great museums and performance spaces of downtown and Midtown. When the New York Times described Detroit as "the last stop on the L Train,"[194] imagining a long transit line from hipster Brooklyn to funky Corktown or trendy Eastern Market, it focused not on the DIA and Symphony Hall, but on working artists of the sort who apply for Kresge Artist Fellowships and perform "radical interactive works in unique spaces" (Sidewalk's phrase) such as Old Redford, North End, and Banglatown.

It's worth noting that the hipster chic that lately attaches to Detroit rankles many artists who have spent their whole careers in the city. The long-timers point out, correctly, that their creative environment was rich in biodiversity long before the New York Times (or the legions of restless émigrés from Brooklyn, Los Angeles, or Boston) ever heard of Corktown. Their resistance to some of this hype is more than a matter of local pride – it illustrates the complex metaphor that

Kresge is constantly invoking in trying to explain and promote the idea of an ecosystem for the arts in Detroit: This is not about "building" an arts scene. It's about drawing together and enriching, diversifying, and sustaining a continuous array of cultural resources, many of which are *already present*, whose roots in Detroit run deep, but that have for too long occupied separate realms, cut off from one another, without the fortifying interaction that nourishes and preserves a flourishing, self-sustaining whole.

All the Rachel Carson imagery behind this metaphor can easily become heavy-handed. But for Rip Rapson, it has its whimsical side. In one of the many richly illustrated diagrams that he uses to capsulize his thinking for the Foundation, he has depicted four sub-environments of what he considers a healthy, diverse, creative ecosystem. Between what he has labeled "the Wilds" of the Heidelberg and Alley projects and the "Big House" museums and performance halls, the drawing depicts two intervening habitats. One is "the Greenhouse," a step up in age, scale, and budget from the Wilds, but still populated by relatively small organizations. These include spartan but respected operators like Mosaic Youth Theater of Detroit, which offers training and mentoring to hundreds of young people in the theatrical arts, or the Sphinx Organization, which cultivates young black and Latino classical musicians. The next step is "the Garden," populated with more prosperous institutions with stable (if still tight) finances and enough name recognition to attract support from at least some businesses, prominent donors, and foundations. These include the Charles H. Wright Museum of African American History, the Detroit Historical Society, and MOCAD.

The point of separating these four clusters is not to draw invidious distinctions among them, but just the opposite: to illustrate how the work of each of them can enrich and inform the others', and how certain kinds of support — festivals, individual fellowships, organizational operating support, real estate improvements, professional development for artists, outreach to bring in other funders — ought to benefit *all* of them, and encourage more interaction from the ungoverned wetlands to the great estates.

The full flux and flow envisioned in this scheme is still largely a dream in Detroit. But there are signs of progress and growth. Ryan Myers-Johnson pointed out, for example, that the Sidewalk festival is fomenting more and more interaction with the boldface-name institutions from the Garden and the Big House. "Part of our goal," she said, "was also to create a junction or a pathway for major institutions to engage with regular people on the people's own turf." So they brought the DIA and MOCAD and the Cranbrook Academy of Art, an elite graduate fine arts and architecture school, to present exhibitions at the festival. "And they brought these great, interactive experiences that a lot of people would never have gone all the way to Midtown or Bloomfield Hills to see."

Cultivating audiences, encouraging philanthropic support, reaping the benefits of culture and creative expression for highly stressed communities, and capitalizing on a sense of excitement and wonder in a hardscrabble city — these are fruits of a creative environment that can grow in every habitat. Drawing them into a coherent system that collectively constitutes Creative Detroit is a natural role for philanthropy — one that has been embraced by foundations in cities such as Cleveland, Pittsburgh, Philadelphia, and Minneapolis, to dramatic effect. Can it work in Detroit?

Kresge's conviction is that it should work *especially* in Detroit — a city with so many distinctive places (neighborhoods, parks, commercial strips, prime thoroughfares, ethnic and cultural hubs) that can and need to be returned to life in newly imagined form. For Kresge, the arts and culture are increasingly seen as the creative spark in the making of places — a process in which imagination, planning, and community mobilization weave together. The result, if done properly, should be a reinvigorated community that encourages people to visit, entices residents to remain, lures others to move in and repopulate empty blocks, and prompts them to connect with one another, make improvements, and re-establish a conscious reason to live and do business *here* — in these buildings, on these streets, amid these neighbors.

That is, of course, a different vision from the one some Detroiters see unfolding in Midtown and Corktown, where the concentration of creative energy and trendiness have sparked rising real estate prices and a noticeable change in the economic, racial, and age mix of the population. Can the arts make attractive places that are not also uprooted? Can places be made richer and more creative without also being made wealthier, more exclusive, or more homogeneous?

In its support for "creative place-making" — a central theme of Kresge's national grantmaking that is now taking center stage in its Detroit arts initiatives — the Foundation is betting that the answer to these questions is Yes. But more than that, it believes that the question is fundamentally misplaced. The issue is not so much whether the arts may become a driver of gentrification (yes, sometimes they can) as whether efforts to *preserve* communities from gentrification — to mobilize and engage residents in preserving and protecting diverse neighborhoods — are likely to be stronger, subtler, and more durable with the arts built into their core.

The Foundation is a prime backer of the national funding consortium called ArtPlace, a collaboration among multiple foundations, federal agencies, and financial institutions to incorporate art into the preservation and development of disadvantaged communities. When the goal is to revive depleted commercial strips, vacant property, and run-down common areas, ArtPlace suggests, the solution need not be just to import a new "creative class," as some economists and planners have recommended. Instead, it can be to cultivate the community's own cultural and creative elements as elemental assets of its redevelopment.

Jamie L. Bennett, executive director of ArtPlace, argues that "What's powerful about the arts is that they exist everywhere. Not every neighborhood has waterfront access. Not every neighborhood has a major university. But I've never come to a neighborhood where there isn't music, where there isn't painting, where there isn't textile work. So it's an asset that everyone has. Why not activate it?"[195] To date, ArtPlace has made roughly a dozen grants to Detroit arts organizations in all four of Rapson's sub-ecosystems, from neighborhood start-ups to MOCAD and the DIA.

For now, in civic discussions about Detroit's economic recovery, the arts do not draw nearly as much attention as do real estate development, city services, crime, education, and transportation. That is probably to be expected in a city just a few years out of bankruptcy, with so much lost material wealth still to be regenerated. But as befits a city with a strong foundation of arts and culture in its history, popular support for artists and cultural institutions runs high. A 2015 report by the National Endowment for the Arts found that metro Detroiters' attendance at live performing arts events and festivals runs far above the national average.[196] After turning thumbs down on a property tax increase for the arts at the beginning of the century, voters in Wayne, Oakland, and Macomb counties at least partly reversed course a decade later and approved a $23 million annual increase to support the DIA. In exchange, residents of those counties now enjoy free admission to the museum, along with longer operating hours and several areas of expanded programming.[197]

Attendance at other "Big House" arts institutions is strong and, in some cases, rising. The opening of the QLINE now lets visitors make several stops in the cultural district, stroll the waterfront, and continue on for lunch or dinner at one of the multitude of new restaurants that are making Detroit a gastronomic travel destination.

Funding for the arts from local and national foundations has also begun to spread — even beyond the massive philanthropic investment in the "Grand Bargain," which preserved and strengthened the DIA. The Knight Foundation alone contributed more than $20 million between 2007 and 2016, including grants to 171 projects through its Detroit Knight Arts Challenge. Bloomberg Philanthropies has supported more than two dozen Detroit organizations in its Arts Innovation and Management Program, and the Connecticut-based Emily Hall Tremaine Foundation, which supports career development for artists and curators, has given major support to Creative Many Michigan. All of these have become major funders of arts and culture in Detroit since Kresge launched its arts initiative, and several have drawn inspiration and guidance from Kresge's experience. Locally, the Fisher and Hudson-Webber foundations also maintain active grantmaking programs for the arts.

None of this yet constitutes a mature "ecosystem," in Rip Rapson's expansive sense of the phrase. But it is a strong sign of life, around which the rest of the vision may yet coalesce. And in the meantime, the contribution of creative Detroiters to the resurgence of their city is unmistakable and growing.

The role of art, of course, is not principally to rebuild cities or boost economies or widen the palate of urban planning. Art serves its own ends, whose value is not measurable in purely physical or economic terms. Nevertheless, creativity unavoidably serves other purposes beyond its own, as is becoming increasingly obvious in both the polished enclaves of central Detroit and the freewheeling hinterlands where new forms and audiences are coming to life.

The national art world's current patron saint for this theory of the multiple purposes of urban creativity is the Chicago performance and installation artist Theaster Gates, who has advised Kresge on its arts programs. His creation of the Stony Island Arts Bank, among many other projects on Chicago's South Side, has made him an icon for adaptive, transformative creativity in neglected urban spaces. "Theaster's bringing art into a neighborhood where there's not a lot of resources devoted to those sorts of questions," curator Sarah Newman told the New York Times, "and he's bringing labor and craft traditions into the National Gallery. It's a kind of circular economy." Only a small step in disciplinary jargon separates the economist's "circular economy" from the environmentalist's "self-sustaining ecology." The idea, by whichever metaphor, is essentially the same.

"There is a double duty being performed here," Rip Rapson said, referring to this combination of pure artistic expression and ancillary benefits to the city's neighborhoods, economy, and image. Alongside the core purposes of their work, he noted, artists are "creating the buzz, creating an atmosphere, creating a receptivity to new ideas and forms of expression, creating a sense of possibility — and, sometimes very intentionally, they are contributing to a reimagined sense of place, in the community where they live, and where their audience lives, and where their work grows."

Looking back, more than a decade later, on the work she helped launched, Barbara Kratchman believes that the change in Detroit's reputation for edgy creativity has been not only healthy for the city's economy and neighborhoods, but a jolt of fresh energy for its artists and arts organizations as well. "One of our objectives was to make artists know that they're wanted and they're welcome here," she said. "And it happened, even better than anyone expected. We worried, at the beginning of the fellowships, that we might go through all the arts talent, and then what were we going to do? Well, we haven't gone through it all, because there's more and more of it. People keep coming; young Detroit artists keep emerging. It's exciting, it's different, it's energizing."

Chapter 6

BACK TO LIFE

"When all else is said and done, often it is love — love of a place, love of a neighborhood, love of a team or a landscape or family or just a moment in time that is boundup in the experience of Detroit — that can prompt this city of 714,000 to stand its ground and face its bitter truths, willing to work and hope for the days of change. ... What Detroit needs now are strong leaders who love what it stands for and what it can become, residents who have a voice in their neighborhoods and can imagine the possibilities for the entire city, and the best possible knowledge that comes from hard facts and deeply felt personal experiences — and yes, from an enduring love and understanding of Detroit."

— From "Detroit Future City"[198]

The Joe Louis Fist, a sculpture by renowned artist Robert Graham, placed at the crossroads of Woodward and Jefferson avenues in downtown Detroit. Photo Credit: Ryan Southen

Catastrophes — including those like Detroit's, of the political and economic kind — pose a triple threat to philanthropy. First, their sheer mass can quickly overwhelm the resources that even a large foundation has at its disposal, threatening to make any intervention seem puny in comparison with the need. As Laura Trudeau pointed out in a 2013 paper on Kresge's efforts in Detroit, the city's loss of property value just between 2008 and 2012 instantly "dwarfed" The Kresge Foundation's entire contribution to the city over the previous nine decades.[199] The Foundation's total annual grant outlays nationwide would not fund the cash-starved Detroit Public Schools for even three months.[200] Strategic foundations like Kresge that strive for "coordinated, integrated solutions" (Trudeau's phrase) to massive public needs can easily end up buried by the size and complexity of the problems they are confronting, unless they can rally the backing of other, larger players, or target their investments to points of maximum leverage — or, most likely, both.

Second, great crises generally draw the attention of many public, corporate, and philanthropic actors with disparate ideas about how to solve problems. Picking which ideas to support, or what alliances to make, and for what purpose, is therefore even more of a challenge for foundations in extreme circumstances than in normal ones. The choice among different approaches and points of view will eventually tie the foundation to some subset of the competing interests and advocates — and thus likely place it in conflict or disagreement with others. In the worst case, if its preferred course of action is solely its own, the foundation may find itself in the middle of the crossfire, a convenient target for all sides. This is usually a manageable problem — the crossfire is not literal, after all — but it can be an exceedingly uncomfortable position for institutions dedicated to social harmony and cooperation. Laura Trudeau summed up the difficulties this way: "Cross-sector collaboration is imperative, but foundations need to protect their work against other sectors' limited capacity or conflicting priorities."[201]

Third, a catastrophic landscape usually features a panoply of different needs whose urgency cries out for immediate attention. Focusing on just one or two of these cries for help means making painful, invidious choices. But the temptation to tackle everything at once — to find "comprehensive" remedies or, as Robert F. Kennedy famously put it in 1966, to "grab the web whole" — can mean aiming at too many targets and diluting the chance of being effective at any of them. In Detroit, where Rip Rapson explicitly envisioned "taking on [an] entire" city, and where Kresge has sought "to change the trajectory of Detroit," the number of different fronts on which the battle can be waged is enormous. For the sake of clarity and simplicity, Rapson's framework for Re-imagining Detroit 2020 comprised nine fields of effort — but even that list encapsulated dozens of sub-areas, each demanding different skills, answerable to different constituencies, subject to different systems and rules, and likely to progress on profoundly different timelines.

To move on so many fronts at once, Kresge has acknowledged, means choosing a smaller number of areas on which to concentrate the Foundation's own time and money, and playing a supportive role in others. But even so, that has meant immersing itself — and mining the skills of its staff and advisers — in areas as diverse as urban planning, transportation, capital formation, leadership development, neighborhood revitalization, the arts, and early childhood education, among others.

It has also meant forging constructive but complex alliances — with big corporations and individual investors, for whom civic and business interests inevitably intersect; with state and local public officials who rarely see eye to eye, and who often focus on conflicting issues; with grassroots neighborhood leaders and downtown elites who live and work in different social strata (and, most often, in markedly different physical places); and with foundations and donors who, no matter how absolute their dedication to the public good, are bound to draw disparate conclusions about the most important needs and the most promising solutions.

A result of all this can be a formidable challenge of priority-setting and diplomacy. But even more, it's a complex strategic and organizational puzzle whose stakes are no less than the survival of a still large and important American city. There is no pattern or precedent for this type of philanthropy *in extremis*. No great American city has fallen so far, so fast as Detroit, nor brushed so close to financial and political ruin, nor struggled against such ferocious headwinds in its efforts at recovery. No foundation, before Kresge, has tried to "change the trajectory" of so large and complex a place. Detroit is not the kind of "Gray Area," teetering but still vigorous, on which the standard playbook of urban philanthropy has been based for some 60 years.

Nor are Detroit's woes purely economic, and thus correctable primarily with money, as might be the case if the problems had been limited to underfunded pensions, poorly distributed taxes, or mismanaged debt. Decades of racial segregation, white flight, disinvestment, industrial decay, and racially charged hostilities between the city and its suburbs have contributed to a dangerous erosion of the fundamentals of urban well-being: the physical integrity of neighborhoods, the viability of their commercial strips, the ability to control crime or provide other essential public services, and — some might say worst of all — the quality of the schools. Grants alone cannot reverse such things. It takes collective will, civic bonds of trust, and patient perseverance over several decades — all of which are virtues in short supply in contemporary America, and none of which can be summoned into being by any amount of philanthropy alone.

Yet for all its difficulties, Detroit has held on to a reservoir of strengths that make it possible not only to persevere, but to imagine a different, more equitable, and more resilient city taking shape on the horizon. Its community and religious leaders, a new generation of political and administrative talent, a growing cadre of private investors and young entrepreneurs, and most of all, a bedrock of resolute Detroiters constitute a solid platform on which to continue building. It may even be reasonable to hope that the younger generations of the new century, on both sides of the 8 Mile Road city limits, may find the barriers of race less sturdy than did their elders, and may find new ways to breach them.

In the meantime, however, are urgent practical challenges — acres of empty or crumbling real estate, overstretched municipal services, failing schools, meager economic opportunity, neighborhoods fearing oblivion — that cannot wait for further generational shifts or an upsurge of public confidence and trust. It is on these fronts that the "trajectory of Detroit" must shift, and soon. "Re-imagining" the city means, in essence, mapping an upward path on all these issues and generating a lasting momentum, even if the process takes decades — as seems probable.

A philanthropy of 'entire cities'

What makes this abundance of different challenges so difficult is not just that there are so many, but that they are interdependent. Neighborhoods depend for their survival partly on the quality of their schools, and vice versa; economic opportunity depends partly on transportation; city services depend partly on property values and the tax revenue they generate; and on and on. Focusing on just one or two of the big issues, to the neglect of others, runs the risk that the neglected areas may ultimately undermine any progress on the ones where the work and money are concentrated. Seen in that light, Rapson's contemplation of "taking on entire cities" is not so much an act of visionary audacity as a simple confronting of reality. Even if Kresge can't play a leading role in all these areas — and in some cases shouldn't — it must be a deliberate part of a web of effort that touches the entire city, with some overarching plan or vision holding all the effort together.

In Detroit, such a broad, encompassing vision has been lacking for more than half a century. At least since the violence of 1967 — which, as Coleman Young later wrote, "put the city on the fast track to economic desolation"[202] — Detroit's struggle to regain its footing has tended to be transactional and particular, focusing on big projects like the Renaissance Center, the People Mover, sports stadiums, and casinos that were somehow supposed to reverse the cycle of decline, depopulation, and decay. Philanthropy was as much a part of this transactional, big-project approach to revitalization as was government and the corporate civic establishment. Kresge itself, in its early years, preferred to award its support project by project, based mainly on the merits of each individual transaction (though, to be fair, the underlying objective of many of these transactions was to strengthen the organizations that sponsored them — arts institutions, the Riverfront Conservancy, Eastern Market — and equip them to accomplish more things over time).

Even among the foundations embedded in Detroit, the pattern was much the same: Each one had its specialties and signature projects, and while executives met periodically to exchange information and solicit one another's help, each foundation essentially pursued its own business its own way. One person who regularly attended these meetings described them as "very cordial and often quite interesting," but concluded that they "never challenged anything or changed anyone's basic direction."

What Rapson had called "the absence of a shared community vision," which he identified as "*the* defining problem" of Detroit, was not just a failure to conjure a goal beyond the next big project. It was an inability to draw the city's — and the region's — many factions and interests into a single discussion, transcending sectors, geographic boundaries, racial divisions, and political or ideological leanings. To weave the various lines of effort into a coherent (if still pointillist) picture of overall recovery for Detroit was a job that, in Kresge's view, fell disproportionately on philanthropy's shoulders. "Philanthropy," Rapson said at a gathering of urban experts in 2011, "has emerged as the sector best able to provide the long-term vision and investment of capital the city needs to right itself." As the region's largest foundation, Kresge embraced the challenge.

Why philanthropy? First, because it carries an exclusive legal mandate to serve the public interest. And second, because it bears fewer of the perceptual and political burdens that restrict the maneuvering room of other sectors. Unlike businesses and private investors, philanthropy has nothing to gain materially from public improvements, and thus is less likely to be suspected of self-serving motives. Unlike elected officials and their appointees, it is not at the mercy of election cycles, political factions, or campaign contributors, and so is freer to explore unfamiliar and even unpopular ideas. Unlike government administrators and regulators, it is not confined to particular silos of responsibility or rulebooks of permissible action. Unlike financiers, whether public or private, it is comparatively free to accept risks and losses if it deems the possible benefits great enough.

But when it comes to setting public goals and elaborating big visions, these considerable assets are also liabilities. Unlike businesses, investors, and lenders, foundations are relatively undisciplined by the market and may not suffer materially if their visions prove unrealistic. Unlike public officials, foundations wield no popular mandate and have no formal accountability to voters or their representatives. And, as Trudeau has pointed out, the very fact that foundations stand outside the daily rough-and-tumble of business and politics means that they are often poorly understood by people whose lives are spent mainly in those two realms. "Foundations are not always known quantities as partners," she has written, "which can create distrust."[203]

Still, it is reasonable to ask, in the dire circumstances of Detroit in the early years of the 21st century: Who might have assembled a complete plan for recovery if philanthropy — and Kresge in particular — had not asserted a role? With local government overwhelmed by accumulating crises ("everything was a fire," as a former city aide put it), and with business interests held in suspicion by some powerful elected and community leaders, a prominent foundation would seem the logical player to step forward with an attempt at a unifying agenda. Kresge's ability to put significant amounts of money behind key initiatives (greenways, the arts, Eastern Market, and the RiverWalk in the early years, with the later addition of the Woodward Corridor and M-1, Eastern Market, Detroit Future City, LISC and other capital-aggregators for neighborhoods, and a host of housing and economic development investments) made its leadership not just persuasive but sometimes decisive.

Its size — roughly three times that of the next-largest regionally based private foundation[204] — combined with its national mission and high profile in the foundation world, made Kresge unique in southeast Michigan as a voice for the public interest. While the Community Foundation for Southeast Michigan might be expected to take a leading role in Detroit affairs — and frequently does — it was itself created partly by Kresge and is barely one-fifth as large. In most years, Kresge's aggregate donations and investments in Detroit alone have been greater than the Community Foundation's total giving. As the Kresge board concluded in the late 1990s and early 2000s, *not* putting its scale and stature to use as a force for galvanizing a public agenda would have been a wasteful sin of omission, the equivalent of leaving an enormous institutional asset under the mattress.

By asserting not merely leadership but an overarching vision, a complete "re-imagining," of Detroit, The Kresge Foundation crossed another standard boundary of conventional philanthropy: the principle that it is better to stick to a few issues and make a profound impact on them than to take on whole tapestries of social, political, and economic complexity. Although the word "comprehensive" has become ubiquitous in latter-day philanthropy, most foundations use the word to describe multifaceted interventions in relatively small, precisely delineated fields of endeavor. A "comprehensive" community development initiative, for example, might encompass many aspects of life for lower-income families, but in just a handful of neighborhoods. Or a "comprehensive" program might take on several kinds of systemic reform, but in just a slice of some larger system — focusing on certain grades or curricula in public education, for instance, or certain diseases or medical practices in the health care system. To change the "trajectory" of a whole municipality of about 700,000 people — a trajectory 60 years or more in the making — is a rare and risky proposition. Call it "audacity," "courage," or "hubris" (all three words come up now and then); it is certainly an unconventional and provocative conception of a foundation's role in public life.

'Private legislatures'

Among the risks of that kind of broad ambition — apart from the risk of outright failure, which is ever present — is the danger of being resented, and thus discounted, by other sources of leadership and authority. Seeing itself described by the Wall Street Journal as "grabbing the wheel in the Motor City" stung some at Kresge, as has the occasional jab from its philanthropic colleagues for playing the "big dog," "throwing their weight around," and "blowing their own horn," as nonprofit leaders put it in 2016 interviews. When the Journal described Kresge's approach as a "foundation-knows-best attitude," it undoubtedly was drawing on sources among Detroit's political and civic leaders who saw the Foundation's intentions in just that way.

Much of a foundation's ability to guide or influence public debate depends on a reservoir of goodwill: the perception that it is acting as a partner in the public interest, and not for self-aggrandizement. Kresge has labored, not without success, to preserve that reputational asset, even — perhaps especially — at its moments of greatest assertiveness. Many people in both elite and grassroots leadership, including those who disagree with the Foundation on some important issues, share the opinion of one top corporate executive who said in 2009 that "Kresge is at the center of everything positive going on in Detroit at this time." Admittedly, it is hard to tell whether that opinion is widely shared today, or limited to an influential and knowledgeable few. But the point is that the boldness of Kresge's approach to Detroit has met with plaudits as well as resistance, and has not, at least yet, hurt its ability to build its arguments on a fundament of goodwill.

A Detroit civic leader who has not always seen eye to eye with Kresge described the Foundation's balance of assertiveness and collaboration by comparing the atmosphere among local foundations before and after Rip Rapson came to Detroit:

> Pre-Rip, you had the larger foundations in town that got together regularly and liked each other, and we had lunch three or four times a year and talked about projects we were all working on, and it was us pitching to each other. When Rip came in and started pushing some other buttons, those meetings were a lot less pleasant. Suddenly we were arguing and disagreeing, and there was a lot of tension. And they also became a lot more productive. ... I firmly believe that by creating the tension, by calling some questions, by not agreeing to go along with some things, and by pushing hard on some others, Rip changed the discussion to one that produced more fruit.

This same observer added, pointedly, that whatever the disagreements or tensions may have been, "Kresge was at the table, debating and listening, not on the outside sniping or ignoring the rest of us." Its leadership in the Detroit Neighborhood Forum, this observer added, was another signal that Kresge, for all its strong views, was eager for discussion and debate and in fact welcomed a frank exchange of ideas on critical issues.

The need to project collegiality and supportiveness is especially critical in the implementation of Detroit Future City. Kresge's prominence in the conduct of the planning process and the completion of the published framework has posed the constant risk of making it a "Kresge product," too thoroughly identified with one foundation to be embraced by City Hall, other funders, and the leaders and residents of neighborhoods across the city. It didn't help that the plan was published just as Detroit was about to be placed under the control of an emergency manager and as Mayor Dave Bing was preparing to end his term without seeking re-election. There was little opportunity, at that moment, to engage elected city government in the rollout of the report or to cultivate a sense of ownership of it in the mayor's office. With the imposition of emergency management in 2013, Mayor Bing and the City Council were about to be stripped of nearly all power, and it was not yet clear when that power would be restored, or who would be sitting in the top municipal offices when it was.

Yet nothing better exemplifies the expansiveness of Kresge's concept of philanthropy in Detroit, and its role as a partner of public and private actors, than Detroit Future City. As Rip Rapson noted in 2011, the whole nine-part framework of Re-imagining Detroit "pivots on land use." The whole "shared community vision" the Foundation was seeking to engender would depend on achieving some common understanding, some widely accepted principles and priorities, about what to do with the city's vast landscape of underused real estate. "Detroit simply has to shrink in order to grow," Rapson said in a 2009 speech. "That's a complex undertaking. You have to repurpose land. You have to re-imagine how you deploy resources. You have to engage residents in all aspects and at every stage."[205]

But if Detroit Future City is the product of philanthropic leadership, can it also be a keystone of the city's *political* leadership? As this is written, Mayor Mike Duggan has not formally embraced Detroit Future City as an element of city policy and in fact has taken occasional steps to put distance between the framework and his official vision. Yet supporters of Detroit Future City argue that the mayor's actual decisions often tend to be in harmony with tenets of the published plan, rhetoric notwithstanding, and that there is plenty of time and latitude to build cooperation and mutual support between City Hall and Detroit Future City. Given that the latter is now in the hands of a new, independent nonprofit, supported by but independent of Kresge, the odds of integrating its ideas with those of the elected government could improve.

Maurice Cox, the city's planning director, credited the Detroit Future City plan in 2015 with "refram[ing] the conversation that Detroit was having about its development."[206] Concurring, another senior Duggan administration official said that "most of DFC we can agree with." But he underscored in an interview that the "primary role" in evaluating its recommendations has to be "played by democratically elected government." The foundations operating in Detroit "had planted important seeds we're harvesting now," and Kresge, he said, is "incredibly central among foundations, not only in the volume of their spend and how they leverage their money, but in the ideas they have and their partners. When looking for philanthropic input, Kresge is always at the top of our list."

Still, the fact that something so fundamental to local governance as city planning has been carried out under the aegis of private philanthropy highlights an uncomfortable fact about Detroit in the first decades of the 21st century: Some of its essential public functions — from combating blight to building a rail line to developing signature public spaces downtown — have been handled, in one way or another, outside City Hall. That is not primarily Kresge's doing. As John Gallagher, the veteran urban affairs reporter for the *Detroit Free Press*, explained in a recent book about Detroit, "spinning off pieces of the municipal government into a series of private conservancies, public authorities, and nonprofit corporations" had been progressing on multiple fronts for many years. To note that Kresge has supported a great many of these spinoffs in one way or another is not to say that it created the trend. But for better or worse, the Foundation has become one of the trend's visible symbols.

As Gallagher noted, the absorption of essential public functions into nonpublic or quasi-public entities — a practice opposed by Mayor Duggan — unavoidably knocks some stones out of the foundations of urban democracy. The results may be efficient and effective; they may hasten development and contribute to public confidence that even severe problems can be remedied. But eventually, Gallagher wrote, to ensure legitimacy "the city needs to balance the potential for service improvement with the potential for diminished accountability or democratic control."[207]

Those who see an erosion of democracy and accountability underway throughout the country — a concern not hard to find among community leaders in Detroit — take a wary view of the more assertive brand of philanthropy favored by Kresge, at least when it places foundations on traditionally public turf. Attending a presentation by Rip Rapson on Detroit's recovery from bankruptcy, the journalist and nonprofit scholar Rick Cohen was reminded of a statement by Paul Ylvisaker, an architect of the Ford Foundation's urban grantmaking in the 1950s: Philanthropy "over time has become a recognized social process ... in effect, a set of private legislatures defining public problems, setting goals and priorities, and allocating resources toward the public good." Cohen, who died in 2015, feared that "'private legislatures' making decisions toward what might constitute the public good is a critical concern of contemporary philanthropy across the nation, but particularly in Detroit," where government was not yet strong enough to defend its ground, and where citizens had too long been relegated to the sidelines when great decisions about their future were being made.

Rapson acknowledges the concern but is not intimidated by it. In a 2015 speech, he argued that "in uncommon times, you need to do uncommon things. We're not always staying in our lane. We're sometimes butting into the public sector, butting into the private sector." But that, he said, is a necessary adaptation to circumstances that have placed extraordinary demands on every segment of society. As a result of those exceptional demands, and for as long as they persist, "the kind of reshuffling of roles and responsibilities in Detroit may be unique in America."[208]

Public benefit, private wealth

One further aspect of Detroit's recent successes has exacerbated local fears that private forces may be usurping democratic authority. It is impossible not to notice how much of the surge in construction, enterprise, and employment in central Detroit touches on the business interests of a handful of companies and investors. Most prominent among these is Dan Gilbert, whose control of some 100 buildings totaling more than 12 million square feet of downtown real estate[209] makes him an obvious beneficiary of the city's recovery — and specifically of philanthropically sponsored projects like Campus Martius and the QLINE. His extensive personal philanthropy and civic leadership, including his creation of the nonprofit Bizdom, which supports small, local, and start-up businesses, has not entirely eased the suspicion among some Detroiters that public and philanthropic investment in downtown and Midtown Detroit are, in effect, subsidies for Gilbert's business ventures.

The reality is far more complicated than that, and close observers of urban redevelopment would argue that Gilbert's early investments in what was then still a largely devastated downtown were far more of an economic lifeline to the city than the other way around. If these properties are now starting to prosper financially, it can only reinforce the message that Detroit is an inviting place to invest and do business. The city's hunger for tax revenues can't be satisfied without a recovery in property values; those in turn will surely benefit from the successful preservation, conversion, and construction of prime real estate in the urban core. More generally, it's fair to ask how convincing the city's message of optimism would have been if one of its biggest corporate boosters had *not* staked some of his personal fortune on Detroit's recovery, and then prospered from doing so.

The same points might be made in the case of the Ilitch family, whose new hockey arena for the Detroit Red Wings rose on part of the long-fallow strip just north of downtown. This new arena is shared with the Detroit Pistons, returning to the city after decades in the suburban "Palace of Auburn Hills." The QLINE will now link to all the other commercial growth areas along Woodward, from the river to New Center — including the baseball stadium where the Ilitches' Detroit Tigers play. Other private investors have similarly been drawn to the New Center area at the streetcar's northern terminus, and to properties stretching east and west of Woodward, where Kresge and other foundations have helped to fertilize the market with new housing, retail space, and hubs of creative and technological innovation. If private investors reap profits from this improved environment, that will be at least partly a result of market activity returning to this portion of Detroit — an indispensable first step in reviving confidence in the city, and a clear, early reality test of Kresge's long-term strategy.

That is a complex argument to advance, and some Detroiters remain unconvinced. Where Kresge and other foundations see a cluster of successful efforts at creating market incentives and resuscitating a once nearly comatose urban core, some critics have seen what Rolling Stone editor Mark Binelli described as an "unelected oligarchy" planting gardens of personal enrichment in the city's small nucleus, while the comparatively powerless residents of the remaining 130 or so square miles wait for some benefit to trickle their way.[210]

The merits of the critics' arguments can be debated, but in some respects they are beside the point. Persuasive or not, they illustrate the reputational risk for philanthropy in being associated with private wealth and corporate power — even when those are precisely what is needed to revive the local economy. Far more than in most other American cities, as we've seen, Detroit is a place that has suffered from massive and swift movements of industry and capital — starting with the city's rapid rise on the strength of a surging auto industry, creating an explosion of new, low-density neighborhoods fanning out in all directions, and followed by the dizzying fall as wealth, business, jobs, and residents fled the city pell-mell in the last half of the 20th century. When Detroit politicians or activists warn that wealthy outsiders are "taking the city away from us," the threat may seem fanciful to anyone observing only the data, but the fear rests on generations of distrust and bitter experience of developments whose promise was exaggerated and whose benefits tended to flow elsewhere, while the failures and obsolescence remained behind.

From downtown to our town

At least since the beginning of Detroit's population decline in the 1950s, a consistent theme of local politics has been residents' perception that too much civic and governmental attention was being lavished on the central business district, to the exclusion of outlying residential neighborhoods. Successive mayors have had to contend with the accusation that they "care only about downtown," even as they struggled to explain that downtown's unraveling was a threat to the overall health of city budgets, services, and competitiveness — and thus to the survival of its neighborhoods. Their message only grew harder to deliver in the 1970s and '80s, as several major downtown initiatives absorbed massive amounts of money without doing much to rescue either the core or the rest of Detroit.

The financial collapse of 2008 and the ensuing wave of foreclosures and failed city services transformed what had been a perennial civic complaint into a desperate and heartbreaking cry of anguish. In the ruins of the Great Recession lay huge barren tracts that had once been leafy streets, trimmed lawns, gardens, shops, scenes of street life that defined what it meant to be a Detroiter. A Detroit News survey in 2012 suggested that 40 percent of city residents would leave within five years if they could, for fear of crime and lack of municipal services.[211] In fact, at the turn of the 21st century, hundreds of thousands actually did so. Between 2000 and 2010, the city's overall population dropped 29 percent, the largest decrease in the nation. Most of this exodus was from the city's African-American population: Having remained steady between 1990 and 2000, it fell by 23.9 percent in the succeeding decade.*

During his campaign for mayor in 2013, Duggan pledged to stem, then reverse, this population outflow in his first term. While the outflow has not reversed, it does appear to have slowed. According to population figures from the Census Bureau's American Community Survey, between 2010 and 2014 the city averaged annual population declines of roughly 1.2 percent per year. Population loss for the lastest two years, however, lessened to approximately half a percentage point per year, resulting in an estimated 2016 population of 672,879.[212]

While Detroit's median household income increased in 2016 from $26,308 to $28,099, it is still half the national median, and the city's poverty rate — now about 36 percent — remains among the highest in the nation.[213] In particular, African-American median income continues to lag significantly behind that of white and Hispanic Detroiters.

*By comparison, Chicago lost 17 percent of its black population in that decade. Nationwide, a majority of African-Americans in large metropolitan areas, particularly among the middle class, now live in the suburbs.

Amid the unyielding hardship, it has been hard to persuade residents, as urban planners and civic leaders bravely tried to do, that recovery would come gradually, over many years, emanating from the core outward. Mayor Bing's suggestion that some areas would unavoidably have to "depopulate" proved too harsh for voters to accept, but Mayor Duggan's later promise that "every neighborhood has a future" has struck many observers as either naïve or misleading. Much depends on what that "future" entails. The future of some neighborhoods, as one urban researcher pointed out, distinctly off the record "will come in some cases 30 years from now, and may be a forest or a meadow. Is that a future? I guess."

In the spirit of Detroit Future City, Kresge and several of its corporate and philanthropic partners have sought a middle ground — between a mere surrender to devastation and a dream of resurgence on every city block. In 2016 the Foundation chose, as Rapson put it, to "pivot into the neighborhoods and carry into them the entire toolbox that we've deployed over the last decade in the central business district and its major arterial."[214] Declaring that "it's the neighborhoods that will determine if Detroit's comeback has staying power,"[215] Kresge has now trained its strategic gaze more intensely north of Grand Boulevard and to the east and west of the urban hub.

Treading gently on this sensitive terrain, the Foundation has taken the view that neighborhood development in Detroit, to use a favorite Rapson metaphor, is likely to be "syncopated" — strong beats alternating with weaker ones. As stronger neighborhoods draw population, business, and physical upgrading, more opportunity will arise in the weaker areas to reduce density and create alternative forms of green and blue conservation. In this vision, no area needs to be deliberately "depopulated"; market forces and individual preferences will create these rhythms naturally. The process can — and, the Foundation believes, should — be helped along by civic investment in strategically chosen places that hold natural strengths, that are drawing or retaining residents, and that have strong enough neighborhood organizations and leaders to put investments to productive use (or, at least, promising organizations and leaders, whose strength can grow over time). Support can also go to cultivating green and blue uses where population declines create the best opportunities.

"All Detroiters," the Foundation has written, should "have pathways to opportunity." By emphasizing "all Detroiters" rather than "all neighborhoods," the statement stakes out a kind of intermediate position in which the city's physical makeup and civic energies serve its people, rather than its land mass.

To anyone who would prefer that philanthropy concentrate on the neediest or hardest-hit places first — a disaster-relief approach rather than a long-term development approach — Kresge's choice may seem unresponsive, even cold. Many neighborhoods have suffered terribly: friendly surroundings turned empty and menacing, the value of family homesteads wiped out, businesses shuttered, leaving behind little or no residual value with which to finance a move elsewhere. It is hard to regard that depth of loss without wishing to provide some kind of near-term relief.

But a strategy that embraces syncopation means, in effect, assigning priorities: making the most of the places with the clearest options. And, given the Foundation's limited money and staff capacity, it means starting with just a few of those, priming market forces, cultivating community organizations, and supporting residents' visions for the future until progress is far enough along so that it becomes possible to shift emphasis elsewhere. Thus far, that has meant a particular Kresge concentration on three or four neighborhoods with unmistakable assets, such as the center of immigrant construction and entrepreneurship in southwest Detroit's Mexicantown; the spread of development east of downtown, drawing energy from Eastern Market, the riverfront, and proximity to the core; the historic North End/New Center area just north of Midtown; and the Livernois-McNichols neighborhood.

In places such as these, Kresge's Detroit team wrote in 2016, "we will have an ample opportunity" to help attract capital and cultivate assets for local improvement. "We can assume the first level of risk in transactions too risky for the private markets to undertake without help. We can invest in amenities — parks, open space, greenways, and other civic assets — that signal stability and long-term value. We can strengthen the channels of capital deployment and absorption" by helping to strengthen community development organizations and to nurture civic leadership among neighborhood residents.[216]

Apart from the need to make difficult strategic choices among many needy residential and commercial areas, Kresge's targeted neighborhood strategy also amounts to an altered approach to thinking about its relationship to the "entire city." In Detroit's 130-plus square miles of neighborhoods, it would be impossible for an institution of Kresge's size (or of 10 times Kresge's size) to invest constructively in a large percentage of the territory. Nor is it necessary for the Foundation to be a hands-on investor throughout the city, now that there is a restored, fiscally healthier, and better-performing city government to assume command.

In other words, Kresge's service to the "entire city" now must flow through a partnership with City Hall, based on a shared vision of what's possible, equitable, and sustainable, and on a platform of shared values. It must also continue to work through private investors and market forces, which the Foundation sees as increasingly drawn to some residential areas outside the downtown/Midtown core. Supporting, encouraging, and guiding these mainstream drivers are effectively the Foundation's only realistic means of influencing neighborhood life citywide. In the meantime, as those partnerships progress, Kresge will concentrate on a "few opportunity areas to create 'proof points' and help the city and other funders understand what it takes" to re-imagine Detroit's neighborhoods.[217]

The danger of success

Sooner or later, almost every community recovering from abandonment and economic decline runs into a concern that, in the darkest times, might have seemed like the most remote of its worries: the fear that a growing, wealthier population and rising property values will force current residents out of the neighborhood. Beyond downtown and the neighborhoods immediately surrounding it, an out-of-town visitor might be astonished to learn that anyone is concerned about Detroit's turning into the next SoHo, Southie, or Mission District. And for now, it's true, the deluge of spectacular wealth that overran New York, Boston, and San Francisco remains a far-off danger in Detroit.

Yet the resurgence of Midtown, for example, where some residents say they already feel priced out, and where the upscale conversion of some residential buildings has forced out former tenants, has begun to clarify the debate: How should redevelopment be managed — with how much of a brake on market forces, or with what amount of protection and provision for longtime residents — to avoid turning a recovery for Detroit into (yet another) hardship for Detroiters.

The debate is easy to caricature — "are we really worried about an army of one-percenters taking over Detroit?" a former city resident asked in 2015 — but even more analytical observers consider the prospect of widespread displacement remote, at least for now. For example, Sue Mosey, head of Midtown Detroit, Inc., told Bridge Magazine in 2014 that even in trendy Midtown, "there is affordable housing everywhere. Is the market-rate [housing] going up? Yes. But that's going to happen. ... You have to have an economic base to make a neighborhood work. You have to have a mix."[218]

Still, from the perspective of very low-income Detroiters — with 36 percent of city residents living at or below the poverty line, twice the statewide figure[219] — rents or property tax bills do not need to rise dramatically to make them unaffordable. This might seem, at first glance, to be a threat mainly for renters, given that homeowners experience rising prices as a boost to their net worth. But in Detroit, with its comparatively high property tax rates, owners may face above-average risks from increased valuations: Tens of thousands of property tax foreclosures in 2014 and '15, with many more threatened, seemed to illustrate what can happen to those living closest to the economic margin when housing values rise even slightly. For at least two-fifths of the city, "gentrification" has nothing to do with one-percenters; it can be a matter of even relatively small increments that push families from barely hanging on into homelessness.

As with most social and economic issues in Detroit, the fear of gentrification is also a question of race. There is no mistaking the change in complexion of central Detroit in the 21st century, from predominantly black and older to a mix of white and black professionals and hip millennials, interspersed with a remnant of older residents, even in places where the change in average incomes is not dramatic. An influx of white graduate students, artists, and start-up techies may not bring in much wealth or high disposable incomes at first, but their presence can change the character of a place, and may unintentionally create an impression that older and African-American residents of long standing are now somehow unwelcome, out-of-place, passé. That is not a change measurable in tables of income or property values. But it is real, and it can easily undermine community members' confidence that development is benefiting them.

In any event, the best time to formulate a strategy to control gentrification is well before it begins. Acknowledging that hard-learned lesson, in a review of its earlier work in Detroit, Kresge staff resolved that its next stage of work would have to address unintended consequences like displacement and alienation of longtime residents head-on. "We are, among other things, exploring a wide variety of tools to explicitly promote the multiple dimensions of 'inclusive recovery' — avoiding displacement, ensuring neighborhood access to capital, pursuing asset-building strategies such as small business formation, and many others."[220]

Out of school

Amid an expansive program born with a vision of "taking on entire cities," the most noticeable gap in Kresge's approach to Detroit's overall recovery is public schools. Apart from its initial support for Excellent Schools Detroit, and its willingness to "back-fill" behind the leadership of other foundations in this area, particularly Skillman, The Kresge Foundation has not staked out a primary role in any aspect of Detroit's K-12 school reform efforts. Instead, it is concentrating on early childhood development — not only early education, but medical care, family and community supports, nutrition, child care, and other services that open a path for the healthy, successful development of young children before they start traditional schooling. The new Hope Starts Here plan, and the broader KEYS:Detroit program, cornerstones of that effort, represent a broader strategy that, the Foundation says, "'doubles down' where we have gained traction"[221] — meaning, in effect, that it zeros in on a single field where the staff is confident of its approach and believes it has begun making a visible difference.

Kresge's past efforts to support the K-12 system evidently fail the "traction" test. "For us," Wendy Lewis Jackson said in early 2016, "the issue is always, 'What do you lead with?' It's a question we are always asking at Kresge. And we knew that the issues around student achievement start a lot earlier than high school, and in fact earlier than kindergarten. So that's what we felt we needed to lead with."

That assessment, in the long term, is compelling: The pressure on city schools to improve student achievement would surely be lightened if more students arrived in kindergarten healthy and ready to learn. This is a critically important aspect of the overall challenge of educating children — particularly children in very-low-income families, living in troubled neighborhoods with too few amenities, in a city poorly equipped financially to provide them the care, safety, and enrichment that most parents would wish for. There is no disputing the need.

But it would be hard to find any extensive commentary on Detroit's future that does not dwell at length on the fractiousness, disorganization, and drift in Detroit's K-12 public education system. One might reasonably ask whether it is productive to deliver a cadre of better-prepared, healthier, better-cared-for 5-year-olds into the embrace of a school system that repeatedly is ranked at or near the bottom of urban school districts on academic achievement, surrounded by physical conditions that the Washington Post has described as "appalling,"[222] in "classrooms where not even the pretense of education takes place," according to the 2016 federal lawsuit,[223] and managed by a system the Citizens Research Council of Michigan described in 2016 as "failing academically and financially."[224]

The public education crisis includes many charter schools (publicly funded, but privately operated and more loosely regulated) which have proliferated under the sponsorship of multiple statewide "authorizers." For-profit "management companies" operate 83 percent of these charter schools,[225] competing with the traditional public schools for the brightest students. Yet the charter schools — enrolling more than half of Detroit's students — still often fail to raise the achievement bar, further provoking despair from some of the city's otherwise most enthusiastic civic boosters.*

Where, if at all, does such a desperate circumstance fit in the strategy of a foundation convinced, as Rapson wrote in 2015, that "philanthropy has to be prepared to cut from its safe and secure moorings to embrace a level of risk commensurate with the magnitude of the challenge at hand"?[226] Given the magnitude of Detroit's public education challenge, what would be a "commensurate" foundation response?

The question is nowhere near as easy to answer as it might seem. To counsel Kresge that it ought to invest tens of millions of dollars in school reform would require, first, that there be some local consensus — or a reasonable shot at gaining consensus — on what "reform" would look like, and thus some openness among education funders, public and private, to rallying around a coherent plan of attack. That does not

*The merits of traditional public schools vs. charters is the subject of full-throated debate. In 2015, for the fourth straight time since 2009, students in Detroit's public schools were ranked lowest among a score of cities with populations over 250,000, according to the federal Department of Education's National Assessment of Educational Progress (NAEP). NAEP reported that only 6 percent of students in these Detroit schools were "proficient" or better in fourth-grade reading; 7 percent in eighth-grade reading, 5 percent in fourth-grade math and 4 percent in eighth-grade math — figures "not significantly different" from the start of the biennial review of large urban districts in 2009. Proficient is defined by NAEP as "solid academic performance." Detroit public school students were also generally at the bottom among the big cities in "basic" — or "partial mastery" — reading and math. Comparable figures for charter schools in the cities are not reported by NAEP. The New York Times stated in 2016 that "most [Detroit] charters have failed to improve on the dismal performance of the traditional public schools." However, according to Margaret Raymond, director of Stanford University's Center for Research on Education Outcomes (CREDO), a 2015 CREDO study which looked at test results concluded that, overall, Detroit charter schools showed "significantly more academic progress" over the public schools, in both reading and math.

A separate Stanford study of the nation's 200 largest school districts, measuring academic growth between 3rd and 8th grades on the basis of test scores, ranked Detroit's public and charter schools as No. 132, close to New York City's 129 and Philadelphia's 137. (Chicago, according to researchers at the Stanford Education Data Archive, was No 1.) The typical 3rd-grader in Detroit was 2.1 years below grade level; the typical 8th-grader, 2.6 years below grade level, the study reported. Source: Email to authors from Sean F. Reardon, Stanford professor of poverty and inequality in education, Dec. 15, 2017.

Following page: Prior to the development of the Detroit Future City framework, Rip Rapson created a drawing mapping the land-use considerations for the plan.

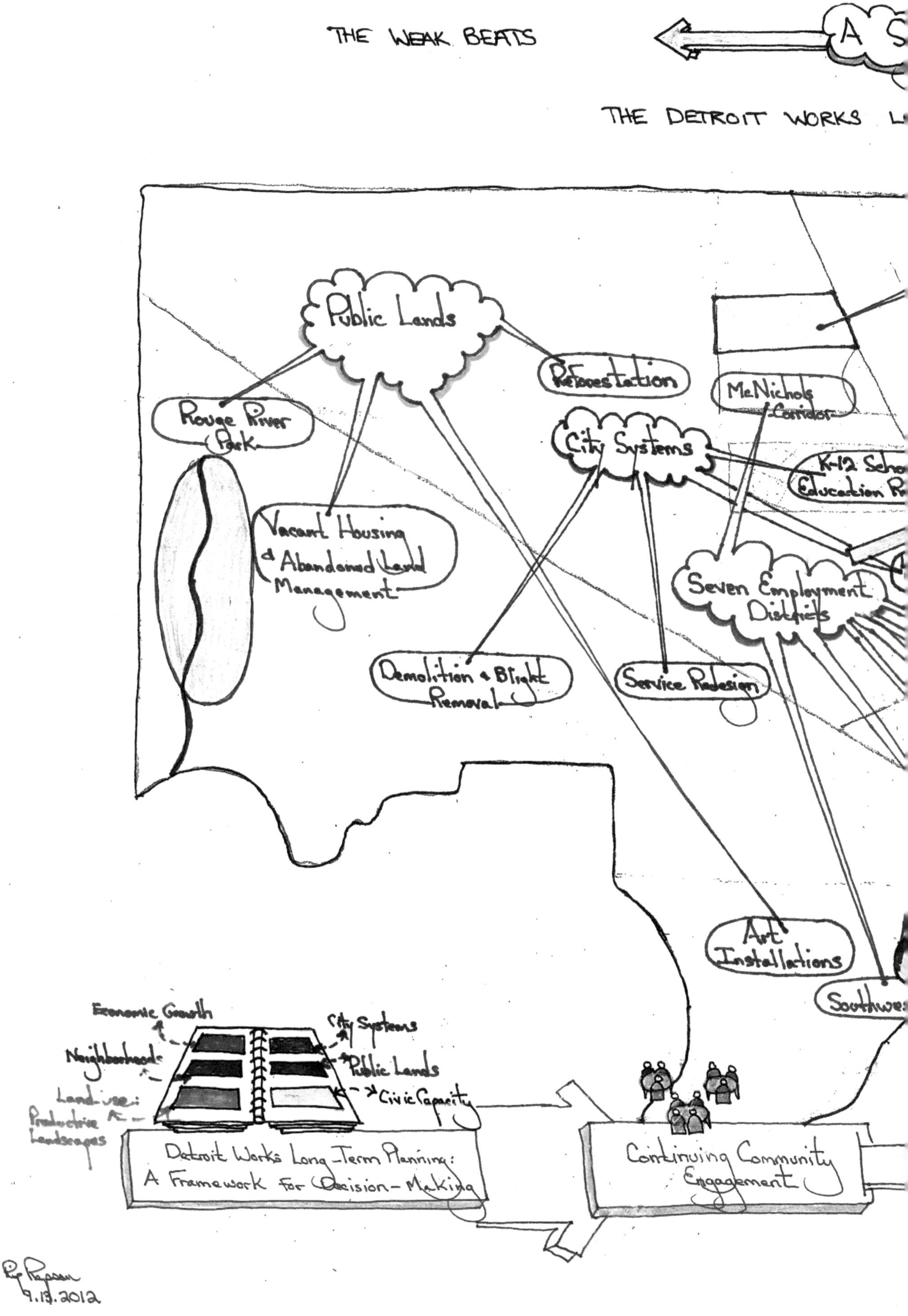

THE DETROIT WORKS
Public Lands
Reforestation
Rouge River Park
Vacant Housing & Abandoned Land Management
City Systems
McNichols Corridor
K-12 Scho
Education R
Seven Employment Districts
Demolition & Blight Removal
Service Redesign
Art Installations
Southwes
Economic Growth
Neighborhoods
Land use: Productive Landscapes
City Systems
Public Lands
Civic Capacity
Detroit Works Long-Term Planning: A Framework for Decision-Making
Continuing Community Engagement
9.13.2012

on Strategy → THE STRONG BEATS

n PLANNING & INVESTMENT FRAMEWORK

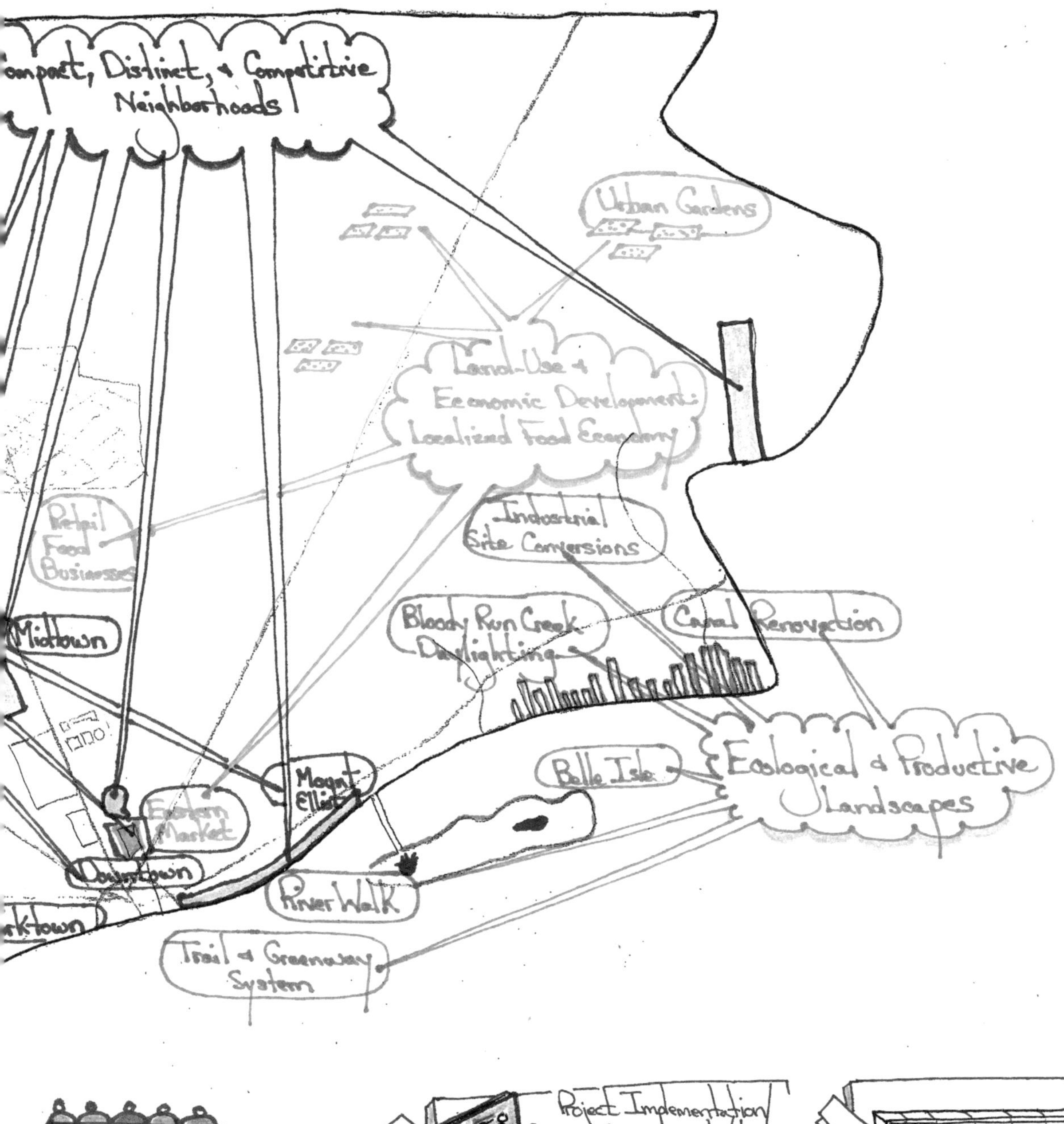

- Broad-based civic consortium
- Held outside of city government
- Responsibility for Plan stewardship
  - → Resources
  - → Implementation oversight
  - → Evaluation/tracking success
- Communications

- Coordinated by Detroit Economic Growth Corporation - quasi-public entity
- Delegation of plan elements
  - → LISC/CDC's
  - → Private sector
  - → Other CBO's
- Close coordination with public sector

- Capture & align work underway
- New short- and intermediate-term investments
- Investments in community capacity & engagement

exist, at least so far, in Detroit. Nor does the wreckage of so many other American school reform efforts — many of them in environments less daunting than Detroit's public schools — offer an inviting proposition for a giant Kresge intervention at this moment.

Precisely because the frustration is so deeply felt by so many leaders at so many levels of Detroit's public and civic life, a multitude of reform advocates are all holding tenaciously to their own, competing ideas about the best way to proceed. The Coalition for the Future of Detroit Schoolchildren is seeking to draw these ideas more tightly together into something like a consensus, but that goal remains elusive for now. Amid this contentiousness, a foundation would need supreme confidence in its formula for success, powerful allies, and a plausible route to amassing significant public and private dollars before embarking on a full-bore school reform initiative. At least at this moment, Kresge does not see those requisites lining up, or even lying plausibly within its reach. As a result, it has chosen to focus on an aspect of the problem where the stars are more favorably aligned, and where a positive result will still unquestionably be helpful in meeting the larger challenge.

Whether that constitutes "embrac[ing] a level of risk commensurate with the magnitude of the challenge at hand" is a hard question to answer. For a foundation that took on the overwhelming needs of a desperate city heading for bankruptcy, and stuck with its commitment through years of crises, political brushfires, and worsening conditions, it is reasonable to wonder whether Kresge would find so much greater a challenge in the Detroit public schools.

But in this case, Kresge would have to tackle the complexity of Detroit school reform *on top of* the continuing challenge of supporting the city's recovery and redevelopment, including the ongoing struggle to rebuild neighborhoods and create a regional transportation system. This is a body of work that still stretches many years into the future with perhaps hundreds of millions of future dollars in aggregate yet to be spent. Piling another massive challenge onto that already weighty agenda might seem less a case of "embracing risk" than of forsaking reason. For now, the Foundation has chosen an unquestionably safer, but perhaps also saner, course.

Tales of the city

Among the most intangible yet crucial assets of any city is its reputation: *What kind of place is this* in which to live, invest, work, network, raise children, retire, have fun? As the urbanist Richard Florida has argued, a good reputation can be self-perpetuating: Buzz draws youth and talent; talented people create or lure businesses and jobs; media pick up the trend; and all of that in turn burnishes the city's reputation still further. A bad reputation works the opposite way.

For many years, Detroit's reputation — aggravated by a proliferation of articles and photos wallowing in devastation, which Detroiters derided as "ruin porn" — was the worst in the nation among big cities. So a certain amount of bounce-back was inevitable when conditions started to improve. Florida himself, having once declared Detroit all but unsalvageable ("As its population density dips further," he wrote in 2009, "the city's struggle ... will only intensify"[227]), experienced at least a partial conversion in 2013, resulting in an upbeat Atlantic Cities article headlined "Don't Let Bankruptcy Fool You: Detroit's Not Dead." There, he spelled out what has by now become the standard synopsis of the city's rebound: "Detroit's downtown urban core is seeing more investment, economic activity, and an influx of talent than it has in decades. This revitalization is concentrated and spotty, and it is far from inclusive, but it is certainly something positive, generating jobs, revenue, and much-needed hope and optimism that provide a foundation to build upon."[228]

The "influx of talent," at least in the trendy precincts of greater downtown, has lately helped make the city a media darling around the country. But it rankles many Detroiters. In a LinkedIn blog post that briefly went viral in 2016, titled "Why I Hate Detroit," a city native and branding consultant, Eric Thomas, lamented "every single new $10-per-cup coffee shop and trendy restaurant that only serves chicken skins and not actual chicken." The media fixation on central Detroit, he complained, has created an Oz-like image that actually pertains only to a small fraction of the land mass and that is all but irrelevant to the vast majority of Detroiters. "To say you love 5 percent of Detroit is like ordering a hamburger, eating the sesame seeds on the bun, and claiming you love hamburgers."[229]

The problem with so much enthusiasm about the resurgent core is that it creates a countervailing narrative about the rest of the city —as if it were a kind of giant Red Zone where the cosseted gentry of Corktown and Midtown ought not tread. The reality of many struggling neighborhoods no longer matches either the old or the new story of Detroit — they are neither beyond hope nor resurgent; they struggle with the aftereffects of abandonment and blight, but they are keen to fight back, persevere, and assemble their own micro-level version of the government and civil society that deserted them. Community groups that patrol streets, clean and mow empty lots, clear snow, provide safe recreation for kids, and tend communal gardens and farms all attest to the resilience of rank-and-file Detroiters in the face of a near collapse of the bigger systems that were supposed to provide for them but couldn't.

To tell a story that benefits these neighborhoods, the city needs not just a better reputation, but a more accurate and complete one, a version that accounts for both the hardships and the gains, the new residents and the old, the longtime African-American majority and the white and Latino minorities, the repopulating areas and the still-shrinking ones, Shinola and shuttered storefronts, the *joie de vivre* and the *cris de coeur.* Building up Detroit, beyond the central hot spots, depends on an understanding of the future that includes all Detroiters and that encompasses a plausible story of how decimated places and weary residents can re-create a desirable, vibrant city.

For Detroit's civic leadership, including Kresge, this final challenge transcends and envelops all the others. The Foundation's "pivot to neighborhoods" is in some ways a recognition that the successes of the past 10 or 15 years have to be understood as the first chapter of a much longer and more expansive story that radiates outward from the core.

When, despite much effort led by Dan Gilbert, Detroit failed in early 2018 to make the cut for Amazon's second headquarters, Gilbert argued that the "elephant in the room" — "the single largest obstacle" to Detroit's success — was "this lingering negative perception that has unfortunately survived our impressive progress." One remedy, he said, is to "bring people HERE to see, touch and feel the excitement, opportunity, growth and reality" of Detroit now. "Once we get them here, we've got them."

"Selling" a new perspective, both to Detroiters and to outsiders, is an express part of the mission Kresge has adopted in the city. As the Detroit team wrote to the board in September 2016:

> Kresge has historically been a promoter of Detroit — what Rip refers to as the "seller" function. We have shown deep commitment to our hometown and have effectively contributed to shifting the national narrative of Detroit from one of failure to one that highlights Detroit's resurgence and the potential for greater prosperity. But that is only a partial narrative, and we have spent considerable energy over the last year trying to thread the needle of recognizing the continuing challenges Detroit residents face while maintaining a positive vision for the future. Going forward, we will ... create multiple platforms for elevating the visibility of good work occurring in low-income communities and communities of color outside of Detroit's economic core.[230]

The hope for "narrative change" has become a fixture of 21st-century philanthropy in all sorts of areas, from the environment to poverty to health care to criminal justice. It remains, at this point, a dream more honored in the poetry of annual reports than in the prose of impact evaluations.

Following page: As the Foundation's strategic efforts in Detroit solidified, the Detroit Team determined that they would concentrate their work in several of the city's neighborhoods, as illustrated in the 2016 working drawing by Rip Rapson.

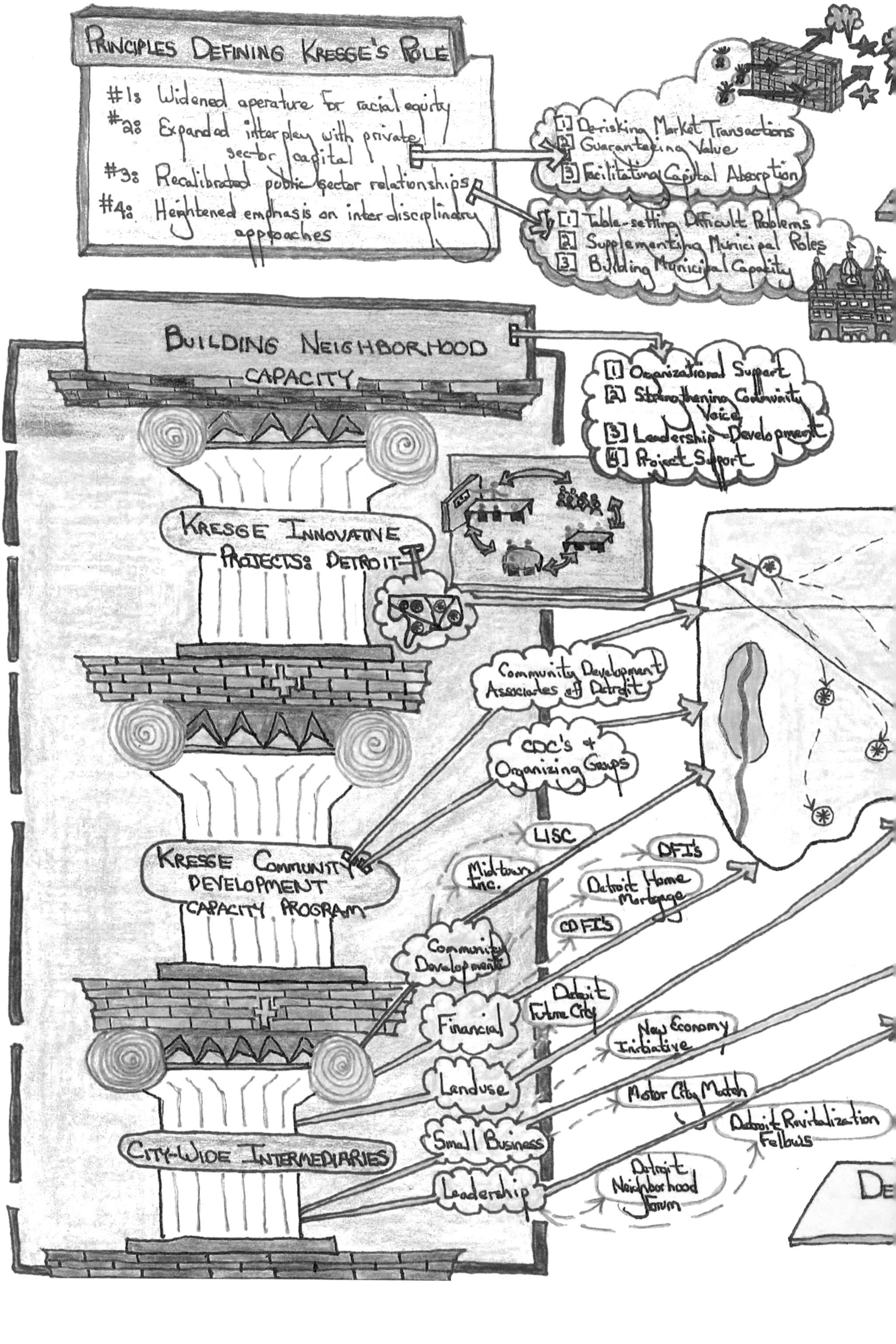
PRINCIPLES DEFINING KRESGE'S ROLE
#1: Widened aperature for racial equity
#2: Expanded interplay with private sector capital
#3: Recalibrated public sector relationships
#4: Heightened emphasis on interdisciplinary approaches
[1] Derisking Market Transactions
[2] Guaranteeing Value
[3] Facilitating Capital Absorption
[1] Table-setting Difficult Problems
[2] Supplementing Municipal Roles
[3] Building Municipal Capacity
BUILDING NEIGHBORHOOD CAPACITY
[1] Organizational Support
[2] Strengthening Community Voice
[3] Leadership Development
[4] Project Support
KRESGE INNOVATIVE PROJECTS: DETROIT
Community Development Associates of Detroit
CDC's & Organizing Groups
KRESGE COMMUNITY DEVELOPMENT CAPACITY PROGRAM
LISC
Midtown Inc.
DFI's
Detroit Home Mortgage
CDFI's
Community Development
Financial
Detroit Future City
New Economy Initiative
Landuse
Motor City Match
Small Business
Detroit Revitalization Fellows
CITY-WIDE INTERMEDIARIES
Leadership
Detroit Neighborhood Forum
De

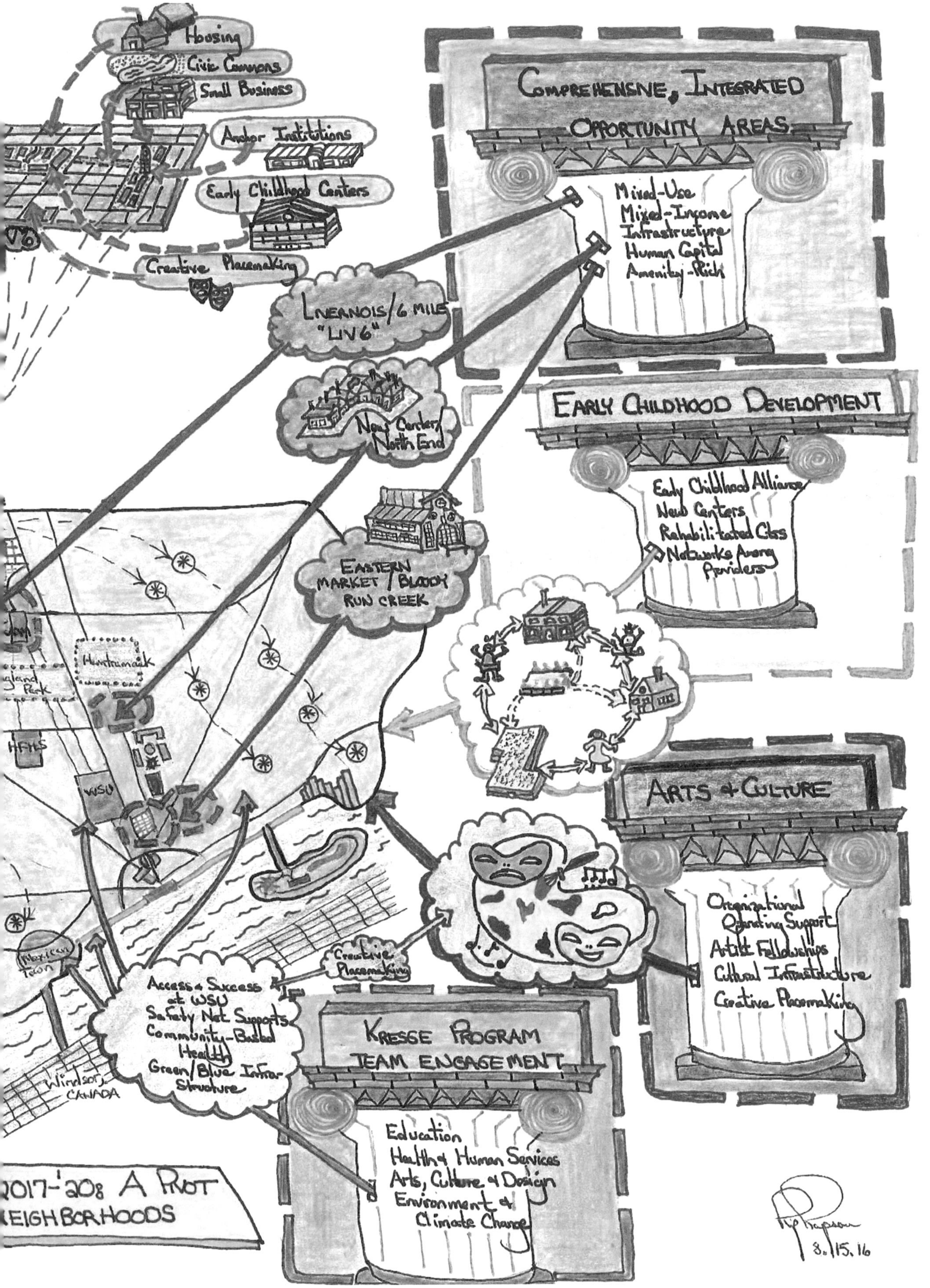
Housing
Civic Commons
Small Business
Anchor Institutions
Early Childhood Centers
Creative Placemaking
Comprehensive, Integrated Opportunity Areas
Mixed-Use
Mixed-Income
Infrastructure
Human Capital
Amenity-Rich
Livernois/6 Mile "LIV6"
New Center/ North End
Early Childhood Development
Early Childhood Alliance
New Centers
Rehabilitated Ctrs
Networks Among Providers
Eastern Market/Bloody Run Creek
Hamtramck
HFHS
WSU
Mexican Town
Arts & Culture
Organizational Operating Support
Artist Fellowships
Cultural Infrastructure
Creative Placemaking
Creative Placemaking
Access & Success at WSU
Safety Net Supports
Community-Based Health
Green/Blue Infra-Structure
Windsor, CANADA
Kresge Program Team Engagement
Education
Health & Human Services
Arts, Culture & Design
Environment & Climate Change
017-'208 A Pivot
EIGHBORHOODS
8.15.16

Apart from funding films and television shows, or trying to pump constructive messages through YouTube and Twitter, foundations have found few practical levers to move the mass of public sentiment or puncture the fortified camps of political ideology.

But even as Kresge embraces the fervid language and lofty hopes of the "narrative change" trend, it has recognized a very concrete, immediate strategic opportunity at this moment in Detroit: The story and image of Detroit are *already* evolving, and as a result, the direction of their evolution can probably be influenced. Achieving that influence and getting it right are as much a strategic imperative as anything else in Kresge's plan of action. Much of the Foundation's work in Detroit — especially its rising emphasis on outlying neighborhoods — is unlikely to succeed unless the buoyant tales of greater downtown merge into a more realistic, balanced, and inclusive story about *all* Detroiters and their increasingly hopeful future.

A foundation, on its own, cannot make that happen. But it can contribute, prod, raise its voice, and support others with even more influential voices. With the eyes of so much of the country on Detroit, the time to enrich the city's image is surely now, when news about the city draws ears and eyeballs, and when a diverse core of Detroiters, old and new, seem eager to talk about their history, their struggles and hopes, and the city their children will live in. "This," Rapson said, "is our moment."[231]

Even Eric Thomas, the blogger who "hates Detroit," demonstrates the force behind this narrative energy. After many paragraphs of invective about today's Detroit, he concludes with a question that perfectly frames what the authors of Detroit Future City, quoted at the top of this chapter, consider fundamental about the city's future: "So, why do I stay?"

Above: Sherita Smith, center, executive director of the Grandmont Rosedale neighborhood in Detroit, and work colleagues. One of many young leaders, and organizations, the Foundation has invested in as a "catalyst for growth and beacon of opportunity." Photo Credit: Lon Horwedel

He answers:

> Because I love the people. I hate the place, but I love the people. I want to be a catalyst for growth and a beacon of opportunity for the next generation of Detroit-born leaders that need to know that there's a better way. ... I am a product of Detroit, and I've seen firsthand how bright and resilient the people are. There are diamonds littered throughout the landscape, and I'm not talking about historic homes. I'm talking about brilliant youth and passionate grassroots activists that have been doing the best they can with what they've been given.

"What Detroit needs now," said the concluding section of Detroit Future City, in a surely intentional evocation of Diana Ross, a North End native, "are strong leaders who love what it stands for and what it can become, residents who have a voice in their neighborhoods and can imagine the possibilities for the entire city."

Foundations can't create love any more than they can conjure narratives. But they can invest in the "brilliant youth and passionate grassroots activists," in the "catalysts for growth and beacons of opportunity." And those, in turn, can take responsibility for the narrative, and ultimately for the love.

CHAPTER 1 ENDNOTES

1 Quoted in: Charles Moore, "Daniel H. Burnham, Architect, Planner of Cities." Volume 2, Chapter 25, Houghton Mifflin & Co., 1921, p. 147.

2 See, for example, the Robert Wood Johnson Foundation evaluation of the Urban Health Initiative ("some measurable gains ... but the gains were small") at http://www.rwjf.org/en/library/research/2013/06/urban-health-initiative--working-to-ensure-the-health-and-safety.html; and the Annie E. Casey Foundation's evaluation of "Making Connections" ("did not achieve the desired population-level change in its neighborhoods") at http://mcstudy.norc.org/publications/files/LessonsfromMakingConnections.pdf.

3 Mitchell Sviridoff and Louis Winnick, "Communities and Neighborhoods: A Possible Private Sector Initiative for the 1980s," Division of National Affairs, the Ford Foundation, Jan. 2, 1979, p. 14.

4 Interview with David Littman, January 2006.

5 Tony Proscio, "Detroit," confidential report to the Pew Charitable Trusts, 1998, p. 22.

6 John E. Marshall III, "President's Statement," Annual Report of The Kresge Foundation, 2000, p. 7.

7 Ibid., p. 8.

8 Detroit GreenWays Coalition Website, "History," at http://detroitgreenways.org/history.

9 Mitch Nauffts, "John E. Marshall III, President/CEO, Kresge Foundation: Building Nonprofit Capacity Through Challenge Grants," Philanthropy News Digest, June 21, 2006, at http://philanthropynewsdigest.org/newsmakers/john-e.-marshall-iii-president-ceo-kresge-foundation-building-nonprofit-capacity-through-challenge-grants.

10 John E. Marshall III, "President's Statement," Annual Report of The Kresge Foundation, 2003, p. 8.

11 Federal Bureau of Investigation, "Public Corruption: Inside the Kwame Kilpatrick Case," Nov. 8, 2013, at https://www.fbi.gov/news/stories/2013/november/public-corruption-inside-the-kwame-kilpatrick-case/public-corruption-inside-the-kwame-kilpatrick-case.

12 "America's Most Miserable Cities," Forbes, Jan. 30, 2008, at http://www.forbes.com/2008/01/29/detroit-stockton-flint-biz-cz_kb_0130miserable.html.

13 Rip Rapson, "Letter from the President," Annual Report of The Kresge Foundation, 2008, p. 18, at http://kresge.org/sites/default/files/Uploaded%20Docs/2008_Ltr_President.pdf.

14 Ibid., p. 20.

15 "Community Development," Annual Report of The Kresge Foundation, 2008, p. 18, at http://kresge.org/sites/default/files/Uploaded%20Docs/2008_Community_development.pdf.

16 Rip Rapson, "From the President," Annual Report of The Kresge Foundation, 2009, p. 17, at http://kresge.org/sites/default/files/Uploaded%20Docs/2009_Ltr_President.pdf.

17 Ibid.

18 Rip Rapson, "The Fifth Sector: Philanthropy's Role in Community Change," address at the College of Design, University of Minnesota, April 7, 2008, p. 12.

19 Rip Rapson, "A Different View of Detroit," closing plenary address to the Independent Sector, Detroit, Michigan, November 2009, p. 2.

20 Rip Rapson, "A Decade of Change: Where Does It Leave the Smart Growth Movement? Where Does It Leave Detroit?" Keynote Address to the Funders Network for Smart Growth and Livable Communities, Detroit, Mich., March 24, 2011, p. 7.

21 Rip Rapson, "Letter from the President," in "Today & Tomorrow: The Kresge Foundation Annual Report: 2010 and 2011," p. 16.

22 Jonathan Oosting, "Detroit Has More Vacant Land Than Any City in Nation Except Post-Katrina New Orleans," MLive, Sept. 29, 2009, at http://www.mlive.com/news/detroit/index.ssf/2009/09/detroit_has_more_vacant_land_t.html.

23 "Detroit Future City: 2012 Detroit Strategic Framework Plan," Detroit Economic Growth Corp., May 2013, p. 98. For a discussion of oft-cited larger estimates, see Kate Davidson, "Detroit Has Tons of Vacant Land, But Forty Square Miles?" National Public Radio, April 18, 2012, at http://michiganradio.org/post/detroit-has-tons-vacant-land-forty-square-miles#stream/0.

24 Oosting, *op. cit.*

25 Rip Rapson, "Re-Imagining Land Use in Detroit: Is It Really Possible?" Remarks to the American Assembly, Detroit, Mich., April 15, 2011, p. 4.

26 Rip Rapson, "A Different View of Detroit," address to

the Minnesota Society, American Institute of Architects, Minneapolis, Nov. 3, 2010, pp. 7-8.
27 Rick Cohen, "A City in Remission: Can the 'Grand Bargain' Save Detroit?" Nonprofit Quarterly, January 2016, p. 34.
28 Rip Rapson, "Re-imagining Land Use in Detroit: Is It Really Possible?," address to the American Assembly, April 15, 2011, unpublished manuscript, p. 5.
29 Annual Report of The Kresge Foundation, 2008, p. 18.
30 All amounts are from the Annual Report of The Kresge Foundation, 2012, pp. 48-62.
31 Robin Hacke, David Wood, and Marian Urquilla, "What Can Foundations Do to Foster Community Investment: 10 Roles for Philanthropy," The Kresge Foundation and Initiative for Responsible Investment, December 2014, p. 6.
32 Nathan Bomey, "Detroit Resurrected: To Bankruptcy and Back," W.W. Norton and Company, 2016, Kindle edition, location 1358.
33 Ibid., loc. 1910.
34 Ibid., loc. 2222.
35 Laura Trudeau, "Capital Absorption in Detroit 2010-15: What Has Changed?" PowerPoint presentation, The Kresge Foundation, April 2, 2015, slide 7 (on the Book Cadillac hotel and "no predictable model") and 13 (on collaboration).
36 United States District Court, Eastern District of Michigan, Southern Division, Civil Action No. 16-CV-13292, Gary B. et al. v. Snyder et al., class-action complaint filed September 13, 2016, pp. 77-78 and ff.
37 Information on Detroit Early Childhood Innovation Fund is from Wendy L. Jackson, "Detroit Early Childhood Innovation Fund: The Community Foundation for Southeast Michigan — Narrative Questions," part of a grant recommendation to the Kresge Board of Trustees, June 13, 2013, pp. 1-2. Information on other activities is from an interview with Wendy Lewis Jackson.
38 "Kresge Foundation Introduces $20 million Initiative to Improve Early Childhood Outcomes," press release, The Kresge Foundation, Jan. 7, 2016.
39 Rip Rapson, Kresge website letter: "Hope Starts here: Detroit's Early Childhood Partnership," Nov. 10, 2016.
40 Judge Steven Rhodes, "Oral Opinion on the Record: In re City of Detroit," U.S. Bankruptcy Court, Eastern District of Michigan, Nov. 7, 2014, p. 3.
41 Figures are taken from the annual reports of each foundation for 2014. It should be noted that two local contributors, the William Davidson and Hudson-Webber foundations, pledged a higher percentage of their assets to the Grand Bargain: 2.5 percent and 5.7 percent, respectively. But unlike Kresge and other national donors, their entire endowments are committed, in their missions, solely to local causes.
42 U.S. Bankruptcy Court, Eastern District of Michigan, Souther Division, transcript, Oct. 2, 2014, p. 211.
43 City of Detroit, Comparative Budget Summary, 2010-2011 Mayor's Recommendations, first column under "Appropriations," showing the 2009-10 budget, at http://www.detroitmi.gov/Portals/0/docs/budgetdept/2010-11_Budget/Executive%20Budget%20Summary%2011/EBS_2010-11_Section%20B_Summary%20All%20Funds_stamped.pdf.
44 Matthew Dolan, "Revival Bid Pits Detroit vs. Donor," Wall Street Journal, July 2, 2011, at https://www.wsj.com/articles/SB10001424052702304887904576397760319014524 (subscription required).

CHAPTER 2 ENDNOTES

45 George Galster, "Driving Detroit: The Quest for Respect in the Motor City," University of Pennsylvania Press, 2012, p. 21.
46 Mike Duggan quoted in John Gallagher, "Five years in, and Dan Gilbert's just beginning," the Detroit Free Press, Aug. 16, 2015.
47 June Manning Thomas: "Redevelopment and Race: Planning a Finer City in Postwar Detroit," Wayne State University Press, 2013, p. 249.
48 Ze'ev Chafets, New York Times Magazine, Sept. 2, 1990.
49 Time Magazine, Oct. 5, 2009.
50 Rip Rapson, "Detroit's Bold Urban Future: Connecting Downtown and the Neighborhoods," Address to the International Downtown — Midwest Urban District Forum, June 2, 2015, p. 6.
51 Detroit Program Staff Memorandum to Kresge Board of Trustees ("Detroit Program Staff Memo"), June 2015.
52 Anonymous interview, January 2016.

53 John Gallagher, "Revolution Detroit: Strategies for Urban Reinvention," Wayne State University Press, 2013, p. 42.
54 Ibid. p.47.
55 Dan Carmody interview, April 12, 2016.
56 Detroit Program Staff Memo, June 8, 2007.
57 Detroit Program Staff Memo, September 2013.
58 Robert Long, quoted in National Geographic, May 2015, pp. 74, 78.
59 Olga Stella interview, March 3, 2016.
60 Amazon Detroit HQ2 RFP Response, Oct. 18, 2017
61 Rip Rapson, "The Arc of Community Progress in Post-Bankruptcy Detroit," plenary address at the Center for Community Progress Reclaiming Vacant Properties Conference, May 20, 2015, p. 6.
62 Detroit Free Press, April 27 and 28, 2016.
63 Candice Williams and Nicquel Terry, "Detroit Bid Now Puts MLS Team at Ford Field," the Detroit News, Nov. 2, 2017, at http://www.detroitnews.com/story/news/local/detroit-city/2017/11/02/detroit-bid-mls-soccer-franchise-ford-field/107274674/.
64 "Today the number of renters in Detroit has surpassed homeowners for the first time since 1950 and numerous neighborhoods that were once homeownership strongholds continue to see an influx of renters." Detroit Future City Implementation Office Special Report, March 6, 2017.
65 "HUD Median Family Income Documentation System" for Detroit-Warren-Livonia, Michigan, at https://www.huduser.gov/portal/datasets/il/il2015/2015MedCalc.odn.
66 Ibid, p. 6.
67 Detroit Program Staff Memo, September 2013.
68 Sue Mosey interview, Oct. 1, 2015.
69 Detroit Corridor Initiative/Capital Impact Partners, "Toward Inclusive Growth in Detroit," Fall 2015, pp. 12 and 15.
70 "139 Square Miles, Detroit Future City," August 2017, p. 23. According to the U.S. Census Bureau's 2016 American Community Survey, the city's white population is estimated at roughly 10 percent and Hispanic at 7 percent.
71 "Midtown Detroit Anchor Strategy," U3 Advisors Final Scan, October 2014, p. 13.
72 Detroit Program Staff Memo, March 2011.
73 Mosey interview, op. cit.
74 Sue Mosey interview, Nov. 12, 2015.
75 Graig Donnelly interview, May 4, 2016.
76 Ibid.
77 Email to authors from Anthony Holt, Wayne State University police chief, Sept. 26, 2017.
78 Erica Raleigh interview, Jan. 21, 2016.
79 Anthony Holt interview, Jan. 21, 2016.
80 Detroit Program Staff Memo, June, 2015.
81 Duggan quoted in the Detroit Free Press, Sept. 17, 2015.
82 Detroit Program Staff Memo, June 2015.
83 Ibid, September 2015.
84 Anonymous interview.
85 Detroit Program Staff Memo, September 2015.
86 Thomas Sugrue, "The Origins of the Urban Crisis: Race and Inequality in Postwar Detroit," Princeton University Press, 2014, p. xxiii.
87 Stella interview, op. cit.
88 Lauren Hood interview, Jan. 26, 2016.
89 Brad Frost interview, Jan. 24, 2016.
90 Walter Robb, Detroit Economic Club, April 13, 2012.
91 Walter Robb to authors; email, May 12, 2016.
92 Rip Rapson, "Post-Bankruptcy Detroit: Where Do We Go From Here?" Meeting of the Minds annual summit, Richmond, California, Oct. 22, 2015, p. 6.

CHAPTER 3 ENDNOTES

93 "Detroit's Bold Urban Future: Connecting Downtown and the Neighborhoods," address to the International Downtown Association – Midwest Urban District Forum, June 25, 2015, p. 4.
94 "The Kresge Foundation: 75 Years of Philanthropy, 1924-1999," The Kresge Foundation, p. 3.
95 Detroit Program Staff Memorandum to Kresge Board of Trustees (Detroit Program Staff Memo), September 2006, p. 8.
96 Ibid., p. 8.
97 Detroit Program Staff Memo, March 3, 2007, p. 121.
98 Detroit Program Staff Memo, March 2013.
99 Detroit Program Staff Memo, December 2008, p. 132.
100 Edward Egnatios Interview, Feb. 1, 2016.
101 Detroit Program Staff Memorandum to Kresge Board of Trustees ("Detroit Program Staff Memo"), September 2013.

102 Wendy Lewis Jackson, "Rebuilding From Strength: Strategies to Safeguard Middle Neighborhoods in Detroit," undated, p. 2.
103 Laura Trudeau, "Testimony Prepared for Robert Wood Johnson Foundation Commission to Build a Healthier America," June 2013, p. 2.
104 Jackson, op cit., p. 1.
105 Rip Rapson: "A Different View of Detroit," Independent Sector and Council of Michigan Foundation's 2009 Annual Conference, Nov. 6, 2009, p. 1.
106 Kimberly Kinder: "Guerrilla-style Defensive Architecture in Detroit," International Journal of Urban and Regional Research, Vol. 38, Issue 4, 2014, pp. 1,767 to 1,784.
107 Monica Davey, "Big Dreams, But Little Consensus, for a New Detroit," the New York Times, Sept. 2, 2013.
108 Detroit Program Staff Memo, March 1, 2008.
109 Laura Trudeau, FSG meeting at Kresge Foundation, Dec. 11, 2015.
110 Erica Raleigh interview, Jan. 21, 2016.
111 Ibid.
112 "Every Neighborhood Has a Future ... and It Doesn't Include Blight," Detroit Blight Removal Task Force Plan, 2nd printing, June 2014.
113 Ibid.
114 Timothy S. Thorland interview, Jan. 26, 2016.
115 Thomas Goddeeris interview, Jan. 26, 2016.
116 Rapson, "Detroit: The Sharp Edge of Innovation," Detroit Homecoming, Sept. 21, 2014, p. 4.
117 Martha Potere interview, Jan. 26, 2016.
118 Karl Seidman, Living Cities, "Findings from Baseline Analysis of Community Development Finance System," 2010, quoted in Detroit Community Development Team Report, June 2015.
119 Foundation: "Detroit Engagement Audit Findings," Grassroots Solutions, April 2010.
120 Detroit Program Staff Memo, April 2010.
121 Detroit Future City: Detroit Strategic Framework Plan, December 2012.
122 Detroit Program Staff Memo, September 2012.
123 Dave Bing, quoted in Matthew Dolan, op. cit.
124 Detroit Program Staff Memo, September 2013.
125 Detroit Program Staff Memo, September 2012.
126 Trudeau, op. cit. "Testimony," p. 5.
127 Interview with Sommer Woods, Nov. 13, 2015.
128 Detroit Future City, op. cit., p. 6; on number of meetings and responses, p. 3.
129 Detroit Future City, op. cit., pp. 18-19.
130 Detroit Program Staff Memo, op. cit.
131 Detroit Future City, op. cit., p. 111.
132 Detroit Program Staff Memo, June 2015.
133 Interview with Anika Goss-Foster, September 26, 2017.
134 Detroit Program Staff Memo, September 2013.
135 Detroit Program Staff Memo, December 2013.
136 Foundation press release, Oct. 20, 2014; Detroit Team Report, December 2015.
137 Grant data provided by George C. Jacobsen, March 25, 2016.
138 Erik Howard interview, Jan. 30, 2016.
139 Detroit Program Staff Memo, September 2015.
140 Melena Ryzik, "For Detroit Artists, Almost Anything Goes," the New York Times, July 16, 2015.
141 Detroit Program Staff Memo, September 2015.
142 Marsha Music (Philpot) interview, Jan. 31, 2016.
143 Ibid.
144 "The Kidnapped Children of Detroit" in "A Detroit Anthology," Anna Clark (ed.), Rust Belt Chic Press, pp. 225-231.
145 Jackson, op. cit., p. 2.
146 Kresge Foundation press release, Aug. 31, 2015; Detroit Team Report, December 2015.
147 Ibid.
148 Annual Report of The Kresge Foundation, 2015.
149 Lauren Hood interview, Jan. 26, 2016.
150 Detroit Program Staff Memo, December 2015.
151 Detroit Home Mortgage Press Release, Feb. 18, 2016.
152 Detroit Program Staff Memo, September 2016, p. 13.
153 Ibid., p. 3.
154 Detroit Program Staff Memo, June 2016, pp. 3, 6-7.
155 Cecilia Kang, "Unemployed Detroit Residents Are Trapped by a Digital Divide," The New York Times, May 23, 2016.
156 Interview, Sue Mosey, executive director of Midtown Detroit Inc., Nov. 12, 2015; Ben Austen, "The Post-Post-Apocalyptic Detroit," the New York Times Magazine, July, 13, 2014; Detroit Economic Growth Association, grant request, Nov. 11, 2013.

157 Stephen Henderson, panelist, "How Philanthropy, Business and Government Sparked Detroit's Resurgence," Brookings Institution, April 26, 2016.

CHAPTER 4 ENDNOTES

158 Quoted in Michael H. Hodges, "Troy Nonprofit Steps Up Gifts as Auto Sector Retreats," the Detroit News, June 30, 2009, p. 7-A.

159 Ryan Felton, "Off the Rails: How Detroit Ended Up With the Worst Public Transit," Detroit Metro Times, March 11, 2014, at http://www.metrotimes.com/detroit/how-detroit-ended-up-with-the-worst-public-transit/Content?oid=2143889/.

160 Daniel Denvir, "The 10 Most Segregated Urban Areas in America," Salon.com, March 29, 2011, at http://www.salon.com/2011/03/29/most_segregated_cities/slide_show/7 (Detroit ranked 4th).

161 Ryan Felton, "Throwing Rail Under the Bus: RTA's Bylaws Show a Clear Bias Towad Bus Over Rail," Detroit Metro Times.com, March 11, 2014, at http://www.metrotimes.com/detroit/rtas-bylaws-show-a-clear-bias-toward-bus-over-rail/Content?oid=2144003.

162 Quoted in John Gallagher, "10 Years Later: Detroit Still Glows After Super Bowl XL," the Detroit Free Press, Feb. 5, 2016, at http://www.freep.com/story/money/business/michigan/2016/02/05/detroit-sbxl-downtown-penske/79875020/.

163 Rip Rapson, "How Did Detroit and Light-Rail Transit Appear in the Same Sentence? A Case Study and Some Implications," address to the Rail-Volution Annual Conference, Minneapolis, Sept. 23, 2014, accessed at The Kresge Foundation website: http://kresge.org/library/how-did-detroit-and-light-rail-transit-appear-same-sentence-case-study-and-some-implications.

164 Information drawn from Wikipedia entries on each system. On Minneapolis-St. Paul: https://en.wikipedia.org/wiki/Metro_Transit_(Minnesota); on Portland: https://en.wikipedia.org/wiki/Portland_Streetcar.

165 Rapson, op. cit.

166 Ibid.

167 Ibid.

168 Ibid.

169 Roger S. Penske, Matthew P. Cullen, Dan Gilbert, Richard Rapson, M-1 RAIL letter to Gov. Rick Snyder and Mayor Dave Bing, undated, 2011.

170 Rapson, op. cit.

171 Darren A. Nichols and Tom Walsh, "Development and Construction Inclusion Report: 2013-2017," M1-RAIL, 2017, p. 1.

172 Email to the authors from Laura Trudeau, Feb. 1, 2017.

173 Eric D. Lawrence, "Amid Deluge of Riders, QLINE Announces Free Rides until July 1," the Detroit Free Press, May 19, 2017, at http://www.freep.com/story/news/2017/05/19/qline-cost-detroit-free/333064001/.

174 Bill Shea, "QLine cost $7 million higher than previous estimate," Crain's Detroit Business, Aug. 28, 2017, at http://www.crainsdetroit.com/print/637526.

175 Shawn D. Lewis and Sarah Rahal, "QLine Ridership down 40% after free period ended," the Detroit News, Sept. 21, 2017, at http://www.detroitnews.com/story/news/local/detroit-city/2017/09/21/qline-ridership-fares-detroit/105860766/.

176 Bill Shea, "Regional Transit Authority Will Seek $2.9 Billion Millage in November for Buses, Rail," Crain's Detroit Business, May 31, 2016, at http://www.crainsdetroit.com/article/20160531/NEWS/160539996/regional-transit-authority-of-southeast-michigan-will-seek-2-9.

177 Frank Witsil and Eric D. Lawrence, "RTA Millage Rejected by Metro Detroit Voters," the Detroit Free Press, Nov. 9, 2016, at http://www.freep.com/story/news/local/michigan/detroit/2016/11/09/rta-regional-transit-authority-millage/93535602/.

178 Rapson, op. cit.

179 Rapson, "Six Core Beliefs Have the Power to Reshape the Philanthropic Sector for the Challenges of the 21st Century," special insert in the Annual Report of The Kresge Foundation 2014, p. 2 of the insert.

CHAPTER 5 ENDNOTES

180 "The 15 Most Influential Art World Cities of 2015," Artsy Editorial, Dec. 16. 2015, at https://www.artsy.net/article/artsy-editorial-contemporary-art-s-most-influential-cities.

181 Rip Rapson, "Art X Detroit: Why Art Matters," closing

remarks to Art X Detroit, The Kresge Foundation, April 11, 2011, at http://kresge.org/sites/default/files/library/art-x-detroit-why-art-matters.pdf.

182 Michael Rushton, "Support for Earmarked Public Spending on Culture: Evidence from a Referendum in Metropolitan Detroit," Public Budgeting and Finance, Winter 2005, pp. 72 and 74-75.

183 Barbara Kratchman, "Kresge General Operating Support Grants to Cultural Organizations," memorandum to Alice Carle, The Kresge Foundation, July 21, 2008, p. 1.

184 Barbara Kratchman, "Kresge Creative Artists Fellowship Program," program description prepared for The Kresge Foundation, December 2007, p. 2.

185 Ibid., p. 5.

186 Kresge Arts in Detroit, "Gilda Awards" web page, at http://www.kresgeartsindetroit.org/gilda-awards

187 Sarah Lutman, "A Formative Evaluation of The Kresge Foundation's Grantmaking to Support Individual Artists in Detroit, 2008-present," Report to The Kresge Foundation, working draft, Sept. 30, 2016, pp. 31-32.

188 Miller Dickinson Blais, "Creative Vitality in Detroit: The Detroit Cultural Mapping Project," slide presentation to The Kresge Foundation, October 2012, slide No. 3, at www.kresge.org/sites/default/files/Creative-Vitality-in-Detroit-2012-revised071713.pdf.

189 Rip Rapson, "Art X Detroit: Why Art Matters," speech at the closing of the inaugural Art X Detroit festival, April 11, 2011, at http://kresge.org/sites/default/files/library/art-x-detroit-why-art-matters.pdf.

190 Quotations are from the Burnside Farm website, at http://www.burnsidefarmdetroit.com/about/.

191 John S. and James L. Knight website: Description of the grant is at https://www.knightfoundation.org/grants/7285, and the description of the program is at https://www.knightfoundation.org/challenges/knight-arts-challenge.

192 Final quotation is from Nicole Rupersburg, "Erik Howard Brings the Corner and the Community Together in Unlikely Ways Through the Alley Project," web page of the Knight Foundation, at https://www.knightfoundation.org/articles/erik-howard-brings-corner-and-community-together-unlikely-ways-through-alley-project. Other quotes from Howard are from conversations directly with the authors.

193 Sidewalk Detroit website, at http://sidewalkdetroit.com/about/.

194 Jennifer Conlin, "Last Stop on the L Train: Detroit," the New York Times, July 10, 2015, at https://www.nytimes.com/2015/07/12/fashion/last-stop-on-the-l-train-detroit.html.

195 "Creative Placemaking: A Conversation with Rip Rapson and Jamie Bennett," The Graduate Center, City University of New York, May 8, 2014, video at https://www.youtube.com/watch?v=aLjM85weYQk.

196 Mark Stryker, "NEA Study: High Arts Attendance Rates in Metro Detroit," the Detroit Free Press, Jan. 31, 2015, at http://www.freep.com/story/entertainment/arts/2015/01/31/arts-attendance-high-detroit/22615729/.

197 Patricia Cohen, "Suburban Taxpayers Vote to Support Detroit Museum," the New York Times, August 8, 2012, at http://www.nytimes.com/2012/08/09/arts/design/detroit-institute-of-arts-county-millage-tax-approved.html.

CHAPTER 6 ENDNOTES

198 "Detroit Future City: 2012 Detroit Strategic Framework Plan," Inland Press, May 2013, p. 343.

199 Laura Trudeau, "Detroit Reimagined: A City Where All People Can Thrive," Testimony prepared for the Robert Wood Johnson Foundation Commission to Build a Healthier America, June 2013, p. 142.

200 Detroit Public Schools, "Adopted Operating Budget, Year Ended June 30 2016," at http://detroit.k12.mi.us/data/finance/docs/FY2016_Adopted_Budget.pdf, p. 16: Total Expenditures $772,995,117. Kresge Foundation Annual Report, "2014 Financial Report," at http://kresge.org/sites/default/files/2014-financial.pdf, $138.1 million "paid out to grantees over the course of the year."

201 Trudeau, op. cit., p. 147.

202 Coleman A. Young and Lonnie Wheeler, "Hard Stuff: The Autobiography of Mayor Coleman Young," Viking, 1994, p. 179.

203 Trudeau, op. cit., p. 147.

204 The Ralph C. Wilson Jr. Charitable Foundation, established in 2015, began with an endowment of $1.2 billion, roughly one-third the size of The Kresge Foundation in total assets. But because Wilson intends to expend all its

resources by 2035, it will be able to allocate at least as much as Kresge to Detroit grantmaking. See Sherri Welch, "Ralph Wilson Jr. Foundation Sets Clock to Spend Down $1 Billion in Assets," Crain's Detroit Business, Oct. 2, 2016, at http://www.crainsdetroit.com/article/20161002/NEWS/161009989/ralph-wilson-jr-foundation-sets-clock-to-spend-down-1-billion-in. For the next-largest Detroit-area foundation, at $828 million in assets as of 2014, see Form 990-PF, "Return of Private Foundation: 2014: The William Davidson Foundation, at http://990s.foundationcenter.org/990pf_pdf_archive/203/203899187/203899187_201412_990PF.pdf.

205 Rip Rapson, "a Different View of Detroit," address to Independent Sector and Council of Michigan Foundations' 2009 Annual Conference, p. 5.

206 Bill McGraw, Bridge Magazine, The Center for Michigan, Aug. 18, 2015, p. 8.

207 John Gallagher, "Evolution of Municipal Government," chapter 12 in Bryan Doucet, ed., "Why Detroit Matters," Policy Press, 2017.

208 Rip Rapson, "Post-Bankruptcy Detroit: Where Do We Go Now?" address to Meeting of the Minds, Berkeley, California, Oct. 22, 2015, at https://www.youtube.com/watch?v=ZKnV_0ZozkE.

209 "Detroit Program," staff memorandum to The Kresge Foundation Board of Trustees, September 2016, p. 12.

210 Mark Binelli, "Detroit, the Billionaire's Playground," The New York Times, Feb. 8, 2013, p. A27.

211 C. McDonald, "Detroiters Paint a Grim Picture of City in Crisis," The Detroit News, Oct. 9, 2012, p. A1.

212 Of the 672,829 Detroit residents in 2016, an estimated 78.7 percent were African-American, 10.3 percent were white, and 7 percent were Hispanic. Source: American Community Survey, U.S. Census Bureau, for 2016.

213 Median income data from Kurt Metzger email to authors, Oct. 4, 2017. Poverty rate data from Data Driven Detroit, Detroit Profile, 2016.

214 Rip Rapson, as quoted in "Detroit Program," p. 13.

215 "Detroit Program," p. 13.

216 "Detroit Program," p. 15.

217 "Detroit Program," p. 17.

218 Sue Mosey quoted in Nancy Derringer, "In a Gentrifying Detroit, an Uneasy Migration of Urban Millennials," Bridge Magazine, The Center for Michigan, Aug. 21, 2014, at http://bridgemi.com/2014/08/in-a-gentrifying-detroit-an-uneasy-migration-of-urban-millennials/.

219 2016 36 percent figure from American Community Survey, 2016. Michigan poverty rate from https://www.census.gov/quickfacts/fact/table/MI/IPE120216#viewtop. The 2015 Detroit poverty rate was 40 percent.

220 "Detroit Program," p. 9.

221 "Detroit Program," p. 14.

222 Valerie Strauss, "How Bad Are Conditions in Detroit Public Schools? This Appalling," The Washington Post, Jan. 20, 2016, at https://www.washingtonpost.com/news/answer-sheet/wp/2016/01/20/how-appalling-are-conditions-in-detroit-public-schools-this-appalling/.

223 Tawnell D. Hobbs, "Lawsuit Targets Detroit Public Schools for Failing Students," The Wall Street Journal, Sept. 13, 2016, at http://www.wsj.com/articles/lawsuit-targets-detroit-public-schools-for-failing-students-1473808179.

224 "Detroit Public Schools' Legacy Costs and Indebtedness," Citizens Research Council of Michigan, No. 1138, January 2016, p. 12, at http://crcmich.org/PUBLICAT/2010s/2016/Detroit_schools_legacy_costs_indebtedness_2016.pdf.

225 Email to authors from Tammy Hatfield, Michigan Department of Education, Feb. 15, 2017.

226 Rip Rapson, "Six Core Beliefs Have the Power to Reshape the Philanthropic Sector for the Challenges of the 21st Century," Annual Report of The Kresge Foundation, 2014, Special Insert, p. 2.

227 Alec MacGillis, "Richard Florida Flip-Flops on Detroit," The New Republic, July 24, 2013, at https://newrepublic.com/article/114013/richard-floridas-detroit-flip-flop-save-or-not-save.

228 Richard Florida, "Don't Let Bankruptcy Fool You: Detroit's Not Dead," Citylab, The Atlantic, July 22, 2013, at http://www.citylab.com/work/2013/07/dont-let-bankruptcy-fool-you-detroits-not-dead/6261/.

229 Eric Thomas, "Why I Hate Detroit," blog post, LinkedIn, at https://www.linkedin.com/pulse/why-i-hate-detroit-eric-thomas.

230 "Detroit Program," p. 9.

231 Rapson address to the 2015 Mackinac Policy Conference, May 28, 2015, p. 4.

INDEX

This index is sorted letter-by-letter. Italic page locators indicate photographs on the page.

N

O

P